The EVERYTHING® Zen Book

To
Frank

Dear Reader:

Practicing Zen is a wonderful way to live your life. When you practice Zen, compassion enters your life, and you feel connected to the world around you in a powerful and comforting way.

But Zen practice takes time and patience. You make many sacrifices when you endeavor to undertake a serious Zen practice. Zen is not magic. Like all worthwhile endeavors, it takes work and dedication, sweat and tears.

It is not easy to look into your own heart, to sit and face yourself day after day. But as you do so, your heart starts to open little by little until a wonderful compassionate love enters you . . . and you soften. You have been taught your whole life that something is wrong with you. You are missing something; you are flawed. Through Zen practice, however, you start to realize that what you've always believed is really a fallacy. In fact, you are absolutely perfect, and you have always had everything you ever needed.

We invite you to enter the world of Zen practice. There are teachers waiting to show you a wonderful new way to live. There are practice centers in every state in the country. If you would like to see what Zen is about, the world is ready for you, rooting for you to wake up and see things as they truly are. The world is a wonderful place when you study Zen. Find out for yourself.

The EVERYTHING® Series

Editorial

Publishing Director	Gary M. Krebs
Managing Editor	Kate McBride
Copy Chief	Laura MacLaughlin
Acquisitions Editor	Eric M. Hall
Development Editor	Patrycja Pasek-Gradziuk
Production Editor	Khrysti Nazzaro
	Jamie Wielgus

Production

Production Director	Susan Beale
Production Manager	Michelle Roy Kelly
Series Designers	Daria Perreault
	Colleen Cunningham
Cover Design	Paul Beatrice
	Frank Rivera
Layout and Graphics	Colleen Cunningham
	Rachael Eiben
	Michelle Roy Kelly
	Daria Perreault
	Erin Ring
Series Cover Artist	Barry Littmann

Visit the entire Everything® Series at everything.com

THE

EVERYTHING®

ZEN

BOOK

Achieve inner calm and peace
of mind through meditation,
simple living, and harmony

Jacky Sach and Jessica Faust

Adams Media
Avon, Massachusetts

Jacky dedicates this book to Philip H. Sach,
who sits by the river, breathing love into her heart.

An Everything® Series Book.
Everything® and everything.com® are registered trademarks
of F+W Publications, Inc.

Published by Adams Media, an F+W Publications Company
57 Littlefield Street, Avon, MA 02322 U.S.A.
www.adamsmedia.com

ISBN: 1-58062-973-3
Printed in the United States of America.

J I H G F E D C B A

Library of Congress Cataloging-in-Publication Data
Sach, Jacky.
The everything Zen book / Jacky Sach and Jessica Faust.
    p.   cm.
(An everything series book)
ISBN 1-58062-973-3
1. Zen Buddhism. I. Faust, Jessica. II. Title. III. Series: Everything series.
BQ9265.6.S23 2003
294.3'927—dc22
2003014349

This book is available at quantity discounts for bulk purchases.
For information, call 1-800-872-5627.

Contents

Top Ten Pearls of Wisdom Found in This Book / x

Introduction / xi

The World of Zen / 1

What Is Zen? **2** • The Face of Zen **6** • Why Zen? **6** • Practice Makes Practice **8** • Enlightenment **9** • Showing the Way **11**

A Look at Zen History / 13

Siddhartha Gautama **14** • Search for the Truth **18** • Enlightened Mind **19** • Buddhism After the Buddha **21** • From India to China **22** • Zen's Arrival in Japan **25**

Zen Comes to America / 27

American Zen **28** • D. T. Suzuki **29** • Shunryu Suzuki **32** • The Beat Culture **35** • Zen Literature Today **36** • Where and How to Practice? **37**

Living the Zen Life / 41

Zen Basics **42** • Ethics of Zen Living **44** • The Five Precepts **47** • The Precepts versus the Ten Commandments **52** • Zen's View on Death **52** • Zen and Sexuality **53** • Making Difficult Decisions **53**

Sitting Around: Zazen / 55

What Is Zazen? **56** • Zazen versus Other Meditation Practices **56** • Zazen Supplies **58** • Important Zazen Tips **59** • Sitting Postures **61** • Breathing **63** • Empty Mind **64** • Making Mistakes **65** • Confronting Fear **66**

6

Koan Study / 69

Koan Defined **70** • Zen Stories from the Past **70** • Working with Koans **73** • What Is Mu? **76** • Talking about Koans **77** • Every Moment a Chance for Practice **81**

7

Living Zen in Relationships / 83

Respecting Others **84** • Zen and Your Parents **85** • Zen and Your Children **87** • Friendly Zen **89** • Committing to Another **90** • Marriage and Zen **92**

8

Using Your Teacher in Zen Practice / 95

Who's the Guy in the Funny Robe? **96** • Finding a Teacher **97** • Interacting with Your Teacher **99** • Learning Through Pain **101** • The Student/Teacher Relationship **103** • Trusting Your Teacher **105**

9

Becoming Enlightened / 107

Lighting the Way **108** • The Great Mystery **111** • Sitting as Enlightenment **114** • I'm Awake: Now What? **115** • The Bodhisattva Path **116** • Engaging the World **118**

10

Zen and Troubled Times / 121

Suffering **122** • Worrying **123** • Stressed Out and Sick **125** • Dealing with Sick Family and Friends **125** • Facing Death **127** • Impermanence **129** • Living Through Zen **132**

11

Me, Myself, and I / 133

Who Am I? **134** • Where Did I Go? **136** • If There Is No Me, What about You? **138** • Giving It Up: Acceptance **139** • Where Do I Go After Death? **142** • Reincarnation **142**

12 Living Zen at Home / 145

Setting Up a Peaceful Space 146 • Cleaning, Organizing, Simplifying 147 • Living Peacefully 150 • House Chores Are Practice 153 • The Stink of Enlightenment 155 • Finding the Buddha Within 156

13 Welcome to the Zendo / 157

Introduction to the Zendo 158 • The Altar 158 • Zendo's Headmaster 160 • Zendo Attire 161 • Zendo Behavior 163 • *Gassho* and Bowing 165 • Setting Up Your Zendo at Home 166

14 Working Zen: Practice in the Office / 169

Wherever You Go, There You Are 170 • Taking Zen to Work 171 • Right Livelihood 173 • Empty Mind 176 • Stressing Out on the Job 177 • It's All in the Attitude 178 • Successful Relationships at Work 180

15 Creating with Zen / 181

Art as Practice 182 • Zen Gardening 183 • Calligraphy 187 • Flower-Arranging 189 • Poetry 190 • Unlimited Creativity 192

16 Zen and Your Body: The Zen Athlete / 195

Respect Your Body 196 • The Zen Athlete 197 • The Zone 199 • Zen and Competition 201 • Zen and Martial Arts 202 • Yoga 205

17 Going on Retreats: Sesshin / 209

Retreats 210 • Preparing for Sesshin 211 • Exhaustion 214 • *Dokusan* 215 • *Kinhin* 217 • Meal Practice 218 • Work Practice 219• Sesshin Benefits 220

18 Zen Lives Today: Western Zen Masters / 223

Philip Kapleau 224 • Bernie Glassman 226 • Robert Aitken 227 • Richard Baker 229 • Charlotte Joko Beck 230 • Joan Halifax 232 • John Daido Loori 233 • Rev. Madeline Ko-i Bastis 235

19 **Being Mindful** / **237**
Mindfulness **238** • Thich Nhat Hanh **240** • Miracle of Mindfulness **241** • Practicing Mindfulness Every Day **242** • Staying in the Moment **244** • Mindfulness and Peace **245**

20 **Zen Every Day** / **249**
A Day in the Life of the Zen Practitioner **250** • Waking Up **250** • Breakfast and Other Meals **252** • Leaving for Work **253** • On the Job **254** • Back Home Again **255** • At the End of the Day **257** • An Illness Called Separation **258**

Appendix A • Glossary / **262**
Appendix B • American Zen Practice Centers / **266**
Appendix C • Additional Resources / **273**
Index / **281**

Acknowledgments

We'd like to thank Eric Hall, our editor, for all of his support and guidance. And we thank Kurt, who pointed the way and told us to find the path ourselves. With special thanks to Alex Fernandez and Michael Flynn, who have made so many things possible.

Top Ten Pearls of Wisdom
Found in This Book

1. To study Buddhism is to study the Self. To study the Self is to forget the Self and to forget the Self is to be enlightened by the Ten Thousand Things. —Dogen

2. Our practice should be based on the ideal of selflessness. If you try to be selfless, that is already a selfish idea.—Shunryu Suzuki

3. There are no doors to the hells; you yourself make the doors. —Zen Master Hsuan Hua

4. There has never been an Enlightened Person. There are only enlightened activities. —Bodhin Kjolhede

5. Sentient beings are numberless. I vow to save them. Desires are inexhaustible. I vow to put an end to them. The Dharmas are boundless. I vow to master them. The enlightened way is unattainable. I vow to attain it. —The Four Great Vows

6. In Zen practice, one cannot emphasize enough the vital role of the Zen teacher who has charted the paths of this arduous journey to the core of one's being.—Ruben Habito, *Healing Breath*

7. Enlightenment, for a wave in the ocean, is the moment the wave realizes it is water.—Thich Nhat Hanh

8. Manifest plainness, Embrace simplicity, Reduce selfishness, Have few desires. —Lao-Tzu, *Tao Te Ching*

9. People say "I want peace." If you remove I (ego), and your want (desire), you are left with peace.—The Dalai Lama

10. There is only one time that it is essential to awaken. That time is now. —Buddha

Introduction

▶ ZEN IS NO LONGER A FOREIGN WORD in the Western world. It's no longer a mysterious, exotic practice seen only in small corners of our big cities. Zen centers are found everywhere in the United States, and if we take a close look at one of them, we see that the Zen students as well as the Zen masters represent a cross-section of the American population.

So what's the big attraction? Why are people flocking to Zen practice in record numbers? Why can you find Zen books that cover everything from golf to computer programming at your local bookstore? The answer to these questions comes from Zen itself. Zen is, in essence, a search for self. When we practice Zen, we turn our questioning minds inward to seek answers to that age-old question: Who am I?

People turn to Zen for a number of reasons. They may be dissatisfied, depressed, addicted, on a spiritual quest, or simply restless . . . the list goes on. Many are trying to find answers to questions they don't even know how to ask, or they may be looking for some kind of peace and serenity that they have not been able to find in their lives any other way. Whatever your reasons for seeking Zen, you come with a questioning mind, and this is a wonderful first step.

Zen is simple. All you need to practice it is a quiet space and a cushion. Zen practice is not easy, but it is tremendously rewarding. You can find contentment and serenity in your Zen practice.

You can find happiness in the simple joys of life and, after your lifelong search, you might find that you already had everything you ever needed to be happy. You have probably tried to fill the hole inside yourself with possessions, with love, with attention and acclaim. Zen might be calling to you for a reason you cannot possibly fathom. Listen to that inner voice, and enter into the world of Zen practice.

Zen practice will teach you how to live your life in the *now*. It is not about books, movies, tapes, academics, mind twisters, or brilliant discourses on the nature of reality. Zen is about experience. Reading about Zen is not practicing Zen, but books can show you where to look to find it.

If you were one of those children who was always told you thought too much, then Zen is an excellent practice for you. It's time to stop thinking and start breathing. Zen will help you unclutter your mind and your life so you can enjoy things just as they are . . . and not how you think they should be. What a wonderful way to live! Ⓔ

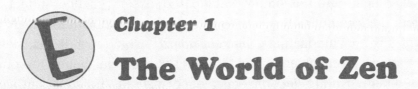

Chapter 1

The World of Zen

Zen is everywhere these days. You can go to the bookstore and find books such as *Zen and the Art of Motorcycle Maintenance, Zen Golf,* and hordes of others. This book is about applying your Zen practice to your life. No matter what you are doing, Zen can change the way you view what you are doing and the way you do it. In fact, Zen practice will change your entire life.

What Is Zen?

Zen is a Japanese word that is actually derived from the Chinese word *Ch'an,* which in turn originated from the Sanskrit word *dhyana,* meaning "meditation." So, in essence, Zen means meditation. Meditation is an important aspect of all forms of Buddhism. It is considered a path to enlightenment, and it is highly emphasized in Zen practice. In fact, Dogen, the founder of the Soto lineage of Zen Buddhism in Japan, taught a way of meditating called *shikantaza,* which means that sitting (meditating) *is* enlightened mind. Contrary to popular belief, the purpose of meditating isn't to *become* enlightened; instead, the goal is to *enjoy* your enlightened mind.

> "Meditation can be practiced almost anywhere—while sitting, walking, lying down, standing, even while working, drinking, and eating. Sitting is only the most familiar form of meditation."
> —Thich Nhat Hanh, *The Blooming of the Lotus*

Zen is a branch of Buddhism. It traces its way back to the Buddha, who lived 2,500 years ago on the border of northern India and southern Nepal. Buddhism started with the enlightenment of the Buddha as he sat under the *bodhi* tree. When Buddha became enlightened, he discovered the true nature of reality. He decided to teach others what he had realized and spent the next forty years sharing his understanding with all who would listen.

It is said that one day the Buddha rose to address his followers. In his hand he held a beautiful lotus flower. Instead of speaking out loud to those who were congregated in front of him, he simply held up the flower for them all to see. Mahakashyapa, one of the Buddha's disciples, smiled in understanding, and so he became the first person to receive dharma transmission from mind to mind, with no speech necessary.

In other words, he understood exactly what the Buddha was trying to teach because the Buddha was able to transmit his beliefs directly into his disciple's mind, without any verbal explanation. This transmission of the Buddha's teachings from mind to mind marks the beginning of Zen.

What Mahakashyapa realized when the Buddha held up the lotus blossom was the interrelationship and true nature of all that is. He woke up.

Self-Realization

The purpose of Zen practice is to realize enlightenment as the Buddha realized it. Zen practice is an effort to awaken to the absolute truth of reality—to achieve self realization. In other words, it is an effort to understand the way things really are, not the way you interpret things through the filters of your egos, your fears, and your notions.

Throughout your life, you have built an image upon your idea of who you are. Ask yourself, *Who am I?* And you might come up with answers such as, "I am kind, I am fearful, I am a baker, I am a failure, I am a father, a daughter," and so on. Zen, on the other hand, is being in the moment without the "I" construct, the "me." Instead of thinking about who you are all of the time, Zen will teach you to just *be.* It will lead you to awaken to your true self—your Buddha-nature.

FACT

Another word for enlightenment is *nirvana.* Nirvana is not a place. It's not somewhere outside ourselves; instead, nirvana lies within each of us. It is the goal of spiritual practice in all branches of Buddhism. Nirvana is a departure from the cycle of unhappiness and an entry into a different existence. It is pausing the activities of the mind in the state of consciousness.

Zen is also something you experience intuitively. It is not about engaging your rational, thinking mind; it is not about your thoughts at all. In fact, any intellectualizing—any thinking you do—will be obstructive to your Zen practice. Now that you've spent your life trying to hone your logical rational mind, you will use your Zen practice to still that mind.

Living in the Moment

So far, Zen probably sounds a little complicated. But the beauty of Zen is that it is not complicated at all. Zen is right now. It is entering the present moment fully and completely and letting go of all else. It is dropping ego, dropping self, dropping past and present. Zen doesn't discriminate: We can all can wake up if we practice hard enough. Zen calls to people. If you are reading this book, you may have the feeling that you have been looking for something you haven't been able to find. You may have felt compelled to turn to Zen.

Zen is also the end of suffering and the end of time as you know it. Using an analogy that might be more familiar to anyone who runs or participates in any energetic or creative activity, you could say that Zen is hitting "the zone." It lies in those moments when you are completely unaware of yourself and your life, when you are completely in the right now. If you have ever driven somewhere and arrived without any recollection of how you got there, you have probably realized that there are parts of your brain you use without ever being aware of them. You dropped your self, your worries, your fears, and your thoughts, but you still continued to function. You hit a zone. You were simply driving, in the here and now. This experience is a Zen experience—the dropping of self.

And as you practice Zen in your life, you will see that living in the present moment is like living heaven on earth. Even though we can all deal with this one moment right in front of us, we rarely live in this one moment right in front of us. We don't know how. We have been conditioned since our early childhoods to live in the future or the past. Through Zen practice, we learn to live in the here and now. This simple lesson will relieve you of the suffering you feel when your mind is allowed to constantly run and jump from moment to moment. You will be free in a way you never dreamed you could be freed.

Quieting the Mind

While Zen itself isn't complicated, living in the present moment is no easy task. Our minds are like monkeys jumping from branch to branch. First we think of this, then we are on to that. Sit still for one minute and notice how your mind jumps around. It can't keep still. Your mind wants nothing more than to escape the present. It is two weeks down the road on your vacation, or way back in the past ruminating about your high school prom. It is off five minutes from now wondering what you will have for lunch; it's stuck on five minutes ago, wondering what your boss meant by that comment.

So how can you possibly experience the present moment if your mind won't sit still? Zen is the practice of learning how to quiet your mind. Like teaching a young child how to sit still, practicing Zen is teaching your mind how to sit still and be quiet. It's not easy, just as getting a three-year-old to sit quietly isn't easy, but it can be done. By slowly encouraging the child to sit still for short periods of time, you'll soon discover that an hour of quiet can be attained.

FACT

Dharma can mean "teachings," "the Buddha's teachings," or "the truth." (All these can be considered as meaning the same.) Dharma is everything. It is truth, the teachings, nature, morality, ethics, and all that helps one achieve nirvana. Dharma is the path to enlightenment.

A common misconception is that Zen means living in a void: no thoughts, no feelings, no pleasure, no pain. But practicing Zen doesn't mean you will never think or experience sensation again. Zen clears you of the monkey mind. It unclutters your jumbled head so that you can experience things on a different level than you have experienced them before. You can learn to still the monkey, make it stop jumping around, and simply enjoy the present moment for once in your life. How many of us feel tormented by our own crazy thinking? How many times have you wished you could just stop yourself from thinking of the same situation over and over again? And how often do you wish you could just stop it and think of something else? Zen practice can help you stop your mind in its pattern of circular, obsessive thinking and let it be peaceful and serene.

Shunryu Suzuki, in *Zen Mind, Beginner's Mind*, tells us that beginner's mind is most useful for Zen practice. It is an amazing gift to have no preconceived ideas and to be willing to be open to new experiences. If you've ever introduced a child to an amusement park, you understand what the beginner's mind can be like. The child sees only fun, excitement, and maybe a little fear. She has no knowledge of the headaches that can come from banging your head on a ride or the nausea that comes from spinning around and around. Because of her beginner's mind, the child also has no notion of the actual thrill of a roller coaster.

If you can bring your beginner's mind to your Zen practice, the world will begin to unfold for you in wonderful ways you never dreamed possible. And if you experience moments of enlightened mind, you will recognize something you have always had and somehow lost. Finding enlightened mind is like going home, and Zen practice is one of the pathways home.

The Face of Zen

Buddhism is considered a worldwide religion, and Zen is a school of Buddhism. However, there is an argument over whether or not Zen is a religion. Ultimately, it is a personal choice whether you consider Zen your religion. Zen can certainly be practiced alongside other religions, and practicing Zen does not mean you are discounting your religion of origin.

So who are all these Zen practitioners? Most likely, not everyone who expresses an interest in Zen Buddhism calls themselves a Buddhist. The truth is that many Americans are taking up Zen practice and incorporating it into their own religious traditions and spiritual belief systems. In the United States, many people make a distinction between spirituality and religion, and some do Zen meditation practice to get closer to the God of their own understanding.

An American Zen center will show the faces of Americans from all religions. While some people who come to a Zen center are devoted to their practice and dedicate much time to it, others are merely curious, trying it on for size.

Why Zen?

According to practitioners of Buddhism, some of the reasons that Americans practice Zen include a need to connect spiritually after illness, addiction, or loss; a desire to end suffering; a dissatisfaction with their faith or religion; or a need to connect with themselves and others through meditation.

Finding Yourself

People turn to Zen to find themselves. Not unlike the people you would encounter in a church or temple, many Zen practitioners first find themselves on a meditation cushion in a Zen center because they are unhappy, unfulfilled, or dissatisfied in some way. They are looking for something more in life, some meaning or perhaps a way out of some pain they are experiencing. Zen centers, like churches and temples, might also see an increase in practitioners after major life-changing events. Whether it's personal, like the death of a loved one, or global, like the bombing of a school, people seek a place to find peace when they aren't feeling peaceful within themselves or with the world around them.

QUESTION?

What percentage of the world's population practices Zen?
Today it is estimated that approximately 6 percent of the world's population is Buddhist. Of those who are Buddhist, approximately 4 percent practice Zen Buddhism.

Confronting Yourself

Zen practice is also a way to confront yourself, to see who you really are. People who know themselves as intimately as Zen practitioners do are on the path to wisdom. Loving yourself means having compassion for yourself and all your foibles. This is a wonderful first step toward cultivating the same feelings of compassion and understanding for others. You cannot truly love another until you truly love yourself.

Sitting absolutely still is a wonderful means of confronting all of you. You cannot escape your thoughts, feelings, and ideas when you sit still and watch them march across your mind. You try to still your mind and stop the thoughts before they arise. But eventually, after failing again and again, you start to wonder where your thoughts could be coming from. If they are coming from you, why can't you control them? So you try harder and harder to still your mind and calm the raging stream of endlessly arising thought.

How brave it is to try to wrestle with your own mind! You start to see that you are no different from anyone else; in fact, you see that nothing is different from anything else. Everything is the same, and everything is connected. You strive for release from the pain of your small self. Eventually, great compassion arises from such practice, and following on the heels of this wonderful new compassion is a deep and abiding love for everything, as well as a wisdom that surpasses any wisdom you have yet imagined possible.

Practice Makes Practice

So what is involved in Zen practice? Zen starts with seated meditation, then you take what you learn on the cushion and apply it to the rest of your life. Zen is practiced at home, in the office, on the road, in our art, in our workouts, on the way to work, and as we prepare for sleep at the end of the day. Zen is a 24/7 kind of practice, and the more you try to incorporate it into your day, the greater the results you will notice.

Following Rules

Zen Buddhists believe that in order to achieve an enlightened mind and reach nirvana, they must follow a set of guidelines to living. These guidelines were passed down to us by the Buddha himself and should be incorporated into every Zen practitioner's life. Included in these principles for living are the following:

- Meditation
- Mindfulness
- Moral action
- Moral thinking

Each of these principles makes up a part of Zen practice. These principles will be covered in detail later on, but it is important to stress that like many religious practices, Zen is an *active* belief system. If you are not taking action, you are not practicing Zen.

The realization of Buddhist practice in daily life is not easy, which is perhaps one reason we call it "practice." It takes a great deal of work to stay in the moment and be present for each moment that arises, even if you only achieve it for a short time. So keep practicing, because practice will lead to more practice. And all of that practice, and your continued habit of practice, is the path to enlightenment—the path to your true self.

Enlightenment

What exactly is enlightenment? Enlightenment, also known as nirvana, *satori,* and *daikensho,* is the cessation of suffering. Unlike the Western belief that suffering is something that occurs because of a life change, such as the loss of a loved one, or physical pain, Buddhists believe that suffering itself is caused by desire. Therefore, we can eliminate suffering by eliminating desire.

The Buddha passed down his teachings on how to eliminate desire, and these teachings are known as the path to nirvana. Anyone who practices Zen is on the path to enlightenment. Living in the present moment is giving up on desire. Living in the present moment means you are not wanting for anything because everything you could possibly need is provided for you in this moment.

"We want more and still more. Instead of quelling the fire, we reignite it. Instead of seeking inner disarmament—the only kind that counts— we multiply our tools of conquest. And we even forget to check whether the fulfillment of our desire is really the one we had wished for." —The Dalai Lama

Ceasing to Desire

Our culture has become one in which we are very attached to the notion of desire. We want so many things in our lives. We want health, happiness, money, a promotion; we want love, serenity, college for our children, a new car, a new house, good teeth, a dog, a candy bar.

Most often we believe that thinking of all that we desire makes us happy and keeps us motivated. Our desire for a new house keeps us getting up in the morning and going to work every day. It keeps us from screaming at our boss and acting like a lunatic at the office. Our desire for love keeps us on the straight and narrow and helps us to treat others nicely. Sometimes we even use our desire for entertainment. When sitting with a group of friends, we'll ask what we'd do with three wishes or if we won the lottery. Every time we want something, every time we either do things for our desires or live for desire, we are living out of the moment and in the future. And when we live in the future, we are missing what is going on right under our very noses. We are suffering.

By giving up on desire, we can enter the moment. Entering the moment is to live in enlightened mind.

Have you ever videotaped a child's play or a friend's wedding? Think about that time. What do you remember about the event? Do you remember the look on your child's face when she stepped on the stage? Do you remember the feeling you had when your friend looked into the eyes of her new husband? Or do you remember thinking this would be a great shot, struggling to make sure the sound was working and the camera was focusing properly? How often do you live life behind the camera, too busy worrying about what it was going to be like later to notice the smile on your child's face or the feeling of love during your friend's wedding?

Enjoying Today

Seconds, minutes, and hours of our life can pass unnoticed when we live in the future. If you're so busy planning for tomorrow, it's hard to enjoy what you have today. When you practice Zen, you give up the future. That doesn't mean you go out and spend your 401(k) money right now. It doesn't mean you get drunk as a skunk because work doesn't matter tomorrow. What it does mean is that you remain mindful of your future and tend to it, but you live your life in the present. You enter the moment as it occurs and you live it with every part of your being. You don't miss out on any of the moments of your life. You live *now*.

Showing the Way

If Zen is so simple, why are you reading this book? If all that really matters is living in the moment, then why not get to it? The answer is that Zen might be simple, but human beings are not. We complicate everything, and finding a way to live in the moment is not as easy as it sounds.

For thousands of years, Zen masters have been passing on the teachings of Zen practice and guiding their students through their practice.

Support Groups

Practicing your Zen is difficult, and practicing alone is even more difficult. With that in mind, it's important to begin your Zen practice by finding a support group. This is a group of people with similar interests and desires who can help you on your path to enlightenment. There is a list of Zen centers in the United States at the back of this book. Check one out, and it will help you keep up with your practice.

There are support groups for many different things in this world. In fact, it seems that everyone has a support group, including recovering alcoholics, new mothers, newlyweds, and college freshman. There is a reason for support groups—they work! So why shouldn't a Zen practitioner seek out a group of his or her own for encouragement to keep striving in the search for enlightenment? If you find a group to practice with, you just might find that sometimes, the only reason you show up is because of your obligation to your group. But that's fine. Your practice continues, and that's all that really matters.

Zen in Your Life

Practicing Zen in all parts of your life is a wonderful way to live. Through your practice and your continued search for enlightenment, you will come to discover fundamental truths not only about yourself but also about the world around you. Suddenly, the things you deem greatly important might seem less so; the things you've wished you had more time for, such as yourself, family, and friends, will take on greater importance. So let this book serve as a guide to taking Zen into all aspects of your life. First learn about some of the colorful history of Zen, then try some sitting yourself. Move on to investigate retreats, and take a look at some Zen masters. Finally, take your Zen practice through your entire day, from exercise to work to family and friends. Incorporate your practice into every aspect of your life, and the world will change from the inside out.

"In all things be a master
Of what you do and say and think.
Be free.
Are you quiet? Quieten your body.
Quieten your mind.
By your own efforts
Waken yourself, watch,
And live joyfully."
—The Dhammapada

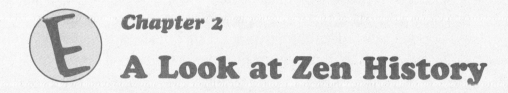

Chapter 2

A Look at Zen History

Buddhism is one of the world's five great religions, keeping company with Christianity, Islam, Judaism, and Hinduism. Zen Buddhism is a branch of Buddhism that dates back to the Buddha himself, having made it to our Western shores from the exotic past of the Far East. Zen practices came out of the Buddha's original teachings. The Buddha passed his teachings down, and they have survived to this day.

Siddhartha Gautama

Sometime around 566 B.C.E., a boy was born to a royal family in the Himalayan foothills, on the border of what is now northern India and southern Nepal. The boy was named Siddhartha Gautama. Siddhartha's mother was Queen Maya; his father, King Suddhodhana. The royal couple had been childless, and the baby boy was a blessing because they would now have an heir to rule over their small but prosperous kingdom.

Soon after Siddhartha's birth, his father held a feast at the palace and invited a group of Brahmins so that they could predict the future of his newborn son. The predictions said that Siddhartha would become either a great and powerful ruler or a wise spiritual guide. Despite how wonderful these predictions sounded, the Brahmins warned that if Siddhartha followed the spiritual path, he would endure many hardships. Eventually, however, if he set out on this path he would become a Buddha. On the other hand, if Siddhartha chose to remain within the palace walls, he would become a great ruler throughout the world. While eight Brahmins predicted that Siddhartha could follow either path, one Brahmin alone was convinced that the young boy would most certainly become a Buddha. His prediction stated that four signs would influence Siddhartha, encouraging him to leave home and begin his spiritual journey.

FACT

In the ancient caste system of India, a Brahmin was a person of high social standing—a priest. The Brahmins were those motivated by knowledge, often viewed as wise men capable of predicting the future.

King Suddhodhana was not pleased with the predictions that his son would become a spiritual leader. He desired a son who would not only take over his role as ruler but who would rule over many lands. He wanted his son to grow to become the most powerful leader the world had ever seen. In the hopes that his dreams would come true, he set out to prevent Siddhartha from taking the spiritual path. He made every attempt to keep Siddhartha cloistered in the palace by giving the boy more luxuries and riches than anyone could imagine.

Luxurious Life

King Suddhodhana's attempt to keep Siddhartha safely within the palace walls by giving him everything a boy could want worked for a long time. Siddhartha was trained by the kingdom's best teachers, and he kept company not only with his friends but also with beautiful girls. He grew into a strong man, making his father proud. As a talented athlete, an intelligent student, and a charming young man, Siddhartha's future as a ruler seemed secure.

At the age of sixteen, Siddhartha married the most beautiful woman in the kingdom, his cousin Yasodhara. And by the time Siddhartha was twenty-nine, his wife was pregnant with their first child. Knowing that the impending birth made her unable to entertain her husband, Yasodhara—in a generous effort to keep her husband happy and contented—suggested to Siddhartha that he look beyond the palace walls for entertainment. For the first time, Siddhartha wandered through the gates of the property in search of the beauty he until now only heard of that lay just outside his comfortable home.

The Four Signs

During his excursions beyond the palace walls, Siddhartha discovered a world he had never known existed. One day, upon seeing an old man with white hair, wrinkled skin, and a staff to aid his walking, Siddhartha asked his trusted companion and servant, Channa, what he was seeing. Channa explained that he was looking at an old man and that someday, everyone—both rich and poor—would age in a similar manner. Saddened and shocked by the revelation, Siddhartha wondered how he would ever again be able to enjoy life knowing that old age would someday befall him and those he loved.

On two subsequent trips outside the palace grounds, Siddhartha was faced with yet more disconcerting revelations. One day he confronted a maimed man. It was up to Channa once again to reassure the young prince: Siddhartha would not face a similar fate—he was healthy and well cared for. Siddhartha's third revelation came upon seeing a funeral procession. It was this sight that left him particularly shaken. Channa told him that death was inevitable but something he should not worry about as it could not be avoided. Overwhelmed by the sights before him, Siddhartha couldn't help but wonder how he had missed all the suffering in life.

The four revelations signified a turning point in Siddhartha's life. The first three signs made him realize that life was subject to old age, disease, and death. However, it would be the fourth revelation that would inspire Siddhartha to leave the world he knew to search for a solution to suffering.

During yet another excursion Siddhartha began to wonder about the privileged life he was leading. During this particular trip, he and Channa came upon a monk wearing yellow robes with shaven head and an empty bowl. Channa praised the man highly and explained to Siddhartha that the monk had renounced all worldly goods. Meeting the monk made Siddhartha pensive, and this time the luxuries of the palace failed to calm him. In fact, they disturbed him deeply. Just as the Brahmins had predicted, the four signs had left their mark. To Siddhartha, the veil of luxury and riches had been removed, and the world had been revealed as a place of suffering and pain.

The Renunciation

Yasodhara gave Siddhartha a son. However, the four signs had revealed to him the constant circle of birth and death, and this circle seemed endless and overwhelming to the young prince. Despite his love for his family and the birth of his new baby boy, Siddhartha decided to set forth out into the world in search of an end to the constant parade of life and death. He left his family behind and made one final journey outside the palace grounds. By shaving his head and donning the yellow robes of the mendicant monk, the young prince began a new life.

From the moment Siddhartha took his first steps in accordance with the Brahmin's predictions, he was following the path of Zen. He was seeking enlightenment. To many, this was a man blessed with everything that equals happiness. He had love, fame, power, money, family, health, education, and happiness. He was safe from danger and even sickness; he had a beautiful wife and now a son. Yet the young prince had seen suffering and just knowing it existed in the world tainted his enjoyment of the life he was currently living. In order to seek enlightenment, Siddhartha needed to leave all of his riches behind, including the riches brought by family.

Siddhartha saw aging, disease, death, and the endless circle of life as suffering and vowed to try to save all beings from it. So he set out in the world to change the repetition of loss. The awareness of *duhkha*, or suffering, had entered the consciousness of the young prince and was to change his life forever.

In Buddhism, *samsara* means the opposite of nirvana. It is the world we live in now. For Buddhists, this is the world of illusion, passion, and attachment to people and things. It means multiplicity and differentiation.

Because seeking a holy life was a worthy cause, many people in the lands surrounding Suddhodhana's castle were in search of a holy or enlightened life. In his yellow robe and with his shaved head, Siddhartha found himself among a group of monks who were seen as adventurers. Wandering far over the Ganges plain, Siddhartha met many truth-seekers who, like him, practiced denial, meditation, self-control, and yoga. By freeing himself from the endless cycle of *samsara,* Siddhartha believed that he could become enlightened—free from rebirth.

Good Company

Siddhartha wasn't long in his journeys when he joined up with five ascetics. Together they practiced the principles of asceticism in their search for enlightenment and liberation. Through their practice, ascetics believed, they could suffer enough in this life to save themselves in the next.

Convinced that external suffering would banish internal suffering forever, Siddhartha and his companions practiced asceticism by wearing little or no clothing, sleeping out in the open in all weather, starving themselves, and even, unimaginably, ingesting their own waste. Not surprisingly, Siddhartha soon became extremely ill. Most upsetting to him, though, was the realization that no matter how much he suffered, he was still plagued with desires and cravings.

Finally, Siddhartha realized that no matter what he did, he wasn't going to be able to quiet his ego. The ascetic life was not working. Despite illness and injury, he was still the same Siddhartha. Frustrated that he had almost reached death and still not discovered enlightenment, Siddhartha vowed anew to find a path that would lead him to the truth.

Search for the Truth

Leaving the ascetics, Siddhartha continued on his journey. While walking, he found himself thinking of little else but his memories of an afternoon spent under an apple tree as a young boy. He relived the moment of sheer joy as his awareness dropped away and left him free of self and able to fully enter the moment. It wasn't long before he realized that the path to enlightenment could not be reached through self-inflicted punishment. In fact, the way to truth could not be discovered through *any* extreme behavior—not ascetic self-denial, and not self-indulgence. The path to enlightenment could only be found somewhere in the middle.

Asceticism is the practice of denying physical or psychological desires in order to attain a spiritual ideal or goal. Through asceticism, a legend says, Siddhartha eventually learned to exist on one grain of rice a day, which ended up reducing his body to a skeleton.

Nursing himself back to health, Siddhartha slowly added weight to his emaciated frame and rebuilt both his body and spirit. During this time, he became conscious of every movement he made and its effect on the world. He paid close attention to his reactions to his environment, watching every thought as it passed through his mind. Over time, Siddhartha became *mindful* of his every gesture and thought, no matter when it was made—while walking, eating, sleeping, or resting. It was amazing to Siddhartha to realize how much and how quickly everything changed. Cravings, thoughts, and even feelings came and went. Just as loss was inevitable, Siddhartha learned that change was inevitable. With change came fear. And with fear came suffering.

Enlightened Mind

Settling under a bodhi tree, the former prince arranged his body into a meditation posture and began to notice how all things, great and small, were interrelated. The fruit attached to the tree gained nourishment from the earth that the tree was attached to and the earth received its nutrition from the sky, which provided rain. He saw that insects and animals ate from the earth and the trees, both nourished by the sky. He realized too that not only would the animals and plants die, but that he would too. No matter where he went or how long he searched, Siddhartha saw that life was filled with interconnectedness and change. He saw that nothing was permanent, but he also realized that while every individual thing would die, another like it would be born in its place.

The bodhi tree is also known as a banyan, bo, or pipal tree. It originates from the Asiatic fig. The tree rejuvenates continuously by rooting its branches in the soil. A descendant of the original tree is still growing at Bodh Gaya in India, and bodhi trees are commonly found in Buddhist centers all over the world.

Finally, after a great deal of searching, Siddhartha reached a moment of enlightenment. While sitting under the bodhi tree, meditating and watching his thoughts drift through his mind, he started to break free of his ego. His thoughts dropped away, and he entered each moment, fully present.

The Arrival of Mara

Despite this great moment, Siddhartha's battles were far from over. Mara, an evil demonic force, arrived in an effort to distract Siddhartha from his path toward nirvana. Mara sent his daughters to tempt the young prince with lustful dances and taunt him with words meant to arouse his ego and pride. When his daughters didn't succeed, Mara sent monsters to arouse Siddhartha's fear, then hurled questions aimed to undermine his motives. As each attack failed, Mara used his powers of evil and destruction to launch another, determined effort to unseat Siddhartha.

When every tactic failed, Mara yelled to Siddhartha: "Rise from your seat. It does not belong to you but to me!"

Siddhartha still did not move. Mara's warriors and demons rose up beside their master and swore that they bore witness to Mara's right to Siddhartha's seat. "Who bears witness to yours?" Mara roared at the still unshaken Siddhartha.

Finally Siddhartha responded by placing his right hand on the earth. The earth instantly roared back at Mara: "I bear witness!"

With that, Mara crumbled in defeat, disappearing from Siddhartha's presence.

The Internal Battle

The evil Mara symbolizes the internal battle that Siddhartha waged within himself as he groped his way toward enlightenment. Mara represented the part of Siddhartha that we all have inside us: those character defects and struggles that everyone faces on the path to enlightenment. Siddhartha, in other words, was plagued by the same defects that plague all of us. He was filled with lust, fear, pride, and doubt. In an effort to rid himself of ego, Siddhartha reached to the earth, symbolizing the connection we all have to the world.

The true nature of the universe is love, and it is the seeker of this truth who is most connected to the earth and the very essence of existence. The seeker of enlightenment is the one most in tune with nature and the truth of the universe, not the evildoers or perpetrators of violence.

Siddhartha's Awakening

Siddhartha had achieved enlightened mind: In this place now sat the Buddha, the "Fully Awakened One" or the "Enlightened One." Siddhartha had awoken to the true nature of the world, and it was as nothing he could have imagined.

No matter how much he wanted to, however, the Buddha could not sit under the bodhi tree forever enjoying enlightened mind. He knew it was time to move on, to speak of his experience, and to help people learn how to reach enlightenment on their own.

QUESTION?

Is there only one Buddha?
No, there have been anywhere from seven to innumerable Buddhas (depending on your source) who have lived at one time or another. Siddhartha is known as "the Buddha" of our time. Many periods of time do not have a Buddha, so we can consider ourselves fortunate to have one in our age. Without a buddha in our time, we would not have the opportunity available to us to practice Zen.

Buddhism After the Buddha

The Buddha's teachings started to spread. As he traveled around India, the Buddha drew students to him who were eager to hear about his experiences. One by one, as these students awoke to the truth, they carried his message all over India, taking it with them on the road into China, Japan, Tibet, Korea, Myanmar, Sri Lanka, Thailand, Cambodia, Laos, and Indonesia. Buddhism started to change over time as each country added its own influences. Slowly, three schools of Buddhism arose:

- Theravada Buddhism
- Mahayana Buddhism
- Vajrayana Buddhism

Theravada Buddhism emphasizes monastic rules and education and is considered the more conservative tradition of Buddhism. It spread south to Sri Lanka, Myanmar, Thailand, Cambodia, Laos, and Indonesia. Mahayana Buddhism headed north, toward China, Japan, Tibet, and

Korea. It is considered a more liberal form of Buddhism. Mahayana Buddhists emphasize intuition and meditation in practice. Vajrayana Buddhism developed out of Mahayana Buddhism. It is also known as Tantric Buddhism and ended up settling strongly in Tibet. Zen Buddhism grew out of the Mahayana tradition of Buddhism.

From India to China

Although groups of Buddhist monks were living in the northern parts of China as early as 65 B.C., it still took Buddhism nearly 500 years to make its way over to China. It is widely believed that Bodhidharma is the one to have brought Zen to China, and he is considered the first Zen patriarch of China.

Although Zen practices were known in China before his arrival, Bodhidharma's Zen teachings differed in that his emphasis was on "pointing directly at mind" to reveal one's true nature (also known as one's Buddha-nature).

Bodhidharma

Bodhidharma was an Indian monk born around the year 440 B.C. His teacher instructed him to go to China and carry the message of Buddhism. When he arrived, Buddhism was already thriving. Many monasteries and monks existed across the country. Eventually, Bodhiharma was invited to visit with the great Emperor Wu, who was known to be a devout student of Buddhism. Emperor Wu had come to power through a lifetime of violence and murder, but he then tried to atone for his past by doing good deeds in the name of Buddhism. He built temples, translated Buddhist texts into Chinese, and considered himself highly educated in the teachings of the Buddha. When he heard that the renowned Buddhist monk Bodhidharma had arrived in China, he quickly requested a meeting. He was pleased with the great works Bodhidharma had done in the service of Buddhism and was eager to ask Bodhidharma what merit the great Wu had accumulated through all his good work in the name of Buddhism.

Emperor Wu was appalled and shocked when Bodhidharma told him he had achieved no merit at all. The emperor had been taught that performing good acts was a way of accumulating great merit; it was a common belief that in Buddhism, good deeds added up like merit points. What was this nonsense Bodhidharma was spouting? Emperor Wu became defensive, and he endeavored to test his visitor.

FACT

Bodhidharma is also credited as the founder of the martial arts. He established a program for the monks involving physical techniques that were efficient, strengthened the body, and could be used in self-defense. The technique proved to be an effective fighting system, which evolved into a martial arts style called Gung Fu.

"What is the meaning of enlightenment?" Emperor Wu asked. "Vast emptiness, nothing sacred," Bodhidharma said.

This too confounded the great emperor. He wondered what the meaning of this could be. "Who is it that faces me so?" he asked Bodhidharma.

And Bodhidharma replied, "I don't know."

Bodhidharma was actually showing the Emperor all that he knew about Zen and the nature of reality. But he was unable to give Emperor Wu the understanding of his teachings because the emperor could not understand what Bodhidharma was telling him. Bodhidharma was trying to show Wu the nature of emptiness, the lack of distinction between things, the absence of self, and the true reality of everything.

And so Bodhidharma departed, leaving the emperor frustrated. He eventually made his way up the mountains to Shaolin, site of the famous Shaolin monastery. It was here, in a small cave, that he sat facing a wall and meditated for nine years. Legend has it that he became so frustrated with himself for falling asleep that he cut off his eyelids to ensure he would stay awake. It is also said that when Bodhidharma cut off his eyelids, he threw them to the ground and tea leaves sprouted. Thus, tea was first grown in China.

Hui'ko

Zen is transmitted from one person to another, from mind to mind. Bodhidharma transmitted Zen to Hui'ko, who became the Second Zen Patriarch of China. Hui'ko was determined to realize the truth. He showed up outside of the cave where Bodhidharma sat for nine years and waited in the snow, hoping to become Bodhidharma's student. In order to show his great sincerity and deepest commitment to realizing the truth, Hui'ko is said to have cut off his arm while standing outside the cave.

Zen legends are full of extreme acts of resolve, such as that of Hui'ko cutting off his arm, and they are a reflection of the culture of the time. It is hard for us in our modern world to dream of cutting off a limb to illustrate religious or any other kind of conviction. These legends are to be understood as a reflection of past culture.

Hui'ko studied at Shaolin with Bodhidharma for many years. Bodhidharma was able to show Hui'ko enlightened mind. Teachers throughout Zen history have used many different means to help their students become enlightened. Enlightenment is understood to be available to each of us in our very still centers, and a teacher can help us find the way back there.

As Zen was passed from mind to mind in China, five different schools of Zen were eventually established in the country. These schools—or Five Houses, as they are called—used different teaching methods. The Five Houses were the following:

- The Guiyang school
- The Caodong school
- The Linji school
- The Yunmen school
- The Fayan school

Three of these five houses no longer exist in the world today. However, the Guiyang school is now what is known as the Soto school in Japan, and the Linji school is now called the Rinzai school, also in Japan. These are the two remaining schools of the original Five Houses of Zen.

Zen's Arrival in Japan

Toward the end of the twelfth century, Zen arrived in Japan. The samurai warrior spirit was running high, and the rigors of Zen practice were welcomed by the Japanese. The two houses of Rinzai and Soto made their way to Japan and thrived. The Japanese monk Eisai brought Rinzai back from China, and Eisai's student Dogen introduced the Soto school. Both schools of Zen emphasized the importance of seated meditation. Over many years, the Soto school became larger than the Rinzai school in Japan (today, it might be as much as three times as large), though both schools are still very prominent. The strictness of practice in the monasteries historically kept many laypeople from practicing Zen. But as Zen headed West in the twentieth century, this would no longer be the case.

FACT

The samurai were Japanese warriors who were members of the military class. A samurai was near the top of the social hierarchy and had many privileges. However, he was also required to be a good example to the lower classes by following *Bushido*, or the way of the warrior. Some of a samurai's most important values were loyalty to his master, self-discipline, and respectful and ethical behavior.

The Two Schools of Zen

Rinzai Zen and Soto Zen differed in their view of the way one came to enlightened mind. Rinzai followers believed that enlightenment happened all at once in one great moment, called *satori*. Soto followers believed that enlightenment occurred in little flashes, called *kenshos*. Both schools imposed rigorous requirements on their followers, but the practices of Rinzai are probably a better reflection of the dramatic samurai spirit.

Rinzai practitioners are known to seek sleep deprivation. Their beliefs state that being deprived of sleep helps the mind to open. Soto Zen emphasizes silent seated meditation, while Rinzai adds the practice of koans, which are questions that cannot be answered by the rational mind but are answered as one pushes closer to enlightenment.

> "To study Buddhism is to study the Self.
> To study the Self is to forget the Self and
> To forget the Self is to be enlightened by the
> Ten Thousand Things." —Dogen

From Japan, Buddhism headed West, where it took a firm foothold in the United States. Today, Zen centers are found in every state, and American Zen students take many different forms. Though different schools of Buddhism have added to the original teachings of the Buddha, Zen remains simple. There is little emphasis on text and great emphasis on the deceptive simplicity of seated meditation. Zen teachers recommend that you do what the Buddha did: Sit and find enlightened mind yourself. The Buddha believed that each person needed to find the truth for him- or herself. No one can show you the truth: It is a discovery you must make all on your own. Ⓔ

Chapter 3

Zen Comes to America

Zen headed West in the last years of the nineteenth century. The United States was known for its welcoming shores, and immigrants from all over the world headed there in search of a good life. The country also became the melting pot of various religions, and Buddhism was just one of the many to flourish. The simplicity of Zen, in particular, slowly took root in the lives of many American spiritual seekers.

American Zen

In 1893, the first formal gathering of representatives from the world's religions—both Eastern and Western spiritual traditions—was held in Chicago. It was a momentous occasion called the Parliament of the World's Religions. Today, that parliament is seen as the foundation of the continuing formal dialogue between the world's great religions. One can imagine the incredible moments in history when representatives from religions all over the world got together to educate each other and celebrate the diversity of human spiritual practices.

The Invitation

Attending the Parliament in 1893 was Zen Master Soen Shaku, a renowned Rinzai Buddhism Zen Master, who spoke for the first time on Western shores. Until that time, Zen was not commonly known in the United States, and very few people were familiar with most Eastern spiritual practices, except perhaps for academics and scholars. Few books were also available on these subjects. In fact, it wasn't until after World War II that Zen writers attracted a readership in the West.

QUESTION?

Does the World's Parliament of Religions still take place today?
Today, we have the Council for a Parliament of the World's Religions (CPWR), which officially started in 1988. After that, two monks from the Vivekananda Vedanta Society of Chicago decided to organize a centennial celebration of the 1893 parliament, which took place in 1993 in Chicago with 8,000 participants.

Upon hearing Soen Shaku speak, Americans opened to the possibilities of Zen, and a connection was made. After the parliament, the publisher of *Open Court,* a journal focusing on ethical and religious issues, asked Soen Shaku to invite a Japanese Zen scholar to the United States to work with him. So it was then that D. T. Suzuki, Soen Shaku's student, came West and landed in America. More than any other figure in history, D. T. Suzuki is credited with opening the minds and hearts of the

Western world to Zen with his wonderful writings. Suzuki communicated to the Americans the experiential aspect of Zen, and he explained Zen in a way that left them hungry for more.

It is interesting to note that seventeen years after Soen's visit, in 1910, there were only 3,165 known followers of Buddhism in the United States. Today, statistics on American Buddhism vary from 2.45 million to between 3 and 4 million American Buddhists. Obviously, Buddhism has taken hold of the American spiritual heart, and it appears the religion is here to stay. The number of American Buddhists practicing Zen is difficult to estimate, since many American Zen practitioners continue to practice the religions they were born into while maintaining a regular Zen practice.

D. T. Suzuki

One of the most influential figures in American Zen has been Daisetz Teitaro (D. T.) Suzuki. As Mr. Christmas Humphries, founder of the Buddhist Society, says of him, "D. T. Suzuki has been called many things by many people: the greatest Zen man in the world, a great Buddhist philosopher, a brilliant religious thinker, an eminent speaker on Eastern philosophy and so forth."

Suzuki's influence on American Zen cannot be underestimated. He explained Zen to Americans in a manner that gripped them. In order to practice Zen, one must be gripped by it; it must take hold of every fiber of one's body in order to lead one through the maze of practice to enlightenment. Without being absolutely gripped by Zen, the student cannot muster the dedication to practice and break through the learned behavior of a lifetime of Western thought and action.

FACT

The first school of Buddhism to make it west to America was Mahayana, in the form of Zen Buddhism. In Buddhist philosophy, the Mahayana school is called the "Greater Vehicle" in reference to the Mahayana notion of salvation. According to this notion, it is possible for all people to reach enlightenment under the guidance of a dedicated teacher, or bodhisattva.

The Student

D. T. Suzuki was born in Japan in 1869 to a physician and his wife. He was the youngest of five children. He found an interest in Zen at an early age and followed it through high school and eventually into university. At that time, he started studying at an important Zen temple in Kamakura with Ksen Imagita. But Ksen died soon thereafter, and Suzuki continued his studies with Ksen's successor, Soen Shaku. When Soen Shaku was invited to the World Parliament of Religions in 1893, it was Suzuki who translated into English the speech that Soen Shaku would give at the parliament.

When Soen Shaku called for Suzuki to go to the United States to help Paul Carus, the publisher of *Open Court,* Suzuki redoubled his efforts at practice, determined to reach enlightenment before crossing over to the United States. The winter before his departure, he was successful in solving his koan and achieving enlightenment. Soen Shaku subsequently gave him his Zen name, which means "Great Simplicity."

To study Zen is to study that which is real and concrete. Zen is not the world of ideas, although sometimes it seems to be all about riddles and verbal evasions. To understand Zen is to experience the world as it really is. If when you eat you only eat, and when you dress you only dress, you can understand what Zen begs to show you.

The Teacher

Suzuki was a scholar, but he never became a Zen master or monk. His writing served as a bridge between the East and West, opening the minds of Westerners to ways of life they had not previously encountered. He showed Americans that Zen was experiential—Zen could not be understood in words or concepts but had to be experienced instead. It had to be known wholly by the body, mind, and spirit to be comprehended. He explained how Zen always deals with concrete facts and that which is real. It is not about generalizations and vague notions, but rather about change and the nature of being finite. In order to comprehend Zen, we have to go through a tremendous struggle, as Suzuki says, a struggle "that is sometimes very long and exacting constant vigilance. To be disciplined in Zen is no easy task."

D. T. Suzuki married an American woman and lived in the United States for twelve years. He then went abroad, translating ancient sutras and a wide variety of texts in Paris and London. He went back to Japan for many years, where he was a lecturer and then a professor. In 1921, he and his wife began publishing *The Eastern Buddhist,* an English-language journal whose audience was mainly Westerners. He traveled his entire life, teaching at the University of Hawaii and then Columbia University in New York. He died at the age of ninety-six and his last words—a testament to the wonders of Zen practice—were reportedly, "Don't worry. Thank you. Thank you."

The Legacy

To relate the facts of a life is never to capture the essence of that life. D. T. Suzuki had a profound and lasting effect on the lives and hearts of many Westerners. He was able to give the West the gift of Zen practice and open those lives to the possibility of knowing life in a real, intimate, and ever-evolving way. As he said in one of his writings, *The Sense of Zen,* "The truth of Zen can never be attained unless it is attacked with the full force of personality. The passage is strewn with thistles and brambles, and the climb is slippery in the extreme. It is no pastime but the most serious task in life; no idlers will ever dare attempt it. It is indeed a moral anvil on which your character is hammered and hammered. To the question 'What is Zen?' a master gave this answer, 'Boiling oil over a blazing fire.' This scorching experience we have to go through with before Zen smiles on us and says, 'Here is your home.'"

FACT

Some of the people who were influenced and attracted by the teachings of D. T. Suzuki include such great thinkers and creative geniuses as John Cage, Allen Ginsberg, Martin Heidegger, Karen Horney, C. G. Jung, Aldous Huxley, Jack Kerouac, Thomas Merton, Allan Watts, and Gary Snyder.

D. T. Suzuki made tremendous contributions to the Western canon of Buddhist literature. He found a way to express the inexpressible. A list of some of his writings can be found in the bibliography at the back of this book.

Shunryu Suzuki

Another Suzuki was also to have a tremendous impact on Western Zen. Shunryu Suzuki, the revered author of *Zen Mind, Beginner's Mind,* was one of the most influential teachers of Zen in the West. He was born in Japan in 1904 to a Zen priest and his wife. On his thirteenth birthday, Shunryu Suzuki was ordained as a novice monk in a temple in a small village in Japan. His life at the temple was harsh, but the small boy threw his heart into every action he performed. He started as a novice with eight companion boys but eventually, because the teacher was so harsh, Shunryu was the only boy left. His teacher, So-on, nicknamed Shunryu "Crooked Cucumber," telling him that crooked cucumbers were useless—no one wanted them and that he would never become a teacher himself. But Shunryu was to prove the teacher wrong. When he came westward, he blossomed into one of the greatest Zen teachers the West would ever know.

Beginner's Mind

An early encounter with a Westerner would have an enormous impact on the young Shunryu. The Westerner was Nona Ransom, his English teacher at Komazawa University. Miss Ransom believed that Buddhists were idol worshippers and not worthy of her study and interest. She had received a gift of a Buddha statue and kept it on display, though she insisted to Shunryu that it was solely for decoration and had no other value whatsoever. Shunryu would enter the room with the Buddha and *gassho*—a bow with palms together—to the statue. This went on for some time, and Miss Ransom started to tease him about his actions. Shunryu remained silent through the teasing until one day Miss Ransom finally asked him about his worship.

Shunryu told Miss Ransom eloquently how we, ourselves, are Buddhas and offering respect to the statue was to recognize our own Buddha-nature, the nature of all that is. He explained how our own nature was so easy to forget. He also told her briefly about some Buddhist teachings. Shunryu showed his teacher that to understand Buddhism, one didn't think or talk about it much. Instead, one had to experience it through meditation, chanting, or offering respect; one experienced Buddhism in the body, through experience and action.

Miss Ransom was astounded by the young Shunryu's eloquent explanation, and she immediately stopped teasing him. Shortly thereafter she asked him to instruct her in some of the ways of Zen. Shunryu showed her how to sit zazen, and he shared information on Buddhism with her. By biding his time and waiting for the right moment, he was able to open her eyes to another way, and her mind unfolded. This was a turning point in the young Suzuki's life. He realized that her beginner's mind—her complete ignorance of Buddhism—had enabled her to understand very clearly what Buddhism was about. A desire rose in him to go West and teach Zen to the minds of so many who had the potential to have such a beginner's mind. Shunryu later said that his experience with Miss Ransom resulted in his decision to go to the United States.

According to David Chadwick's biography of Shunryu Suzuki, *Crooked Cucumber: The Life and Zen Teaching of Shunryu Suzuki*, when people confused Shunryu Suzuki for D. T. Suzuki, he would say, "No, he's the big Suzuki, I'm the little Suzuki."

Westward Bound

Suzuki came to San Francisco in 1959 to head a small congregation of Zen practitioners, mostly Japanese-Americans. He believed that Westerners would embrace Zen, and he was absolutely right. His simplicity, his kindness, and his way with people made him a wonderful teacher to those who were fortunate enough to stumble upon him. In 1962, he founded the San Francisco Zen Center, which is reputed today to be one of the largest Buddhist *sanghas*, or communities, outside of Asia. The Center is made up of three Zen practice places: Beginner's Mind Temple in San Francisco, Green Gulch Farm in Marin County, and Tassajara Zen Mountain Center, the first Zen training monastery in the West.

There are many stories of encounters with Shunryu Suzuki. David Chadwick's biography, *Crooked Cucumber: The Life and Zen Teaching of Shunryu Suzuki,* is a wonderful story of this influential Zen master. When asked how much ego one needed, Suzuki answered, "Just enough so that you don't step in front of a bus." When asked if he could reduce Buddhism to one phrase, Suzuki laughed and actually complied. "Everything changes," he said with a smile. He was loved by his students and opened the eyes of the West to a spiritual tradition that flourished.

The Two Zen Traditions

Shunryu Suzuki was from the Soto tradition of Zen Buddhism. D. T. Suzuki, on the other hand, was from the Rinzai tradition. As we saw in the previous chapter, the traditions differ in their approach to enlightenment, and these two men were wonderful examples of these differences. D. T. Suzuki focused on koan practice and was the more rigorous and dramatic practitioner. Shunryu Suzuki was more ordinary. He believed that *daikensho,* or final enlightenment, was not the end path or reason for practicing. He believed in "only sitting," or meditating as enlightenment. Shunryu Suzuki taught that sitting itself was enlightenment. Once you entered into a meditative position and sat, enlightenment was present.

*"Our practice should be based on the ideal of selflessness.
Selflessness is very difficult to understand.
If you try to be selfless, that is already a selfish idea.
Selflessness will be there when you do not try anything."
—Shunryu Suzuki*

Before he died in 1971, Shunryu Suzuki passed on his leadership of the San Francisco Zen Center to Richard Baker, his beloved student. Baker was a leader of the center until a terrible sex scandal rocked the center's world in 1983, when he was accused of abusing his spiritual authority. The scandal is a reminder that people who practice Zen, even those who achieve enlightenment, are still human and can reach enlightenment with some serious personality flaws intact. Zen masters have been active alcoholics, sex offenders, and powermongers. They can be downright mean and nasty sometimes. Not everyone can extend their practice into every aspect of their lives. As Shunryu Suzuki said, "a garden is never finished."

The Beat Culture

The years following World War II found Americans still largely ignorant of Zen. A few academics and intellectuals knew something of Eastern spirituality and Buddhist philosophy, but many were in the dark when it came to Zen Buddhism. Things began to change, however. The postwar years brought much prosperity to many Americans, and with material wealth, discontent set in. Americans wanted something more than physical, material wealth. They wanted something to feed their spirit as well.

One area of American culture that absorbed Zen and welcomed it with open arms was the "Beat" culture of the 1950s and 1960s. Known as the "Beat Generation," it was the first to challenge America's tendency toward over-consumption and indulgence. Such famous Beat figures as Jack Kerouac, Allen Ginsberg, Gary Snyder, and Phil Whalen found Zen in the libraries, bookstores, lecture halls, and universities. The freedom and spontaneity of Zen appealed to these free-spirited young people, and the allure of enlightenment called to them like a drug. Another way to reach an ecstatic state had presented itself, and many of the Beat poets and writers signed on for Zen study.

However, the Zen practiced by the Beat poets was not the same Zen being practiced in most monasteries and Zen centers across the country. Absorbed in the art, literary, poetry, and music scenes, the Beats tainted their practice by binging on alcohol and drugs. Despite this different way of practicing, books, such as *The Dharma Bums,* and poems, such as *How,* reflected the impact of Zen on the authors and left their mark on American literature. The Middle Way was hardly the way chosen by this crowd. However, because of their outspoken nature, their irreverent ways, and their popularity, members of the Beat Generation brought Zen into the consciousness of a wider American audience.

Alan Watts was another influential Zen figure to come out of the Beat Generation. Although not a Beat himself, he was a very popular figure in the group's San Francisco world. Watts never maintained a dedicated meditation practice—Zen was mainly an intellectual interest to him. Alan Watts was read widely by members of the generation, and his book *The Way of Zen* still sells very well today.

FACT

It was Jack Kerouac who invented the phrase "Beat Generation" in 1948. The phrase was first introduced to the public in 1952, when Kerouac's friend John Clellon Holmes wrote an article, "This Is the Beat Generation," for the *New York Times Magazine*.

Zen Literature Today

Go to a bookstore, and you will most likely find a variety of books on Zen. Zen has permeated our culture, and the reader has much to choose from. Magazines, books, and tapes abound, promising us that Zen is here to stay.

There is a good selection on meditation, Zen gardening, and Zen and psychotherapy. You can also find Zen cookbooks and books like *Zen and the Art of Motorcycle Maintenance*.

Many of the great Zen masters in the United States have written books that enjoy long lives on the shelves of your local bookstore. Here are some of the wonderful authors you can look out for:

- Robert Aitken
- Paul Reps
- Shunryu Suzuki
- D. T. Suzuki
- Alan Watts
- Peter Matthiessen
- Thomas Merton
- Philip Kapleau
- Cheri Huber
- John Daido Loori

Some of the greatest American authors have Zen themes in their words as well—check out Walt Whitman, Henry David Thoreau, and Ralph Waldo Emerson.

Where and How to Practice?

So what now? If you decide to try Zen practice and introduce the Zen way into your life, what can you do? Well, first and foremost, you should know that practicing alone can be a frustrating and lonely experience. Continuing to practice alone sometimes seems like an insurmountable task, especially in the beginning. Finding a group to practice with is a very worthwhile gift to bestow on yourself.

The Location

We have compiled a list of Zen centers from nearly every state—take a look at the back of this book to see if there is an organized Zen center by you. However, Zen centers are not your only option. You might be able to find a Zen sitting group in your area, no matter how remote your location. Check your local newspaper or community posting boards. Check the grocery store postings, and ask around with friends who are like-minded.

The Internet is also a terrific source of Zen sitting groups. Go to a popular search engine, such as *www.google.com*, and in the search field enter "[YOUR LOCATION] Zen meditation groups." For instance, if you entered "Northern New Jersey Zen meditation groups," a nice selection would pop up. You can also check out different Buddhist Web sites, such as *www.buddhanet.net*, which usually have lists of local sitting groups all around the country.

Once you find a center or group, request a newsletter if they have one, or ask if you may talk to a staff person. Ask whatever questions you need to feel comfortable before showing up in person. Here are some questions you might want to ask:

• What kind of people practice with the group (age, ethnicity, monastery residents, and so on)?

- Is there a teacher? If so, what is the lineage of the teacher?
- How long has the teacher been teaching?
- Is it part of a larger organization—worldwide or countrywide?
- Do I need to bring a cushion, or will one be provided for me?
- What are the hours of practice?
- What do practitioners normally wear?

You will want to make sure that you can reasonably make sits on a regular basis, so try to find a center or group whose meditation hours work around your schedule.

The Attire

Now that you've found a place to go, you might wonder how you should dress. When you show up at the center for the first time, you should wear comfortable, subdued clothing. Don't show up in provocative clothing or clothing that is bright and colorful. It can be distracting to others. We recommend sweats or workout pants, such as you would wear to the gym or to a yoga class. Make sure your trousers are loose-fitting and are preferably a dark color.

If there is a Zen priest or teacher leading the group, it is possible the teachers will wear robes during practice at the monastery or center. However, most people who practice will appear in casual clothing, unless perhaps you sit with monks.

ALERT!

Remember, this is a meditative, quiet environment. You do not want to attract a lot of attention to yourself and distract others from their practice. Make an effort to wear clothing that respects the occasion.

The room where you meditate is called a zendo. You should take off your shoes before entering the zendo, so you might want to be prepared with socks if the idea of going around barefoot with strangers causes you discomfort. There is usually an area outside the zendo or practice area where you can put your shoes. You should leave personal items outside as well. Do not take in backpacks, books, water, purses, cameras, or other extra items. There will most likely be a meditation cushion waiting for you, but you can always call ahead to verify. You will enter a safe environment where people are consciously trying to let go of judgments. Do not be fearful of making mistakes: You are surrounded by a supportive and encouraging group!

The Benefits

Western Zen has taken on a life of its own. We can be grateful for the early pioneers who brought Zen to our shores and provided us with an opportunity to wake up to life as it really is. Because of such people as the two Suzukis and many others, we have a chance to find out who we really are and to change the way we live our lives. We can become kinder and gentler, as well as more centered and calm. We can feel confident and have great mental health. We can learn to cope with anxiety and fear. We can realize to the depths of our being that the world is a wonderful place, and there is nothing at all to fear. All we have to do is find a place to sit!

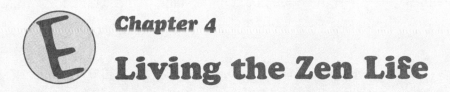

Chapter 4

Living the Zen Life

So far you've taken a look at the Buddha's life and early Zen history. You've seen how Zen made it to the shores of the United States and how it came to be what you find in Zen centers and sitting groups today. You also know how to find a meditation group or Zen center and set up a practice for yourself. So what next?

Zen Basics

Ninety-nine percent of Zen is your sitting practice. Once you have some sitting under your belt, you will see how it infiltrates your entire life. You will see that you are changing in subtle but important ways. Sitting will change you from the inside out. But beyond sitting, there are principles, ethics, and ideas that you should understand before going forward. Let's start with the very basics of Zen.

FACT

In Zen, when we refer to our meditation, we call it "sitting." If you ask someone about his or her meditation, you might say, "How was your sit?"

After he arose from sitting under the bodhi tree some 2,500 years ago, the Buddha revealed what are known as the Four Noble Truths. The Four Noble Truths are:

1. Life is suffering, or *duhkha*.
2. The cause of suffering is desire.
3. Desire can end.
4. The way to end desire (and therefore suffering) is to follow the Eightfold Path.

Suffering

Now, the Buddha wasn't a gloomy, pessimistic man. He didn't mean that life was terrible, that it was unbearable, or that you might as well throw in the towel now. Many people misunderstand the First Noble Truth to mean that Buddhism is just negative. Does "Life is suffering" mean that everyone is sick, poor, irritable, filled with pain and anguish, ugly, deformed, in trouble, forever being tortured? No, suffering comes in many different forms. Even happiness can be a form of suffering, the Buddha tells us.

Your reaction when you first hear this might be to say, "I am *certainly* not suffering. I am happy a great deal of the time!" But right now, consider being happy. What are you happy about? Maybe you are feeling particularly happy because you are going to pick up your brand-new Mini Cooper tonight, and you are planning to take it to your milestone high school reunion this evening. You can't wait to show it off. You've been dreaming of riding up in your shiny new car, showing everyone how happy and successful you are. Suddenly the phone rings and it's the car dealer. The Mini didn't come in after all and it won't be in until next weekend. Suddenly you are angry and disappointed. *You are suffering.*

Another way of looking at this concept of suffering is to say that everything is *impermanent.* The leaves on the trees are impermanent, your loved ones are impermanent, the seasons are impermanent, your job, your dinner, your Mini Cooper, your very life is impermanent. We humans have a hard time wrapping our minds around impermanence. We want things to remain the same. Impermanence causes us to suffer.

QUESTION?

What is meant by practice?
When we talk about our meditation in Zen, or when we talk about the precepts, we talk about our *practice.* We are practicing the principles, actions, and lifestyle of Zen. Even after someone realizes enlightened mind, practice does not end.

However, impermanence gives us great variety as well. The seasons change, we change, our friends change, our bad hair days change. Change makes life interesting and good. If we can fully accept impermanence and change all the time, our suffering will stop. In order to stop our suffering, however, we must stop having desire. Once we stop desiring things to stay the same, we stop suffering.

Desire

Our desires in life blind us to the Truth. Have you ever found yourself desiring something so strongly that it took over every thought or action you committed? Addiction is this type of desire. It's destructive. It takes over your life and blinds you to the truth. However, blinding desire doesn't have to be as strong as an addiction. A person's desire for success in business, love, or happiness can take over their thinking and control the way they act. Desire can blind you to Truth. But all desires are ultimately harmful. They distract us from life in the moment—life right here, right now—and lead us away from an enlightened state, our natural state, our Buddha-nature. When we want something, we are usually consumed with thoughts about getting the object of our desire. We are very far from life in the moment when we are gripped by desire.

You can think of the Four Noble Truths like a diagnosis and a prescription from a doctor. The sickness is suffering *(duhkha)*, the cause of the sickness is desire, and the medicine for the sickness is the Eightfold Path. If we follow the Eightfold Path, we will recover and be well!

But how can we possibly stop wanting things? Buddha tells us the answer: We can follow the Eightfold Path. The Eightfold Path is the path to end suffering, and the end of suffering is enlightenment itself.

Ethics of Zen Living

The Eightfold Path is the path that leads to enlightenment. It is the Middle Way. Zen ethics come to us from the Eightfold Path as outlined by the Buddha himself. Just as the Buddha learned that the path to enlightenment could not be achieved through extremes, the Eightfold Path does not promote excess, whether it's excessive pleasure or excessive denial. By taking a moderate road, you are traveling on the Eightfold Path—you are traveling toward realizing nirvana. The Eightfold Path consists of the following actions, wisdoms, and disciplines:

1. Right Understanding
2. Right Thought
3. Right Speech
4. Right Action
5. Right Livelihood
6. Right Effort

7. Right Mindfulness
8. Right Concentration

The eight steps laid out here are not meant to be practiced sequentially, but are to be practiced simultaneously, all the time. Each day you wake anew is an opportunity to practice these steps. If you look back at the Four Noble Truths, you will notice that they are not actions you can take. The Eightfold Path, on the other hand, is a path of action.

Picture the steps on the Eightfold Path as if they were spokes on a wheel. In order for this wheel to turn, all the spokes must be in working order. They must be straight, strong, and well oiled. Once you understand each of the parts on the Eightfold Path, and each part is strong and properly used, the steps will be like the strong spokes of the wheel, and the wheel will be able to turn, moving you forward toward enlightenment.

You will notice that each of the steps on the Eightfold Path contains the word "Right." The word "Right" here can be taken to mean "appropriate." Each of these steps falls into one of three categories: wisdom, morality, or mental discipline.

FACT

The image of the wheel is frequently used in Buddhism. In Zen we refer to the "dharma wheel." Dharma is the Buddha's teachings, or anything that can teach us about the true nature of the world. When Buddha first gave his sermons on the Four Noble Truths and the Eightfold Path, we say he set the dharma wheel in motion.

Wisdom and the Eightfold Path

Falling into the category of wisdom on the Eightfold Path are the steps of Right Understanding and Right Thought. Let's take a look at what is meant by Right Understanding and Right Thought. It might help to exchange the word "appropriate" for the word "Right."

Right Understanding and Right Thought are the hardest disciplines to master on the Eightfold Path. Wisdom is gained not through textbooks and lectures but through experience and time. You attain wisdom through the insights you gain in your practice. Right Understanding means that we see things not through the lenses of our own glasses but exactly as they are. Right Understanding can only come through the mental discipline of meditation. Right Thought comes through our *intentions*.

In order to attain Right Thought, it is essential to look at the spirit in which we approach things. A spirit of kindness, compassion, and harmlessness to our fellow beings will help us move away from ego toward a life where our actions and thoughts are not ego-driven but selfless instead. You will live a life devoted to service—not because you gain something personally from it, but because it is. In other words, you will not rescue an injured bird because it makes you feel good but, instead, because it is the right thing to do.

Morality and the Eightfold Path

The category of morality includes the steps of Right Speech, Right Action, and Right Livelihood. Morality in Buddhist practice comes from our compassion—from loving kindness. Morality is expressed through our actions, our words, and the occupations we choose. Right Speech means we do not lie, slander, curse, or use abusive language. We do not raise our voices unnecessarily, use harsh words, speak too long or too loudly. We do not gossip or create enmity through our speech.

Right Action means we do nothing that will cause harm to others. We do not steal. We are not sexually irresponsible. We do not take life in any form, destroy property or become disruptive, and we do not overindulge in anything—moderation in all our affairs is important. Right Action also precludes the use of alcohol and illegal drugs. Right Livelihood makes us turn an eye to our profession. Do we do work that is harmful in any way? Do we perhaps make artillery for a living? Do we work in a slaughterhouse? But Right Livelihood also goes beyond the harmful professions and asks us to participate in occupations that affect the world in a positive manner. It requires that we live an honorable life.

Mental Discipline and the Eightfold Path

Finally, the steps of Right Effort, Right Mindfulness, and Right Concentration fall under the category of mental discipline. Mental discipline consists of our meditations on these steps.

Right Effort asks us to consider whether or not we are putting in the appropriate amount of effort toward living our lives. It asks us neither to overdo the way we live nor underdo the way we live. In other words, we aren't lazy, but we also aren't workaholics. Right Effort also asks us to end all improper attitudes and thoughts. Part of living with Right Effort is using our efforts to stop unproductive and unsavory thoughts and instead work toward harmony.

FACT

Mindfulness is present-time awareness. It takes place in the here and now. If you are remembering your second-grade teacher, that is memory. When you then become aware that you are remembering your second-grade teacher, that is mindfulness. If you then conceptualize the process and say to yourself, "Oh, I am remembering," that is thinking.

Right Mindfulness requires that we live our life in the moment, mindful of everything we do. When we wash the dishes, we only wash the dishes. When we clean the house, we focus entirely on the task at hand. For example, while polishing the table, do not think of your workday as you are polishing the table. Notice the wood, the cloth, the way your hand moves. Be present for every moment of your life. Do not live three weeks from now on your yearly vacation. We do not live in the past recollecting childhood arguments.

The way we achieve this ability of Right Mindfulness is through Right Concentration. By concentrating appropriately on our meditation we can learn Right Mindfulness and move toward enlightened mind.

The Five Precepts

In Buddhism there are precepts, much like there are commandments in Christianity. The precepts are our ethical requirements for living a good life. These precepts are the absolute minimum we need to do to balance any negative aspects of our character.

Here are the Five Precepts:

- Do not destroy life.
- Do not steal.
- Do not commit sexual misconduct.
- Do not lie.
- Do not take intoxicating drinks.

In Buddhism, one can take the precepts and consider oneself a Buddhist. There is no formal initiation into Buddhism, but it is traditionally accepted that if you take refuge in the Three Jewels and practice the Five Precepts, you are a Buddhist.

Let's take a closer look at each of the Five Precepts.

FACT

The Three Jewels of Buddhism are the Buddha, the *sangha,* and the dharma. The *sangha* is the group with which you practice. The dharma, we have seen, is the teaching of the Buddha. The Buddha, the dharma, and the *sangha* are the basic components of Buddhist belief.

Do Not Destroy Life

Living by this precept might seem like the easiest of all. Do not commit murder. In truth, destroying life can take on much greater meaning than just taking another life and, according to Buddhism, goes well beyond just human life. The reason so many Zen practitioners are vegetarian comes from the belief that every life is important, whether human or animal. In fact, some follow the precept so closely that they even believe it's wrong to kill bugs. That might be a bit much for most of us to swallow. After all, what are we supposed to do when a wasp nest has taken over our patio or a mosquito is feasting on our arm?

If that's the case, is it even possible to live this life and follow this precept? Yes. What you can do is take reasonable precaution to avoid killing anything, and consider your intentions when and if you do so. Killing for sport or entertainment—such as a bullfight or deer hunt—would not be living by the precept. It is important that we approach all living things with kindness and compassion and not hatred, anger, or greed. One of the beautiful things about Zen is that how you approach it and practice it is entirely up to you. For example, you might choose not to purchase products from companies that use animals for testing, but you may still wear leather shoes. Or perhaps you just can't give up your morning eggs for breakfast, but you choose to eat free-range eggs and meats rather than those that are mass produced. Where you draw the line is entirely up to you.

"There are no doors to the hells; you yourself make the doors." —Zen Master Hsuan Hua

It's also necessary to remember that destroying life does not always mean killing something. You can destroy or disrupt a life simply by disrespecting it. It's important to give people space for their own thoughts, for quiet and privacy. Consider others if you want to play loud music, raise your voice, or bang on the walls.

Do Not Steal

Again, we are given another precept that seems somewhat easy to follow. As children, most of us were taught that it is wrong to steal. In the Zen tradition, however, stealing goes beyond just those tangible objects like gum, a pen, or even borrowed clothing that we fail to return. The concepts of stealing also includes intangibles, like ideas, time, and even energy. In other words, the second precept suggests that we are not to take from others that which is not freely given. We need to develop a sense of generosity toward others and respect others' property and space.

As humans, it is in our nature to demand more than our fair share, whether that means food or money or love. Many of us think we need or deserve two or even three cars, the super-sized fries, or the love of everyone around us. Practice generosity by limiting your consumption. Don't order the giant soda if it's more than you need, and think before purchasing another sweater. Is it something you really need, or do you just want it? If you buy it, can you get rid of an old sweater by giving it to someone in need? Before turning on another light or taking another helping, it's important to remember that you are trying to live a life in the middle, without extremes.

An ascetic believes that spiritual growth can be obtained through extreme self-denial and the renunciation of worldly pleasures. Ascetics might practice poverty, starvation, and/or self-mortification. During the Buddha's lifetime, asceticism was a common spiritual path. The Buddha himself was an ascetic for some time in his life.

When trying to live life without the excesses, it's also important to remember what Buddha learned during his life of asceticism. Just as you shouldn't have more than you need, you shouldn't give away everything you already have. Part of Zen is striving for a moderate, fair existence.

No Sexual Misconduct

The third precept concentrates on living a life of sexual respect for yourself and others. Whether or not you have a life partner, you cannot take your sexual life lightly. You do not cheat on your partner, live promiscuously, or flirt outrageously. You do not participate in prostitution, incest, or rape. You don't sexually harass people or make catcalls or inappropriate sexual comments of any kind.

We are a culture obsessed with sex. Whether it's used to sell underwear, mouthwash, or food, sex is on our televisions, in our movies, magazines, and even on our billboards. The first step toward change is by making changes in your own life. By acting with respect and behaving responsibly, we can foster intimacy in our relationships and create a bond of love, harmony, safety, and enjoyment.

Do Not Lie or Deceive

Very much like the Right Speech step of the Eightfold Path, this precept asks that we don't lie, slander, or act dishonestly in any way.

Lying doesn't have to come from speech. It's also true that something doesn't have to be an outright lie to be deceptive. Speaking with insincerity, promoting falsehood, misrepresenting information, or gossiping maliciously are all as bad as any lie.

Just as you need to be aware of the words you say, you need to be aware of your behavior. Behavior can be just as dishonest as any words. Be truthful in everything you do and say, and you will bring love and kindness into your environment.

Do Not Partake of Intoxicants

Avoiding intoxicants, like alcohol, drugs, and even caffeine and tobacco, allows us to develop inner clarity and keeps our minds free from confusion.

Some take this precept to an even broader level and move beyond just prohibiting intoxicants to prohibiting toxins. Mindful practice requires few distractions, and nothing can be more distracting than a polluted body. Even the smallest amount of an intoxicant can disrupt your consciousness, and it is awfully hard to be present in the moment when you are drunk, high, or even feeling the buzz of caffeine. Mindfulness, concentration, and effort are what drives you toward enlightened mind. Polluting your mind with intoxicants will only thwart you on your journey.

Don't worry unduly about the precepts. As your sitting practice develops, you start to naturally live the precepts. Our sitting makes us slowly aware that we are all connected. Eventually, it becomes unnatural to do harm to any living thing because to do harm to another is to harm yourself.

By closely looking at the Five Precepts, we can better recognize the behavior we have so willingly practiced and strive to end our bad habits. For instance, if all the pens in your home are pens you stole from work, you might realize it's a behavior you need to end. By ending it, you will become a more reliable and trustworthy person. By recognizing the benefits of truth and honesty in every aspect of your life, you will become more trusting and trustworthy. By following the precepts, you will notice how much your behavior affects others. You will become a person who promotes peace instead of negativity and who becomes a positive influence in the world.

The Precepts versus the Ten Commandments

You might notice that the Five Precepts and the Christian Ten Commandments have plenty in common. Many of the world's great religions share similar ethical and moral edicts. In fact, every one of the world's great religions—including Bahá'í, Christianity, Hindu, Judaism, Zorastrianism, Buddhism, Muslim, even Wicca—share the Golden Rule in one form or another: Do unto others as you would have them do unto you.

Both the precepts and the commandments are instructions for ethical and moral living. They share a compassionate center and promote respect for our families and neighbors. They encourage us not to steal, swear, lie, cheat, or desire.

The commandments of Christianity and the precepts of Buddhism do have much in common. However, they take separate paths when the subject of a higher power is approached. Buddhism does not rely on a higher power, and it is here that the instructions differ. If we break our commandments in Christianity, we suffer the wrath of God. If we break our precepts in Buddhism, our suffering is self-inflicted and we live through our own hell on earth.

Zen's View on Death

We do not live in a society that handles death gracefully for the most part. We do not have nearly as many rites of passage associated with dying as we do with marriage or birth. We are surrounded by impermanence all our lives, but when death comes knocking on our door we act surprised, as if we thought somehow we would escape.

Even though we are surrounded by movies of mass destruction, and though we see blood and violence on television and in our theaters, we still feel like strangers when death comes in up-close and personal.

Unfortunately, we are living in a time when we are being forced to become more intimately acquainted with death. From bombings to random snipers, people are dying at the hands of others in what feels like record numbers. However, there is nothing to be afraid of in death, and our practice can help us cope with our fears.

Zen can help prepare you to face your death with equanimity and serenity. In Zen, we die a thousand deaths on the cushion, and impermanence starts to be accepted. In Zen, there is a saying, "Die before you die." By sitting, by practicing our entire lives, we die before we die and are subsequently able to face our own impermanence without panic.

FACT

Zen Master Suzuki Shosan made the word "death" his koan. When someone asked him if he wasn't afraid of dying, he said, "Of course I'm afraid of dying! That's why I made death my koan."

Zen and Sexuality

Interested people often ask if Zen is supportive of gay/lesbian life. The interpretation of what is appropriate is an individual matter. If you are following the precepts and are doing no harm, then you could consider that you are following an appropriate lifestyle.

There are many gay and lesbian Zen sitting groups. A simple search on the Internet will turn up lesbian Zen groups, gay men's Zen groups, and Zen groups of all different types. Regardless of your sexual inclination, if you attend a sitting group, it is doubtful your sexuality will become an issue unless you are making it one. Zen is a personal path.

Follow your heart. If you sit, you will truly know yourself. And to know yourself is to fall in love with yourself as well as the rest of the world.

Making Difficult Decisions

Abortion and euthanasia often come up in discussion on Buddhism. As in other difficult decisions in life, it is best to sit and practice sitting. The answers to the questions that plague you will come, or the questions will cease to matter. You can argue that killing a person goes against the precepts no matter what, or you can argue that it is your *intention* that really matters. If taking a life—whether it be a fetus or a terminally ill person—is the lesser of two evils, then it might be the right choice for you. In the case of abortion, the suffering of both the fetus and the mother could be argued for or against.

We often don't know the exact right thing to do in a situation, but if we listen to our inner voices, we most definitely know the *wrong* thing to do. Listen to that voice. It's your Buddha-nature calling.

According to *The Complete Idiot's Guide to Understanding Buddhism*, in the case of abortion, Zen master Robert Aitken is known to have said, "[The fetus] is given a posthumous Buddhist name, and thus identified as an individual, however incomplete, to who we can say farewell. With this ceremony, the woman is in touch with life and death as they pass through her existence, and she finds that such basic changes are relative waves on the great ocean of true nature which is not born and does not pass away."

The Buddha passed down some basic teachings on how to live life appropriately. He gave us a path to follow that leads to enlightenment. Follow the Eightfold Path: Practice the precepts and zazen to find your way home.

Now that you have a better understanding of the Eightfold Path and the precepts of Buddhism, you can begin, living a better life. In the next chapter, we will get down to the nuts and bolts of Zen meditation. As mentioned earlier, by starting your meditation practice, you will naturally start living the precepts.

Chapter 5

Sitting Around: Zazen

The heart of Zen is zazen: seated meditation. Zazen is just plain sitting. You might wonder what there could possibly be to say about plain old sitting, but entire books have been written about it. When we sit zazen we do not daydream, letting our minds wander wherever they choose. Our objective is to tame that wild and woolly beast we call the mind.

What Is Zazen?

Zazen is meditation. "Za" means "to sit" and "Zen" means "meditation." Zazen is one of the most powerful practices you can undertake in your life. It changes you from the inside out. Zazen can change your perspectives—on yourself, on the world, and on your place in the world. By practicing it, you will slowly learn how to cut down on the clutter in your head. You will begin to know yourself in a truly intimate way. Likewise, you will begin to more clearly understand the world and the people in it. You will achieve serenity, perhaps for the first time in your life. There are endless benefits to sitting zazen. It is a life-changing, powerful force.

In zazen we try to let go of the subjective—the self and the discriminating mind—and experience the world purely. In zazen, the difference between you and the world vanishes. There is no difference.

You don't have to know anything about Buddhism to practice zazen. You don't have to work the precepts or understand the Four Noble Truths. All you have to do is sit and try to follow a few simple directions. As mentioned earlier, it is very helpful to find a teacher or a group to practice with, as solitary practice is hard to maintain. Human nature is such that group effort goes a long way toward sustaining whatever it is we endeavor to undertake. But in the end, all you need is a willingness to sit.

Zazen versus Other Meditation Practices

There are many different types of meditation. Before we take a close look at zazen, let's look at a few other meditation practices.

Western Meditation

Western meditation usually focuses on words. For example, a passage from the Bible will be constantly repeated as one sits with eyes closed. The meditator will focus on the words, the concepts behind the words, and interrelationship of the concepts and the words. Zazen, on the other hand, is beyond words and concepts. In zazen, we let go of ideas and attempt to experience reality as it truly is, without the "baggage" we might bring along. Our subjective interpretations of reality are usually a far cry from the truth. Different schools of Buddhism, however, favor different kinds of meditation.

Mantra

Some meditations focus on the repetition of mantras. A mantra is a mystical incantation. The repetition of the mantra contains the potential for magic and spiritual connection. By repeating a mantra, one can clear the mind, purify speech, and connect to the spiritual. The concentration on the spoken mantra is thought to evoke enlightened mind.

The most famous mantra is *Om Mani Padme Hum*. It originated in India and later moved to Tibet. Tibetan Buddhists believe that saying this mantra, either out loud or silently, will draw the blessings of Chenrezig, the embodiment of compassion.

Creative Visualization

Another form of meditation is creative visualization. In this type of meditation, the meditator focuses directly and wholly on the visualization. Every other sensation, thought, experience, and distraction, is set aside as one completely focuses on the visualization.

Walking Meditation

A wonderful companion meditation to zazen is walking meditation, called *kinhin*. Walking meditations can break up the agony of prolonged seated meditation, giving the body a chance to rest and stretch after getting cramped and sore in a seated position for long periods of time. We will discuss *kinhin* in more depth later on.

Mandala

Mandalas are used as meditation devices in some schools of Buddhism. A mandala is a physical map of the spiritual world. Mandalas are usually represented in artwork as a graphic or a symbolic pattern—

usually in the form of a circle with intricate designs contained within. The patterns are representative of the sacred place where the Buddha or deity abides. Mandalas are designed to awaken spiritual potential, and the meditator focuses on the mandala during seated meditation.

There are many books written on all these types of meditation and more. It might be helpful to try a few different forms of meditation before settling into the practice of one. However many Zen students report being "gripped" by Zen and are called to the cushion to practice zazen.

Zazen Supplies

While you really do not need anything to practice zazen—other than a timing device to mark the beginning and the end of the sitting period— there are a few supplies that can help you be more comfortable.

Zazen supplies might include the following:

- A zafu
- A zabuton
- Comfortable clothes
- Candle
- Incense
- Matches or lighter
- Timer of some kind
- A Buddha statue
- Flowers
- Incense holder
- Incense storage
- Bell

Traditionally in Zen we sit on a zafu. A zafu is a round meditation cushion. The zafu rests on a zabuton, which is a larger, rectangular cushion that protects your legs from what can be an uncomfortable floor. The zabuton is placed on the floor in front of the altar, if you have one. The zafu is then placed on top of the zabuton in the middle of the cushion and toward the back. Your position for sitting is now established.

If you do not want to buy a zafu or zabuton, you can always use a rolled up quilt as your zabuton and a regular pillow folded over to support yourself during zazen. However, if you continue practicing, a zafu is highly recommended.

An Altar

Many people also like to have an altar. On your altar you might have the following: an altar cloth, a bell, incense and incense paraphernalia, flowers in a vase, a Buddha statue, matches, and a candle. Flowers are generally used on the altar to remind us of the impermanence of all things. You can also have optional offerings, which might include tea or rice along with the flowers and incense. The candle is lit before you sit and symbolizes the light of truth that will banish the darkness from your mind. Light the incense from the candle flame, and put it into the incense holder.

After you have burned quite a bit of incense—after many sits—you will accumulate a great deal of ash that can be used to hold up the incense stick in the incense bowl. Until that time, however, raw rice works just as well.

An altar is used for several reasons. First of all, repetition, habit, and ceremony play a large part in meditation practice. The altar is a visual reminder of the importance of practice and is a symbol of your faith in practice.

Important Zazen Tips

Beginning students often ask what the best time and place are to do zazen. It is wonderful to attempt to sit zazen every day, but do it as often as you can, slowly working up to a daily practice. Start out by sitting for ten minutes. Even ten minutes of zazen will seem like a long time in the beginning. Increase your time at your own pace until you reach a time you are comfortable with on a daily basis.

It can be easiest to sit first thing in the morning. As with a regular exercise plan, many find that if they don't do it first thing, they find many reasons to avoid practice, any practice at all. It might be helpful to rise half an hour early to get in a session of zazen. Starting your day with zazen is a wonderful gift to yourself. If nothing else goes right that day, at least you have practiced.

Set aside a room for practice, or if you do not have an entire room to spare, a corner of a room. Make sure it is a peaceful and comfortable place. You will not want to be disturbed, so try to keep others away from the area while you sit. Distractions are part of life and will be dealt with in practice, but allowing yourself as much quiet as possible will make things easier for you.

Sitting zazen is difficult. It is physically challenging—your legs might go numb, cramp up, or become sore. However, the physical challenges are minor compared to the difficulty of keeping your "beginner's mind," that is, of retaining a mind that is open and free from habit.

Regularity of time and place are also highly recommended. Finding a sitting group to practice with will ensure some regularity of time and place if you cannot establish the same at home. If you sit with a group once a week, or even once a month, you will not only find inspiration and community, but you will guarantee yourself regularity you may not be able to achieve on your own.

A Note on Clothing

Clothing for zazen should be very comfortable. You will not want to wear anything constrictive, such as jeans or tight pants. Jeans are usually made of relatively stiff material that can cut off the circulation in your legs. They can also prohibit your legs from falling open into the necessary postures. Skirts can be worn by women, but they should be full-length so that they cover the legs. A loose blouse or T-shirt works well for the top. Make sure you are warm enough and that your top is comfortable. Dark colors are always preferred in a group setting so that you do not distract others with vibrant colors or loud patterns. Zazen is a spiritual and religious practice, and your clothing should reflect the occasion. You can also order traditional Japanese attire from a supply site on the Internet. Some sites for zazen supplies are listed in Appendix C at the back of this book.

Sitting Postures

Posture is important in zazen. As Shunryu Suzuki said, "To take this posture is itself to have the right state of mind. There is no need to obtain some special state of mind."

The Lotus Position

Traditionally, zazen is practiced in the lotus position, so take the lotus or half-lotus position if you can. The lotus position can be assumed by doing the following. Sit on the zabuton or rolled up quilt with legs stretched out in front, slightly apart. Place your right foot on the left thigh with the sole facing up. Your right knee should now rest on the floor. Take your left foot and place it high on the right thigh with the sole facing up. Your left knee should now rest on the floor. This may be difficult at first, but your legs should relax into it with some practice.

Place the zafu under your tailbone so that you are resting slightly on a small portion of the cushion and you are tilted forward. Ideally, your knees will touch the ground. Make sure your feet are resting on your thighs and not your knees or calves.

The lotus position is extremely uncomfortable for many people. However, try to persevere. The lotus is the best position for spine support. Since sitting still for extended periods can negatively affect the back, it is the most highly recommended position. In order to help loosen up your legs and hips, sit with your legs open during a hot bath.

Sway your body gently back and forth from left to right, then front and back, to be sure the body is centered and upright.

Other Positions

You can also try the half-lotus position, which is achieved by placing one foot on the thigh of the opposite leg, as described above, while the other leg remains resting on the floor. If neither of these positions works for you, you can also try sitting Burmese style, which is similar to lotus except that both feet and both calves remain on the floor. You can also try kneeling with the cushion. Put the cushion between your legs, and kneel with the majority of your weight resting on the cushion so your legs don't fall asleep. This position usually works out to be very comfortable for most beginners. If you are still too uncomfortable to possibly sit still, you can always sit in a chair with your back straight and your feet on the floor.

Keep your spine as straight as possible and the top of your head pointed toward the ceiling. Rest your hands in your lap, face up, with one hand cradling the other. Touch your thumbs gently together. You can also rest your hands face up or face down on your thighs. Your mouth is closed, with your lips touching lightly and your tongue gently touching the roof of your mouth. You should be relaxed; your shoulders should be neither tense nor tight. Your eyes can be open or closed. If open, try to relax them and loosen their focus.

Now you can set your timer for the time period you choose. When your timer goes off and your sit is over, be careful that you do not stand up too quickly. It is common for your legs to go completely numb in the beginning of your practice and if you stand up quickly you might fall over. Take your time, shake out your legs, and then stand slowly. Bow to the cushion.

ALERT!

Bowing is a show of respect. In bowing, we pay respect to Buddha-nature. When we bow in Zen, the bow is always accompanied by *gassho.* Place your two hands together, palm to palm, and bow to the cushion and the altar. You can also bow to the cushion and the altar before you start your sit as well. Bowing keeps us humble and checks our ego. It is a recommended practice.

Whatever position you choose, just remember this: The pain will go away quickly once the sit is over. Shake your legs out and stand up slowly. Once you walk around a little bit your legs will return to normal. No one ever died from sitting zazen!

Breathing

When you first start zazen, you will pay careful attention to the breath. Your focus will be on breathing both in and out through your nose. You should also be consciously breathing from your *hara* and not your stomach.

Focus on the *Hara*

The *hara* is located two inches below the navel. It's the physical and spiritual center of the body. Put your entire attention there. As you develop your practice, you will become more aware of the *hara* as the center. Breathe naturally, in and out. While it is difficult at first, try your hardest not to control your breathing.

Count

Once you are comfortably breathing through your nose and from your *hara,* you should start counting your out breaths. Breathe in, breathe out—count "one." Breathe in, breathe out—count "two." Continue breathing and counting until you realize that you are no longer concentrating on the counting but instead your mind has started to wander. Suddenly the counting seems natural and you are thinking of dinner, or your family, or something you could be doing.

Take the time to acknowledge this stray thought, let it go, and go back to your breathing and counting. In and out, one. In and out, two. Continue this practice until the bell rings. As you do this, you will notice how hard it is to stop the stray thoughts and bring your focus back to your breathing. Still that unruly monkey brain. Sitting practice helps you train the monkey and eventually make him still.

Follow Your Breath

When you practice zazen, your mind will always follow your breath. Do not think of breathing, just breathe. If we think, "I am breathing," we are resorting to the dualistic thinking that we are trying to get away from. Saying "I" sets up a "Not I." This kind of thinking is a result of the discriminating mind. We are trying to release and let go of the discriminating mind. Just breathe. In . . . out. If a thought arises about time, let it go. There is no time, there is only sitting. There is only here and now.

Constantly come back to the breath, and let the thoughts glide away. Eventually you will notice a very still blankness at the end of each out breath. That blankness is where you want to be. With practice, you will be able to enter that blankness for a fraction of a second. Keep on practicing.

"Body and mind of themselves will drop away and your original face will be manifested. If you want to attain suchness, you should practice suchness without delay."
—Dogen, on zazen practice

Everything in the world is interdependent. The flower relies on the roots, the roots rely on the earth, the earth relies on the water that comes from the sky, which houses the sun that feeds the flower. Nothing exists independently of anything else. You are not an independent being. This is just an illusion. Zazen will help you to drop the dualistic thinking that makes you believe you are separate. How beautiful!

Empty Mind

It might seem impossible to actually have an empty mind because thoughts are natural for us, and they will never completely stop. However, we can learn to tame our minds in the way we train our bodies for sports. We can tame the mind not to go running after every single thought it wants to. Most of us can feel victimized by our own crazy heads at one time or another. It does not occur to us that we can stop obsessive, crazy, or repetitive thinking. Zazen helps us to control our own minds.

If you sit in the early morning, you will probably hear some birds sing. Your mind will register that the birds are singing. Most of us, by habit, will then think, "Oh, the bird is singing." Then we might think, "That sounds beautiful." We might go even further and think, "That reminds me of my vacation in Florida where the tropical birds sounded so amazing and we had that wonderful fish for dinner . . ." And so on and so on. When you hear the bird, try to catch yourself before you go on a five-minute journey down memory lane. Eventually we will hear the bird and think, "Oh, the bird is singing. That sounds beautiful." Then, later, we might think, "Oh, the bird is singing." Eventually, we will just hear the bird. Empty mind.

Each human moment can be broken down in three parts. First you have an occurrence (the bird singing). Then you have the recognition of the moment (the thought that the bird is singing). Then you have the judgment on the moment (that the singing is beautiful). We aim to stay in the first part of the moment. To stay in the first part of the moment is to truly live in the moment. It is to experience the world as it really is and not as we have been taught to experience it. It is to be *a part* of the moment, completely and wholly a part of the moment. When we judge the moment, we remove ourselves from it. We separate ourselves and create dualistic thinking. Our suffering in life results from our dualistic thinking.

Making Mistakes

In zazen, you can start over at any time, all the time. Go back to the beginning again and again. There are no mistakes; there are only opportunities for practice. If you move, endeavor not to move again. Indeed, you will find that once you move, the urge to move increases and starts to plague you. Sitting still is actually easier than moving. You will survive the sit. You can sit through the pain. Shifting will make you more uncomfortable.

In a group setting, shifting around will be very distracting for your neighbors. If you move, you might cause your neighbor to break concentration. Everyone in a zendo should endeavor to be as still as he or she possibly can.

Sesshin

The physical pain you might experience during zazen is actually helpful. It serves as an incentive to move beyond the pain. Many people who practice zazen attend sesshin. A sesshin is a Zen retreat where zazen is done most of the day. Sesshin is where you can make a great deal of "progress" in your practice. The physical pain can be extreme, but it helps you move beyond into empty mind. You can empty your mind and suddenly the pain will vanish. So sit still. The pain can be beneficial. After all, it is only pain. . . .

QUESTION?

What if my legs go numb during zazen?
Your legs or feet will go numb when you are in an unbalanced position and too much pressure is being applied to your legs. You can try to tense and release your muscles to bring back feeling, but if that doesn't work just sit it out.

Confronting Fear

We all have fears. Our fears can come from many different areas. We are afraid of success, failure, the dark, strangers, aging, getting sick, being alone, and so on. Often our fears are what keep us from living our lives as we would most like to live them.

Fear can be a very, very powerful motivator—both good and bad. It can be the one thing that prevents us from asking our boss for a raise, or it can be fear that motivates us to buy a smoke alarm or get the tires on our cars checked.

If you sit zazen, you will be confronted with fear. It is frightening to sit perfectly still. The first few times some people practice, they can confront a fear that terrifies them. It can feel absolutely scary to sit still without moving. Few of us like to sit with our feelings. We race around our lives, cleaning, working, talking, making love, drinking, smoking, and doing anything and everything we can to avoid looking at the way we feel. Sitting still can be murder.

Zazen is not an opportunity to take out all those feelings and examine them, but the simple act of sitting can arouse the fear of doing so. Just try to take this in: No one ever died from their feelings. No one ever died from sitting still. It can feel as though a terminal void opens up when we plop ourselves down on the cushion. But once you work through the fear with empty mind and breath meditation, you will come to realize how safe you really are in the world. There is absolutely nothing to be afraid of. Zazen can lead to an incredible freedom for those who practice. Once you come face to face with your own mind, you come face to face with your worst demons. Once you realize the reality of empty mind, you realize that all along you were afraid of nothing.

"The practice of Zen mind is beginner's mind. The innocence of the first inquiry—what am I?—is needed throughout Zen practice. The mind of the beginner is empty, free of the habits of the expert, ready to accept, to doubt, and open to all possibilities."
—Zen Master Richard Baker

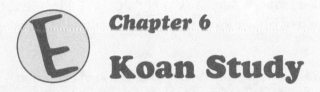

Chapter 6

Koan Study

In the United States today, the lines between Rinzai Zen and Soto Zen have become blurred, with many teachers incorporating elements of both schools in their practices. Koans traditionally came out of the Rinzai school of Zen, which was often considered the more rigorous school of Zen Buddhism. Koans are familiar to many Westerners and are probably the best-known element of Zen outside of meditation practice.

Koan Defined

So, you might wonder, what exactly is a koan? A koan is akin to a riddle or a seemingly impenetrable story that is designed to illuminate the true nature of reality. Koans are tools Zen students can use to push themselves out of their small selves, out of the familiar thinking and ego stance, and beyond into unfamiliar territory. Zen aims to enable the student to drop the self and move beyond what is known and commonly thought of as real.

FACT

An example of a koan might be "What is the sound of one hand clapping?" or "What is your original face, the face you had before your mother was born?" The answer to a koan is as individual as the person seeking the answer, and the answer can be found in Zen practice.

The Zen student works on the koan at all opportunities, trying in essence to actually become the koan. Also, the answer to a koan cannot be found in a book or figured out with your rational mind. You could probably go to an Internet chat board on Zen and find a lively discussion on koans. However, even if you read someone else's answer to your koan, you would still not have yours. Your Zen teacher will let you know when you have found the answer and will help you stumble through the maze on your way to your personal koan answer.

What exactly does a koan look like? Well, it is basically a short text, usually in dialogue form, that contains a Zen teaching. There are collections of koans that have been passed down through the ages. To solve a koan means the student has understood the teaching contained in it. In *The Gateless Barrier: Zen Comments on the Mumonkan,* Zenkei Shibayama tells us that "etymologically the term koan means 'the place where the truth is.'"

Zen Stories from the Past

Teachers throughout Zen history have used great ingenuity in finding ways to impart the truth to their students. Koans existed since the beginning of

Zen, but they were not used the way we use them today until much later. Quite naturally a means of training students in the way of Zen practice arose, and so koan study was undertaken.

The koan texts that have been passed down for centuries were created by Zen masters, who were like scientists of the mind. They understood ways in which they could get their students to move deeper into practice, and they could unlock the firm hold the ego had on the mind, allowing the mind to open, like a lotus flower. Although koans can seem mystical, remote, and impossible to break, students have been solving koans for centuries. With diligence, any student can break the seemingly impenetrable wall of a koan. All the student has to do is completely let go of the self.

There are collections of koans that have been handed down through the years, and several of these well-known collections are frequently used today. These include *The Blue Cliff Record,* compiled by Hsueh-tou in the twelfth century, which contains 100 koans, and the *Mumonkan* (The Gateless Gate), compiled around 1229 by Master Wu-men, which contains forty-eight koans. These collections were eventually taken to Japan and survived the centuries, passed down from teacher to teacher. Koan practice lost strength over the years, but it was eventually revived by Master Hakuin in the eighteenth century in Japan. Hakuin organized the koans in a sequence that enabled the student to move from one koan to another in a systematic way. Koan practice evolves as the student moves from one koan to another.

Master Wu-men called his collection of koans the Mumonkan, which means "The Gateless Gate" or "The Gateless Barrier." The title came from a poem he wrote, and the gateless gate means there is no gate in Zen. Therefore, there is no door to open, no gate to pass through—the only thing keeping us from seeing our true nature is our own self.

There is an old Chinese saying: Nothing that enters by the gate can be a family treasure. What does this inscrutable saying mean? A family treasure is something that remains in the family, that does not come from an outside source. You cannot be given a family treasure by someone outside of the family. Zenkei Shibayama tells us that this can be understood to mean, "Nothing given by others can be really good." Enlightenment cannot be given to you by your teacher or found in words. What is the real family treasure is already inside you. As the saying goes, a fish does not know that it is in water. We do not know that we are already in our true nature. How can we "wake up" to the reality of our own true nature? Koan study is one way we can try.

The Purpose of Koan Study

Koans are designed to teach the student about the true nature of reality: how the true nature of reality functions in the world; how we can loosen our attachment to words and phrases; and about the subtle teachings that deal with understanding the apparent dual nature of the universe. Different lineages of Zen use a different number of koans. Depending on what lineage you are studying under, you might be required to answer a specific number of koans. However, do not get attached to the idea that you must do a certain number of koans in order to be enlightened. Koan practice is a tool, and the student should not have a sense of pride at accomplishing koans. If that is the case, the student must work harder to release the pride and move deeper into the practice. Pride is attachment and attachment, as we now know, leads to suffering.

ALERT!

It is important to remember that enlightenment doesn't come from stories and dialogues. Your true nature is not contained within an ancient dialogue or a few paragraphs handed down from a Zen master who lived a thousand years ago. Your true nature already exists inside you. You already have what you need: You just need help finding it again.

Koan practice is designed as a tool to help you once again discover your true self. It is a means to an end and not an end in and of itself. Once you have solved a koan, it is important to let it go. There is a Zen saying that goes like this: "If you meet the Buddha on the way, kill the Buddha!" In other words, do not hang on to anything. Attachment is not the way to enlightenment. So leave the koans, leave the teacher, leave everything behind once you understand what it has to teach. The Buddha taught us this with the following simple story.

A man needs to cross a great river in order to get to the other side and continue his journey. He fastens a raft together from some nearby trees and uses the raft to navigate the roaring waters. He reaches the other side safely, grateful for the vehicle that enabled him to cross. Now it is time to continue his journey overland. Will he take his raft, strapped to his back and continue on? Or will he leave it behind, eternally grateful for its service, but aware it is no longer of use?

It is the same with our teachings. Once we have learned the lessons, it is time to let the teaching go.

Working with Koans

Koans are very frustrating for Westerners, who typically rely on their logical, rational intellect and love definitive answers to any questions. Westerners usually like to think there is only one answer to one question. People with this mindset often have difficulty accepting answers that are not clear-cut, definitive, and rational. Koan study is a frustrating practice that can arouse deep desperation in a student. Zen is a practice of action, and koans are active practice. They are not to be spoken about, or thought about, but are to be done. When you do a koan, you do not talk about it or banter questions and answers back and forth in conversation, as you would in debate.

While discussing a koan, the teacher may impart information that the student misunderstands. The student might then start chasing a path that will never illuminate the truth. So, keep in mind that anything said in these discussions is not the truth itself but an attempt to describe the truth that can be seen through koan study.

Entering *Samadhi*

In order to undertake koan study, a student must be completely and utterly gripped by Zen. Zen calls to its students, and its students become willing to risk their very existence for the existence of the reality of their true selves. You will be willing to give everything you have to your practice. You must throw yourself at the koan with desperation. You will call your koan with everything that you have.

To start, work on your koan as you sit zazen. Breathe in, and then on the out breath, call your koan with every part of yourself. At the very end of your breath you will eventually find a blank space. The answer to your koan can be found within that blank space. Enter the blank space.

As you move from breath meditation to your first koan, your meditation will become stronger. Initially, you will find with breath meditation that you are able to still your incessant thoughts. Your mind becomes still, and you are fully aware of the present moment. You become able to control your jumping monkey mind, and you will be able to enter *samadhi*. *Samadhi* is a state of deep concentration. It is a meditative state, in which you are aware of everything but in which you are also very deep within the meditation. It is in this state of *samadhi* that you will work on your koan. When *samadhi* has developed to a satisfactory strength, you are primed for your koan practice.

In koan practice, you want to sleep, eat, dream, and live your koan. You want to actually become one with your koan, so call it with everything that you have. As they say, die on the cushion. You will be reborn, and life will take on new meaning.

Realizing the No-Self

Let's take a look at a koan so you get a flavor of what is ahead for you.

The monks of two halls of a monastery were disputing over a cat. Nansen held the cat up for all to see in one hand and with his other he picked up his sword and said, "Monks, if you can say a word of Zen, I will spare the cat. If you cannot, I will kill it!"

Not one of the monks would answer. So Nansen raised his sword over his head and finally cut the cat in two. That evening, Joshu came back to the monastery and Nansen told him of the story. Joshu immediately took off one of his shoes and put it on his head.

Nansen said, "If you had been there, the cat would have been spared."

What is meant by this story? It looks like a load of nonsense to most people. However, Joshu was able, by putting his shoe on his head, to show Nansen that he knew of Zen. We cannot understand this koan with our intellect and cannot rationalize our way through its meaning. But a closer look reveals more than initially meets our limited understanding.

"Of the many devices employed by Ego to keep us in power, none is more effective than language. The English language is so structured that it demands the repeated use of the personal pronoun 'I' for grammatical nicety and presumed clarity. This plays into the hands of Ego . . . for the more we postulate this, the more we are exposed to Ego's never-ending demands."
—Zen Master Philip Kaplean

Nansen and Joshu were both great Zen masters. Nansen asks us to come up with some response that will stop him from killing the cat. As we know from the precepts, killing is abhorrent in Zen, so for Nansen to actually kill a cat must mean that he is trying to impart some extremely important information to the crowd of monks and is willing to do something absolutely awful in order to do so. He waits to see if any of the monks knows anything of Zen and then he kills the cat. The question is: How can you save the cat?

The only way you can answer this question is to be no-self, to kill the self and realize the no-self. The monks were all abiding in their ego-driven small selves, afraid to take a chance, afraid to speak out and be judged by others. Ego raged in the room, and not one monk was a living example of no-self. In order to understand why Joshu put his shoe on his head and satisfied Nansen with an understanding of Zen, one has to work on the koan and give one's whole self to the realization of the koan.

What Is Mu?

Mu is usually the first koan. Mu is known as the "gateless barrier" itself. If you can solve the koan Mu, then you will see what countless Zen masters have seen before you. The koan goes like this.

> *A monk asked Master Joshu: "Does a dog have Buddha-nature or not?"*
> *Master Joshu replied: "Mu!"*

This is an extremely short and extremely valuable koan. It is often the first koan given to a student after passing breath meditation. In the koan Mu, the monk is asking Joshu if all beings have Buddha-nature, even a dog. A simple yes or no answer does not answer the koan. Joshu must illustrate his knowledge of Zen and his own Buddha-nature as he answers the monk. To say yes or no is to be in line with dualistic thinking. So Joshu throws out his answer, "Mu!" Buddha-nature is Mu, Joshu is Mu, everything is Mu.

ESSENTIAL

In order to answer the koan Mu, you must show your teacher what Mu is. What is Mu? You find the answer by calling Mu with all of your being. As you breathe in, you watch your breath, as you breath out, you call "Muuuuuuu." You become Mu. There is no you, only Mu.

Master Wu-men says of Mu, "Don't you want to pass this barrier? Then concentrate yourself into this 'Mu' with your 360 bones and 84,000 pores, making your whole body one with great inquiry. Day and night work intently at it. Do not attempt nihilistic or dualistic interpretations. It is like having bolted a red hot iron ball. You try to vomit, but you cannot."

The question "What is Mu?" makes no sense to us intellectually. We cannot figure out Mu, no matter how much we try. We can go to our teacher and tell the teacher that Mu is nothing, that there is no difference between the student and the dog, the dog and the floor, the student and the floor. But unless the student can demonstrate to the teacher an understanding of Mu, the koan will not be passed. If your teacher asks you, "Does a dog have Buddha-nature?" and you answer, as Joshu did, "Mu!" that does not mean you necessarily have the answer. The teacher will know.

Becoming Mu

Most of us go through life using very little of our human potential. We have vast, untapped realms within us and use only a minuscule portion of our brains in our daily life. How else would a normal person walk on fire or lay on a bed of nails? What is going on with the rest of our minds?

Practicing with the koan Mu is a way to tap into some of that vast potential. Take Mu deep into your *hora,* and let it go with your out breath. Muuuuu . . . Keep at it until all thought is gone, until you become the essence of Mu. You are Mu, the universe is Mu, the moon, the stars, the endless sky become Mu. In the words of Zen Master Wu-men, you cast aside your discriminating mind and join the ancient masters. To understand Mu is to understand the no-self and to embrace the ten thousand things as one. There is no separation, and you realize the true nature of all things.

Talking about Koans

Although we have said that koans are to be done and not talked about, we still talk about them, of course. This is only in an effort to disclose information to the students that may be helpful in pointing them toward greater discovery.

There are traditionally different ways in which a koan may be discussed, including the following:

- *Dokusan*
- *Teisho*
- Dharma combat
- Question-and-answer period

All of the above are encounters in which a teacher will try to move a student ahead in his or her practice, encouraging a mind-to-mind transmission of the true nature of reality. Each kind of koan talk is designed to impart dharma knowledge to the Zen student.

*"To study Buddhism is to study the self.
To study the self is to forget the self.
To forget the self is to be enlightened by
the ten thousand things." —Dogen*

Dokusan

Dokusan is a one-on-one meeting with your Zen teacher. During *dokusan*, a student will try to give an answer to a koan. The teacher will then let the student know if he or she is right or if it's time to go back and try again. When it is the student's turn for *dokusan,* he or she will enter a private room with the teacher and usually bow to the altar and the teacher before sitting in front of the teacher on a cushion that is there, waiting. You, the student, will attempt to answer the koan. It is often necessary to tell the teacher what koan you were undertaking, such as "My koan is Mu," so that the teacher, who may have hundreds of students, can be ready for your answer.

You will then answer the koan to the best of your ability. Answers to koans are not necessarily related in words. You must show your teacher that you have an understanding of your koan. The answer to the koan, when you have reached it, will grip you, and you will be compelled to answer in a specific way. *Dokusan* is not a time for intellectual debates on koans. If you go in and try to explain a koan to your teacher, most likely the teacher will ring a bell and tell you to leave. The intellect is not your friend in koan practice, so try to kill the rational mind and move beyond it into bigger mind.

Your teacher will initially appear very supportive and encouraging, and your first efforts at *dokusan* will most likely be very positive encounters. But as you move into the koan, and the teacher senses that you are getting somewhere, approval disappears. The teacher will then push you further and further into frustration as you hit wall after wall. If you go into *dokusan* and meet with a wall you cannot seem to scale, try again. Try again and again. Try until you are frustrated beyond measure, until you are utterly beaten. It is not until you die on your cushion and give up that you will find the answer.

Koans are difficult to work on outside of a sesshin. A sesshin, a kind of Zen retreat with fifteen hours a day or more of Zen practice, is a time where the student can make the most practice on a koan as all outside distractions are taken away.

Have you ever been obsessed with finding the answer to a problem? You work on the problem, mull it over again and again, but you are completely frustrated when it comes to actually finding the answer. You spend hours, days, weeks, trying to figure the problem out. Finally, completely frustrated, you give up and go out to have some fun. Suddenly, there it is! The answer has just popped into your mind as if it has always been there. This has happened because you have let the answer move into the deeper parts of your working mind. Let it move from the surface thinking to another level, where it can be figured out without the distractions of consciousness.

Teisho

Teisho is a dharma discourse in which the teacher tries to show the student the truth through commentary on a koan. *Teishos* are given to all students present and are not one-to-one encounters. Many modern literary compilations on Zen are actually transcribed and edited *teisho* talks.

During *teisho* talks, the students gather in the zendo and sit very still on their zafus. The teacher might open the dharma talk with some sutras. Then, a koan from one of the koan collections will be presented, and the teacher will offer his or her understanding of the koan to the students. The presentation presumes that the audience of students are enlightened beings. In order to hear the *teisho* and to take it in, the student must shift his or her ability to understand and listen in a wholly different manner.

Dharma Combat

Dharma combat is not a new video game, although it does sound like one. Dharma combat, or *shosan,* is an encounter with the teacher in which the teacher tries to push the student further into the realization of the koan by using a spirited exchange encounter with the students and the dharma community. The teacher presents a koan to the community and encourages the students to test their knowledge of the koan and ask questions. Dharma combat can also take place between senior students or two Zen masters.

Here is an example of dharma combat between two Zen masters.

In the early 1970s, two Buddhist masters met in Cambridge, Massachusetts. One was a Tibetan master named Kalu Rinpoche, and the other was a Korean Zen master named Seung Sahn. The audience was on the edge of their seats as the dharma combat began. Seung Sahn held up an orange and, in the tradition of Zen dharma combat fashion, demanded, "What is this?"

Kalu Rinpoche just stared at him, questioning.

Once more, Seung Sahn asked, "What is this?"

Finally, Kalu Rinpoche looked at his translator and asked, "Don't they have oranges in Korea?"

Mondo

Another form of a koan discussion is the question-and-answer period, known as *mondo.* Everyone in attendance at a *mondo* can ask the teacher questions relating to the koan or other Zen-related topics. It is not as spirited as a dharma talk, and the answers tend to be intellectual and explanatory.

FACT

The *mondo* is a chance for students to get explanations for questions they may have, such as "How do you know when I have the answer to a koan?" The master answers in a way that encourages the student to reach a deeper level of perception.

Every Moment a Chance for Practice

Every moment of your life is a chance to practice your koan. You can take your koan to bed with you, on the train, to dinner, or on a walk. You call your koan whenever you can. All you need to practice your koan are the three essentials of Zen practice:

- Great faith
- Great doubt
- Great determination

The student of Zen needs great faith to continue practice, great doubt in the nature of reality to actually get on the cushion in the first place, and great determination to continue practice in the face of tremendous struggle and frustration.

You have what you need to practice koans. Everything you will ever need resides within you. If you undertake a practice of koan study, find a teacher who can point you in the right direction when you need a gentle (or not so gentle) hand. Koan study is not essential to Zen practice, but it is a way of moving toward enlightenment. The Soto tradition of Zen practices *shikantaza* or "just sitting." You can realize enlightenment with or without Zen koan practice; the choice is up to you.

Chapter 7

Living Zen in Relationships

By now, you have probably started a Zen practice. You are sitting, perhaps trying to work the precepts, and maybe even trying koan practice. But how can you bring your practice out of the zendo and into the world? You can try by taking what you have learned in your meditation practice and practice it outside, before it is second nature for you to do so.

Respecting Others

The precepts in Zen encourage us to be respectful of others. We respect each other's right to privacy, to be quiet, to live free from harm. We respect the other with our actions, our speech, and our thoughts. We live the Golden Rule: Do unto others as you would have them do unto you.

We humans are social creatures. We love to interact with each other even though our interactions often cause us pain and disturb us. How many times have you gone into a store in a wonderful, upbeat mood only to run into a rude clerk or fellow shopper who crushes your good mood and casts a cloud upon your day? We have the power to disturb others greatly. A harsh word, a nasty look, a rude gesture—we have all of these at our disposal. We hold within ourselves the potential for great destruction.

Today, we can see the result of what disharmony can do. We have wars and terrorism of great magnitude around the world. We are living in a time of tremendous divorce rates, overburdened court systems as litigation runs out of control, and talk shows that use argument as entertainment. We look around us and see little respect anywhere. Why should we be any different? Why should we put our necks out?

FACT

Someone once asked Suzuki Roshi: "What is Zen?"
Suzuki held up his hand with two fingers spread open. "Not two," he said. Then he brought his two fingers together. "One."

Promoting Peace and Harmony

Zen changes us. We start to realize that we are connected to the world. We are not separate, as our ego tries to tell us. We are all a part of something bigger than ourselves; we are all interdependent. To harm the soil is to harm the tree. To harm the tree is to endanger the very air that we breathe. To harm the air that we breathe is to harm everyone around us. There is not an unlimited supply of resources, as we seem to believe. Not one of us lives outside of that connection, alone and separate. As this realization grows with our practice, we know that we cannot do harm—to do so will ultimately harm us as well.

If we are affected negatively by that rude store clerk and, in turn, we pass on that negativity to another, we are not messengers of compassion and harmony. We practice Zen so that we can change, so that we can be open-hearted and open-minded. Instead of passing on a negative experience to someone else, we can turn it into a positive experience. We can turn to the clerk in peace, interacting with an open and compassionate heart. If you have ever walked down the street and looked up to find someone calling out a happy good-morning greeting, you know the power of a smile and an open heart. Suddenly, you feel lighter and a part of the world. Someone has flipped a switch inside you, and the light shines on your day.

*"There has never been an Enlightened Person.
There are only enlightened activities."
—Bodhin Kjolhede*

We should respect the world, and we can start by respecting those who inhabit it. The world and everything in it deserves our respect and attention. We can become promoters of peace and harmony. If it doesn't start with us, then who will it start with? Do not wait for others to make the first step of love. That is a coward's way out. To sit in zazen is to be very brave. To face your greatest fears and see inside your heart is to be a very strong and courageous person. To be a person of compassion, love, and attention is to be everything that you can be. It is to be everything you are meant to be. Don't wait until you are enlightened: Start today!

Zen and Your Parents

In *What the Buddha Taught,* Walpola Rahula tells a story about an encounter between a young Indian man named Sigala and the Buddha. At the time, Sigala worshipped the six cardinal points of the heavens, which were east, west, north, south, nadir, and zenith. His father had directed him to do so, and so he did with great faith. But the Buddha told Sigala something entirely different. According to the Buddha, the six directions that should be worshipped were: parents; teachers; wife and children; friends, relatives, and neighbors; servants, workers, and employees; and finally, religious men.

Performing Duties

How can we worship the people in our life? The Buddha tells us we can worship by the duties we perform for others.

So how in your lifetime can you respect and worship your parents? You can speak to them with great respect and listen to them attentively. You can take care of them when they are old. Is taking care of your parents putting them in a nursing home and visiting them once a month? Perhaps it is, but only you can decide. You can visit with your parents and help them with any tasks they need completed around the house. To practice Zen is to practice a humble life. We clean, we cook, we garden. We sweep, we nurse people who are sick, we change sheets, we scrub toilets.

ALERT!

When you visit your parents, don't wait to be asked what needs to be done. Obviously, the lawn needs mowing and the weeds need pulling. The shopping needs to be done, and the windowsills need to be dusted. Listen to them with great attentiveness and with much love in your heart. Be present in your parents' lives and love them in word, gesture, and mind.

Listening

Living Zen practice with family members who are not enlightened is no easy task. Zen practice is, of course, no easy task. You will be challenged to bring your practice to greater heights again and again. How willing are you to sit with your mother and truly listen with an open heart? As the saying goes, our mothers can push our buttons: They created the buttons. In Zen we strive not to have buttons to be pushed. To have buttons is to be a self. To be a self is not the way of Zen. In Zen, we strive not to be.

As Alfred Korzybski, the father of general semantics, said, "The difficulty with the verb 'to be' is that it implies a static, absolute quality, whereas the law of the universe is constant change." Once we say "we are," "that is," or use the verb "to be" in any form, we imagine something static and unchanged. We try to capture the object and stop it from changing. Once we say, "I am," we try to freeze ourselves or others. But the nature of the world, as we know from our Zen practice, is impermanent. Better to stay away from *I am, you are.* Sometimes, it is better not to speak at all. Better, perhaps, to listen.

Zen and Your Children

Children are wonderful. They fill us with joy and love, and they can wake us up again to the wonders of the world as we see things anew through their eyes. Children can also bring out the absolute worst in us, as they frustrate, confound, and bring us to anger. Children are a wonderful opportunity to practice.

QUESTION?

Should I make my children sit zazen?
Show your children the attraction of Zen through your actions and attitudes, but do not force it on them for any reason. If it looks like it works and they want what you have, they will develop a practice of their own eventually.

A friend tells this story: A mother and father arrive home with two gifts for their twin daughters. The gifts were two beautiful dolls, quite different from one another. The parents decided to ask the eldest twin to choose which doll she would like. She was silent for an awfully long time, looking desperately from one doll to the other. Finally, her mother said, "Which one would you like, sweetheart. Just choose."

Her daughter finally blurted out, "I want hers!" and pointed to her sister.

To live Zen practice is to give freely and to always have enough. The poor twin sister was desperate to have what her sister had. She was afraid not to have the right doll, and she knew whatever her sister had would perhaps be the better doll. Nevertheless, she has the ability to have the best doll right inside herself. We always have the best when we live with an open heart. We always have enough. Just enough.

Being Present

When we are with children we can strive to be present with our children. If they are misbehaving, we deal with the misbehavior in the present. We do not project that just because they are crying and screaming now they will be crying and screaming later when your guests arrive for dinner. Just because your child is having trouble reading today doesn't mean she will never learn to read. Live in the present and not the past or the future.

Care for your children. Take care of their health, both physical and emotional. Secure a financial future if possible. Show them good morals by being a living example of love and respect. Do not tell them one thing and do another. Be what you preach.

If you are truly present with your children, you will teach them how to be present with others. If you are distracted by work when you should be listening to your child tell you about her school day, you teach her that it is all right not to be present for others. Our children deserve our respect. Pay attention!

As much as you can, keep your children away from things that can negatively influence them. Give them a good education, and teach them how to care for themselves and the world around them. Keep your children clean, safe, and well-fed. However, do not overfeed them or give them too much. Give your children duties to perform so they can learn the joy of work practice. It is difficult to be present with your family as the world calls out to you. Work, friends, and obligations all call to you as you try to spend time with your family. If you practice your zazen, you will find that you are better able to be present and show up for your life.

Be willing to do what your child wants to do instead of forcing your child to do what you do. Perhaps you want to spend your weekend mountain-biking. You need the exercise and the feeling of the fresh air on your face after being caught up in the office all week. But your child doesn't like to mountain bike and wants to stay home to paint watercolor pictures. Can you forgo your bike ride to paint with your child? Imagine the gift you give your children when he knows you want to spend time with him more than you want to ride your mountain bike!

ALERT!

Teenagers can be particularly difficult as they deal with the changes in their bodies and lives, asserting their independence, and not always in a respectful and loving manner. Now more than ever is the time to be respectful, to listen, and to try to keep your children safe. If you listen carefully, you will not miss the signs of potential trouble you might otherwise miss.

Friendly Zen

There is an old Zen story about two friends that appears in the collection *Zen Flesh, Zen Bones*, by Paul Reps and Nyogen Senzaki.

One of the friends played the harp very skillfully. The other friend listened, just as skillfully. When the harpist played a song and sang about a mountain, the listening friend would say, "I can see the mountain before us."

When the harpist played a song about the water, his listening friend would say, "Here is the running stream!"

One day the listener fell sick and died. The harpist cut the strings on his instrument and never played again.

Interdependence and Kindness

This wonderful old Chinese story illustrates the interdependence of all creatures. Without someone to listen, the harpist doesn't play the same music. Their relationship is interdependent. Realize your interdependence in all of your friendships, and honor the part that you play. Be both a listener and a player at all times possible. To this day, the cutting of harp strings is seen as a symbol of intimate friendship.

*"Moment to Moment, how do you help others?
Not only human beings, but this whole world.
When enlightenment and correct life come together,
that means your life becomes truth, the suffering world
becomes paradise. Then you can change this suffering
world into paradise for others."* —Seung Sahn

The best way to get out of yourself is to do something for someone else. You don't have to have realized what no-self means before you start to practice this way of life. What can you do for your friends, those close to you and those you don't know at all, in a spirit of loving-kindness? Get out of your small self. Practice random acts of kindness, as they say. The way to happiness is straight out of your self.

Committing to Another

Love is a wonderful roller-coaster ride in life. You are extremely fortunate if you find someone to share your life with in a committed relationship. More than in most other kinds of relationships, the propensity for suffering here rears its head. Love often means the possibility of suffering. Practicing Zen in your love relationships does not mean that your love life will be suffering-free and joyous twenty-four hours a day, seven days a week. But practicing Zen in your love life does mean that you accept the suffering and remain open-hearted and compassionate. You sit, and you sit whether you suffer or not.

Finding another to share your life with, however, does not mean that you have found your missing half. You already have everything you need, and perhaps love is just a nice addition. No one else can make you whole. You are already whole. No one else can give you anything you don't already have, and if you are looking outside yourself for completion, you are indeed setting yourself up for suffering.

Live Separately Together

Living Zen in love is living separately together, "alone with others" as Stephen Batchelor says. It is realizing that you alone are responsible for yourself, you alone are accountable for your behavior. No matter how your love life is going, it is up to you to be compassionate, kind, respectful, and diligent. Do not have expectations of another, but be what you want to have. Be the lover you dream you could have. Give your love away as you would like to get it. Expect nothing, and you will live a wonderful life.

Do not look for trouble in your relationship where no trouble exists. Accept what your partner says as truth and let go. Trust your partner as you believe you should be trusted. Be present in your love life, and you will give your partner the greatest gift of all.

Hopefully, you have chosen a mate who is whole all by him- or herself. Hopefully, each of you can walk alone together through life, helping each other and being true friends. Then you will have found a relationship where true love exists and a deep friendship abides. You will have found someone to cut the harp strings with.

Don't Live in the Past

There is a wonderful story about Vietnamese Zen monk Thich Nhat Hanh in Sean Murphy's book *One Bird, One Stone*. An American veteran of the Vietnamese War approached Thich Nhat Hanh and told him that during an ambush in the war, he had killed five children. Now, he was so consumed by grief, he couldn't stand to be in the same room with any children at all.

Thich Nhat Hanh told him: "At this very moment, there are many children who are dying in the world. There are children who die just because they lack a single pill of medicine. If you are mindful, you can bring that pill to that child, and you can save his life. If you practice like that for five times, then you will save five children. Because what is to be done is to be done in the present moment. Forty thousand children die every day because of lack of food. Why do you have to cling to the past to think of the five who are already dead? You have the power to change things by touching the present moment."

Here indeed is a powerful lesson for us all in our relationships. Many people live in relationships where they have sharp past hurts that they hold onto as mantles against possible further pains. Do not live in the past. Forgive, release, and let go. Live in the present; it is all you ever have. Do not stay in a relationship that is damaging and harmful, but do not carry the past around with you like a huge sack of rocks. The past is gone, and all we have is the present moment. Right here, right now. Just breathe . . .

Marriage and Zen

Those who practice Zen throughout the years traditionally stay out of civic matters, so there are few formal, established ceremonial procedures for those life-changing events, such as marriage and divorce, birth and death. Until recently, a Zen marriage ceremony was extremely rare. That is not to say that you cannot have a Zen ceremony if you are getting married—you will most likely just have to come up with the trappings yourself.

"I'm not sitting only for me, or you, or the Minnesota Zen Center. I'm sitting for all sentient beings, all over the world, forever." —Dainin Katagiri Roshi

If you are interested in having a Zen priest officiate at your wedding, check with your local town and state law to make sure the marriage will be legal. In most states you should run into no difficulty. The officiant will sign the marriage certificate, and then the certificate will be filed with the state. Make sure you cover your state's basic requirements in the marriage ceremony, as they are applicable.

A Soto Zen Wedding

There is a wedding ceremony in the Soto tradition of Zen, but there are no formal proceedings in the Rinzai tradition. According to Jiho Sargent, in *108 Answers: Asking About Zen,* a Soto Zen wedding ceremony can include the following:

- Opening words by priest
- Reading of ceremony statement
- Sprinkling of water on the bride's and groom's heads to confer wisdom
- Presentation of Buddhist beads and wedding rings
- Chanting of the Three Refuges
- Vows
- Address by priest
- Chanting of the Four Vows
- Closing

A Rinzai Zen Wedding

A Rinzai ceremony would be similar. One of the authors, who practices with a Rinzai teacher, had a Zen ceremony and it followed a similar pattern, though the priest and the bride and groom arranged the ceremony themselves, like so:

- A short meditation led by the priest
- Readings (selected by bride and groom and read by family and friends)
- Sermon by Zen priest
- Recitation of Four Great Vows
- Personal vows and pronouncement

The personal vows chosen for this ceremony were as follows:

Do you, [bride's name here], promise to love, help, and protect [groom], and to support him on the path to awakening? I do.

Do you, [groom's name here], promise to love, help, and protect [bride], and to support her on the path to awakening? I do.

[Zen priest] Then as [name and title here], a teacher in the tradition of Rinzai Zen, I pronounce you wife and husband.

What Are the Four Great Vows?

Although there are few formal Zen wedding ceremonial procedures, a couple practicing Rinzai Zen sometimes do decide to formally exchange their vows in front of a priest. The Four Great Vows in Buddhism are:

1. Sentient beings are numberless. I vow to save them.
2. Desires are inexhaustible. I vow to put an end to them.
3. The Dharmas are boundless. I vow to master them.
4. The enlightened way is unattainable. I vow to attain it.

Compassion, Respect, and Practice

The stress during a Zen ceremony will be on compassion, respect, and practice. A Zen marriage will be like any other marriage: You must be selfless and kind, compromising and honorable. If you are practicing Zen, you are following the precepts and bringing respect for your spouse into every interaction. You will be faithful, honest, hardworking, and humble. A Zen marriage is no different from any other marriage. Nearly anyone who enters a marriage does so with a hopeful heart and a selfless dedication to making the marriage work. Zen marriages fail, just as other marriages fail.

We are all human, and we all change. Impermanence can apply to marriages as well. Living Zen in relationships basically means practicing respect and awareness at every opportunity. The more you sit zazen, the more natural this will become to you. You will move beyond ego into a wonderful, selfless place where you can truly give to your relationships instead of grasping for more, more, and yet more. If you sit, and if you live in the present, you can show up for your marriage and all of your relationships—contributing to mature, loving, equal relationships that foster growth, harmony, and friendship. (E)

Chapter 8

Using Your Teacher in Zen Practice

A teacher is fundamental to a thriving Zen practice. A teacher will direct you when you lose your way, will inspire and motivate you to keep pushing, will help you keep the faith in your practice. Your relationship with your teacher will be very intimate and unlike anything you have ever known before. It is this person who will first see you as you truly are.

Who's the Guy in the Funny Robe?

If you've visited a zendo or Zen meditation center, you might have entered the room wondering who the person in the funny robe was. That's the Zen teacher, who will become your guide and help you find your true nature, your Buddha-nature.

FACT

The Zen priest is known as the *roshi,* which means "teacher." Another word you might hear for the Zen priest is *sensei,* which also means "teacher."

A Zen teacher can be either a man or a woman—there is no discrimination when it comes to waking up. Although the Buddha was at first resistant to allowing women into his *sangha*—he believed they might be a distraction for the male participants—he eventually invited his aunt Prajapati to become a nun. Five hundred women quickly joined Prajapati as nuns, and the *sangha* swelled with women striving to wake up as well.

The Roshi

It is the Zen teacher's goal to help his or her students reach enlightenment. The teacher can have a position in a monastery, a Zen center, or even a more informal gathering of people with no central location. Most Zen monasteries will have a *roshi* and perhaps another cleric as well, who will be situated to take over the leadership if the presiding priest leaves, retires, or dies.

The *roshi* is usually the hardest worker in the Zen community. He or she will be the first one up, waking the other members of the community in time for early morning practice. The *roshi* will lead sutra practice, sit zazen, work, run any services that are scheduled in the monastery, meet with students, and give lectures.

Qualifications

You might wonder what kind of qualification your Zen teacher will have. Your Zen teacher will have realized enlightenment. The transmission of the lineage from his teacher will pass on to him when his teacher deems him ready. Many Zen teachers will acknowledge that a student has had *daikensho* (the great enlightenment experience) but will require that the student continue to practice for a number of years before taking on students herself.

Not all persons who realize enlightenment go on to teach. In Zen, teaching is following the path of the bodhisattva. A bodhisattva is someone who has realized enlightenment but who defers his or her own final enlightenment in order to help others attain the same. In the United States, most people who practice Zen are lay practitioners. While traditionally the teaching and practicing of the dharma was done by monks, today in the Western world this has changed.

"In Zen practice, one cannot emphasize enough the vital role of the Zen teacher who has charted the paths of this arduous journey to the core of one's being and is familiar with the terrain."
—Ruben Habito, Healing Breath

The Roadmap to Enlightenment

The importance of the role of the teacher in Zen cannot be stressed too much. You can read about Zen but you will not understand it until you start a practice. Zen lives in the practice and the actions you take. You cannot read your way through Zen, as it does not take place in the mind alone but in the body and spirit as well. It is easy to get lost without a teacher to direct you. A teacher has been through the incredible Zen journey and through the labyrinth passages of Zen practice. Your Zen teacher will have the road map that you will attempt to follow to discover your own true nature. He or she has experienced the process of waking up and knows what the journey entails.

Finding a Teacher

How can you find a guide through the maze of Zen practice? Fortunately, Zen has taken a firm hold in the Western world and there are

Zen teachers all over the United States and Canada, as well as Europe.

You can find a Zen teacher at your local Zen center, a community monastery, or you can look online. To find a teacher online, go to a search engine, type in your location and "Zen teacher," and see what comes up. You can also try the Yellow Pages, word of mouth, or local bookstores. You can call your local town hall and see if anyone there knows of local Zen teachers, or try the closest university, which might have a community. Hospitals also can be a good source of spiritual information, as can natural food stores and yoga teachers.

These are all ways in which you can go out and find yourself a Zen teacher. Or, on the other hand, you could just sit back and relax and wait. As the old saying goes, when the student is ready, the teacher appears.

ALERT!

You should not overlook the fact that teachers and lessons are all around us and appear in our lives all the time. Do find yourself a Zen teacher specifically, but do not shut your eyes to the possibilities of lessons all around you. Even the stop sign at your corner has something to teach you.

Don't worry about whether or not you have found yourself a genuine Zen master for a teacher. The most important thing is your practice. Whether your practice is good or bad, whether your teacher is good or bad, this is all part of the practice. Trust the world to provide the lessons you learn. The entire world is your classroom.

Preparing for a Meeting

So what do you need to do to prepare for a meeting with a Zen teacher? Nothing. There is an old Zen story that goes something like this.

A university professor, wanting to inquire about Zen, joins a Zen master for tea. The Zen master pours the tea into the professor's teacup, filling the cup, but then he keeps on pouring. The professor watches the cup overflow and cannot restrain himself from calling out. "It is overflowing! No more will fit in the cup."

"Like this cup," the Zen master says, "you are full of your own opinions and ideas. How can I show you Zen if you are already full? You must first empty your cup."

Interacting with Your Teacher

Your teacher is a mirror for yourself. When your teacher meets you, he meets himself. When you meet your teacher, you meet yourself for the first time. As John Daido Loori says in *The Eight Gates of Zen,* "This intimacy is what the whole process of the teacher-student relationship is about. Ultimately, it is the student meeting himself and the teacher meeting himself; the teacher teaching himself, the student teaching himself. Body and mind fall away and there is a merging." Because of this, a Zen teacher will be hard to define. In fact, the teacher might appear completely unassuming and rather indistinct. When you interact with your Zen teacher, you will come face to face with yourself, and if you are paying attention, you will recognize this.

A student was struggling over whether or not she should make a deeper commitment to her Zen practice.
She approached Suzuki Roshi and said,
"Inside me there is a yes and a no."
"Follow the yes," Suzuki said.

Silence

A student was frustrated with practice and was thinking of giving up. She confronted the Zen teacher with her frustration. "I no longer know why I am just sitting there. I want to give up." She wanted the Zen teacher to talk her into staying, to say what a wonderful job she was doing, and to tell her she would be rewarded for all this great effort. But her teacher sat there in silence. She grew irritated and went home in anger, knowing she was going to give up Zen forever.

Sitting around was a complete waste of time. But the teacher's silence rang in her ears and hung over her for days, echoing in her mind. A realization started to grow deep inside herself. If she was not willing, she had no teacher—the teacher did not exist. If she could not show up for Zen, there would be no teacher to show up for her. The willingness to sit had to come from within. She saw deep into her true nature when she sat with the teacher's silence and had a small awakening. She showed up the next week at her sitting practice with a newfound understanding of herself and completely committed to her practice. It didn't matter how she felt. All that mattered was practice. Silence was a great teacher.

It is important to commit to one teacher in Zen practice. Do not move from teacher to teacher unless it is unavoidable. Teaching styles may vary, and you might become confused. Entrust one teacher with your practice. Constancy can be a great teacher in and of itself.

Silence might be the answer you often receive when you ask questions of your Zen teacher. Sometimes, silence is the appropriate answer to many of our questions. When a student asked the Buddha 2,500 years ago if there was an afterlife, the Buddha told the student that he was like a man who had been shot by a poisoned arrow. Before he will allow his doctor to remove the arrow, he wants to know where the arrow came from, who shot the arrow, what kind of poison was used, why he was shot, and so on. He would most likely die before his questions were ever answered.

Our questions are often about what will happen later, what is to come, what we can expect. Your teacher will help you realize that life is to be lived now. Do not worry about what comes next. Everything happens in the moment. There is nothing else.

Showing the Way

Your true self is revealed to you through the encounters with your teacher. Each encounter you have is a step toward this realization. Whether you meet over tea or over a koan, have a question and answer period, or meet for a brief encounter during the day, every meeting will show your nature to you as you look into the face of your teacher. When you are ready, the realization will come. Your true nature will be revealed, and you will be awake. Your teacher is merely showing the way to see something you already have. She is not giving a gift; she is pointing the way to your true self.

Think of those abstract ink drawings that were popular in the 1980s and 1990s. If you stared at the drawing for a long time and relaxed your eyes, you would suddenly see a three-dimensional lion, or owl, or a monkey staring back out at you. If you blinked, the image would disappear. The image is always there in the drawing, but you cannot see it unless the conditions are right. In the same manner, we cannot see our true selves unless we clear the clutter of our ego away and overcome the conditioning we have had all of our lives.

ALERT!

Enter a relationship with your teacher an open heart, an open mind, and the willingness to practice, no matter whether the practice is good or bad, easy or hard, tiring or invigorating. Your teacher will show you the way if you just keep at it.

The Buddha once said, "You and others like you still listen to the Dharma with the conditioned mind, and so the Dharma becomes conditioned as well, and you do not obtain the Dharma-nature. This is similar to a person pointing his finger at the moon to show it to someone else. Guided by the finger, the other person should see the moon. If he looks at the finger instead and mistakes it for the moon, he loses not only the moon but the finger also. Why? Because he mistakes the pointing finger for the bright moon." In other words, don't mistake the teaching for the truth, don't mistake the teacher for your Buddha-nature. The teacher is only pointing at the moon, the teacher is not the moon itself.

Learning Through Pain

Our greatest teacher in our practice can be pain. While sitting zazen, the student of Zen can encounter quite a bit of pain—both emotional and physical pain. Sitting in one spot for any length of time is initially very disturbing to most people. When we are uncomfortable, we are used to moving about freely to escape the uncomfortable feelings. Sitting through the desire to move can be very difficult.

Physical and Emotional Hardships

Although it wouldn't appear to be the case, sitting zazen requires a tremendous amount of energy. The better physical shape you are in, the less tiring it will be. You do build up a tolerance and capacity for sitting the longer you do it.

Unwavering determination is essential for practice. In order to sit through both emotional and physical pain, it is necessary to be completely determined to do so. There is no indecision or turning back. Once the sit starts, you vow not to move.

It might seem ridiculous to the person who has never tried zazen that it is extremely difficult to sit still. But sit still for a period of time, and you will find your legs going dead or cramping up. Your neck or back might hurt. You will itch, find a stray hair that is bothering you, or want to sneeze or cough. Your nose might run or your toes might start to tingle. You might feel tremendous fear if your legs go numb. But don't worry, most cramps, numbness, and discomfort will disappear within minutes of rising.

However, the emotional hardships can be more difficult. Some students encounter great fear as they sit for the first time. They are faced with themselves and with thoughts they have been avoiding. Sitting through this pain—both emotional and physical—teaches us quite a bit about ourselves and the world. By willingly enduring the pain that arises in zazen, we reconnect with the world and the barriers between ourselves and the rest of the world start to fade.

The Doorway to Buddha-Nature

When you sit, you might find that the pain in your legs actually disappears completely. Keep going in your practice past the pain, even past the no-pain. The longer you practice zazen, you will find the duality you live with disappears. The barrier between you and everything else will start to vanish. So sit through the pain. Find the courage to move past the pain. Pain is a great teacher. You will learn much about yourself as you learn about pain. It will prove an invaluable lesson in your life. Do not judge the pain. Do not say, "The pain is bad. It is hurting me." Just sit with the pain. It is only pain—everything is all right. The pain is a doorway through which you can move into a new world where you will eventually come face to-face with your Buddha-nature. All it takes is courage.

FACT

In some Zen centers, someone walks around the zendo carrying a flat paddle called a *kyosaku*. The *kyosaku* is used to strike the person sitting zazen whose posture is incorrect. Some people request a strike by the *kyosaku* as it can eliminate pain. The *kyosaku* strikes the person across the shoulders.

The Student/Teacher Relationship

When you are starting out in Zen practice, the relationship you have with your Zen teacher will be a new relationship in your life, like nothing you've ever had before. Let it develop naturally, and you will find your feet. However, there are some basics you might want to have under your belt beforehand.

Questions to Avoid

Your Zen teacher is not your therapist. If you approach your teacher with all kinds of questions about your life and your feelings, you are not going to get the answers you might like.

Keep your questions focused on your practice. Do not expect to have a sit-down with your teacher once a week during which you fill him or her in on everything you've been feeling and experiencing in the past seven days. If you have had a rough childhood, a bad marriage, a mountain of debt, if you are unemployed, overemployed, underweight, overweight, obsessive-compulsive, or have a gambling problem, your Zen teacher will most likely not be interested. If you ask your teacher what to do, you might get this answer: "Just sit."

Also, your Zen teacher will not provide you with advice on how to run your life. Do not take questions to your teacher such as: Should I give up my statistics job and do something that benefits society? Shall I drive a car that uses less fuel? Should I become a vegetarian? Should I divorce my husband and enter a monastery? However, if you want to know if your posture is correct, or if you want to ask about your breath meditation or fill your teacher in on the progress of your meditation practice, please do so.

You can work out your life issues in Zen practice, but it will not be done by talking. It will be done by sitting and watching your thoughts as you let them go. Your thoughts rise, you watch them, and then let them go.

Your Zen teacher is not your lawyer (though he may be a lawyer), not your taxi service (though she might drive a taxi), and not an accountant either. In the initial stages of your practice, your teacher might be more encouraging and more open to questions than he or she will be later on. As you progress in your practice, the teacher might become harsher or push you further.

What to Discuss

In *The Three Pillars of Zen,* Roshi Philip Kapleau discusses the different types of individual aspirations students bring to Zen practice. He tells us there are basically four main groups of aspiration:

1. The student who has no faith in Zen and little understanding.
2. The student who undertakes Zen practice in order to improve mental or physical conditions.
3. The student who wants to walk in the footsteps of the Buddha.
4. The student who is wholly determined to realize his true nature.

Roshi Kapleau asks students to tell him which group they think they fit into so he can best help them with their zazen practice and assign them the kind of zazen that will best work for them. This is the kind of discussion that you can have with your teacher. Tell your teacher what you know of Zen, what your level of aspiration is, and what your dedication level is like. Your aspirations might change over time, and you can update your teacher if necessary. Stick to dialogue about your practice. However, your teacher will let you know the nature of the relationship.

Trusting Your Teacher

Your Zen teacher wants to help the world wake up. He or she has vowed to help all sentient beings attain enlightenment. There is a beautiful Zen story that well illustrates this, found in Paul Reps and Nyogen Senzaki's wonderful collection, *Zen Flesh, Zen Bones.*

> *A division of the Japanese army was engaged in a pretend battle and took up residence in a Zen temple while doing so. The cook was told by Gasan, the head of the temple, to feed the officers the same fare as the monks in the temple.*
>
> *This made the soldiers angry, as they were used to being treated much better than this. One went to Gasan and said, "Who do you think we are? We are soldiers, sacrificing our lives for our country."*
>
> *And Gasan replied sternly, "Who do you think we are? We are soldiers of humanity, aiming to save all sentient beings."*

Your Zen teacher will stick by you. He or she will be there to help you realize your true nature and the true nature of the universe. Do not be afraid of your teacher, and do not worry about yourself. Do not hesitate to ask questions if you have them. Just trust in the answers, even if the answer is silence. Especially if the answer is silence! You will show your teacher your truest self. Ⓔ

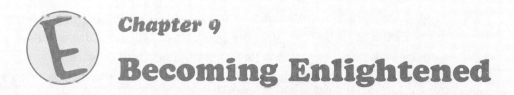

Chapter 9

Becoming Enlightened

There are many different reasons to engage in Zen practice. Some people want to have a more serene and peaceful life. Some are curious about Eastern spirituality, and others seek to discover their true selves. But there are those who get bitten by the Zen bug and want more than anything to see that light at the end of the tunnel: to wake up and realize enlightened mind.

Lighting the Way

The Buddha woke us up to the possibility of a different way of life. We know this different way from all of the people who have gone before us. Many generations of Buddhists practiced the way of Zen and passed it, from mind to mind, down to us today.

It is truly amazing to have the chance to practice Zen. If you are ready to practice, you can consider yourself a very fortunate person. It takes many lifetimes to be born into the position of being a human who can actually wake up. As you practice, that gratitude will grow, and you will be humbled by the opportunity to sit on a cushion and practice your zazen.

Through Practice to Nirvana

Zen practice is a way of life and, as Roshi Suzuki told us, sitting zazen is enlightenment. But as we sit, we start to change, and our zazen changes as we change. Realizing enlightenment is a wonderful possibility if you practice Zen. However, there is no *guarantee* that you will wake up in this lifetime. Does that mean you shouldn't bother practicing? No, of course not. Practicing Zen will have a positive effect on your life, whether you realize enlightenment or not. Learning to live in this moment, right now, is a wonderful way to enjoy your life. Becoming a compassionate, centered, present person is also a gift to yourself, to your family and friends, and to the entire world.

In Sanskrit, the word "nirvana" means to "blow out," to extinguish. Once we extinguish the fire of our desires, greed, delusion, and hatred, we realize nirvana.

The Buddha said: "Nirvana is the highest happiness."

There is, certainly, the possibility that at any time you might attain nirvana. But you should engage in practice here and now, and turn your thoughts away from the future. Do not concentrate on the possibility of waking up, as that day may never come, and in the meanwhile you will have wasted your moments *now*.

Waking Up

As we have seen, some Zen Buddhists believe that enlightenment happens in an instant, while others believe it happens a little bit at a time. Some people believe just sitting is enlightenment itself.

The seeming paradox of Zen is that if you want enlightenment, it is evident you do not have it. If you have it, you do not want it, as wanting it would never occur to you. Zen is so confusing, you say! No, *Zen* is not confusing. It is our minds that confuse us by engaging in dualistic thinking. Let's take another look at the Four Noble Truths:

1. Life is filled with suffering.
2. Suffering is caused by desire.
3. Desires can end.
4. The way to end desire is to follow the Eightfold Path.

So here we are at the Eightfold Path once again. As we saw in Chapter 4, the Eightfold Path is made up of these steps: Right Understanding, Right Thought, Right Speech, Right Action, Right Livelihood, Right Effort, Right Mindfulness, and Right Concentration. If we apply each of these steps to our lives, we can realize enlightenment. So enlightenment means following the way of the Eightfold Path in order to extinguish desire. Once you have extinguished desire, you are released from suffering, and you are truly awake. All boundaries between you and the rest of the world disappear. There is no longer dualistic thinking; there is no separation between you and anything. You want for nothing. Therefore, you see, if you want for nothing you do not even want enlightenment. Simple!

QUESTION?

Where does enlightenment usually take place?
Enlightenment can happen anywhere, at any time. Some students realize nirvana during zazen, some during *teisho,* many while on sesshin, but usually it happens during a time of intense concentration. You can realize enlightenment upon hearing a certain phrase, when seeing a flower, or when watching a bird.

Dropping Ego

In *The Three Pillars of Zen,* by Philip Kapleau, Yashutani-roshi tells a student, "It is true that the majority of people think of themselves as a body and a mind, but that doesn't make them any the less mistaken. The fact is that in their essential nature, all sentient beings transcend their body and their mind, which are not two but one. The failure of human beings to perceive this fundamental truth is the cause of their sufferings . . . We delude ourselves into accepting the reality of an ego-I, estrangement and strife inevitably follow. The Buddha in his enlightenment perceived that ego is not indigenous to human nature. With full enlightenment, we realize we possess the universe, so why grasp for what is inherently ours?"

Some people feel very threatened at the idea of letting go of their ego. During early practice it is not uncommon to get angry at the thought of letting go of yourself. But do not attach to the fear. Watch it arise, acknowledge it, and let it go. It will pass.

Initially, as we begin our Zen practice, it is with great doubt that we encounter the idea that "the ego is not indigenous to human nature." We believe we are entirely our egos. If we do not have "I," then what do we have? Most people have great difficulty imagining the possibility of dropping ego, let alone *wanting* to drop ego. It usually takes great pain to find the way to this determination. And certainly, without great faith, great doubt, and great determination, it is an overwhelming proposition.

Nonattachment

It is very important not to get attached to the idea of enlightenment. Our understanding of enlightenment in our unenlightened minds will turn out to be a far cry from reality. We might expect to be completely transformed, to be godlike, untouchable, unflappable, or capable of magic tricks. We might expect that we can walk across hot coals, lie on a bed of nails, or set ourselves on fire painlessly. We might envision ourselves smiling beatifically at everyone who comes across our path. Or perhaps we might fear we will no longer be in love, that our wives and husbands will just be like anyone else to us, that we will have no desire for the things we hold dear today.

"There simply is nothing to which we can attach ourselves, no matter how hard we try. In time, things will change and the conditions that produced our current desires will be gone. Why then cling to them now?"
—Master Hsing Yun

Whether your vision of enlightenment is a positive one or whether it is one filled with fear, let go of your imaginings and just deal with the here and now. If you reach nirvana, you will have the answers to your questions then. It is impossible to know the unknown now.

The Great Mystery

Enlightenment is a mystery, even to those who have experienced it. Enlightenment is also different for each person. As Sean Murphy says in *One Bird, One Stone,* "In the Zen world, talking about enlightenment experiences is a bit like discussing your sex life. It can be done, under the right circumstances, but it has to be for the right reasons—and it's not for general public consumption."

When we talk about something, sometimes we come to believe what we say, even if it is not quite true. We can freeze a moment in time and make it bigger and bigger until it hardly resembles the original moment at all. Have you ever told a story so many times that you are no longer sure if the story is really what happened or it is just an exaggeration of the truth? If we talk about our enlightenment experiences, we run the risk of attaching to them. We run the risk of losing them by replacing the real experience with an imagined memory of the experience. Live your experiences as they occur; do not try to go back and relive them. Each moment is unique, and you cannot relive it twice. This is one of the wonders of life.

An enlightened person doesn't talk about nirvana. Instead, the enlightened express their enlightenment with every action they take. You *live* your enlightened mind with everything you do. Talking about enlightenment is, to use a now-familiar expression, like a finger pointing at the moon. Talking about anything is forming an idea about something. An idea of something is not the thing. It is an idea of the thing. The idea of enlightenment is not enlightenment.

Hui Neng, who eventually became the Sixth Patriarch of China, realized enlightenment while walking through the market. He overheard someone speaking a line from the Diamond Sutra and it is said at that moment his mind opened like a flower and he attained complete enlightenment instantaneously.

Direct Experience

The only way to reach enlightenment is through direct experience. You cannot reach or understand enlightenment through discussion or conceptualization. Talking about it and thinking about it are not knowing it. When we talk about something, we break it down into pieces.

We can describe our sandwich by saying that it is two pieces of thin white bread with a small crust, with thick, creamy peanut butter slathered in between the slices of bread. We can say the sandwich is stale, delicious, soggy, heavy, pretty, plain, and so on. However, your attempt to describe the sandwich is an attempt to trap that sandwich in a moment in time. What is your sandwich a week from now? Is it the same sandwich? What is your sandwich after you eat the sandwich? At what point does the sandwich stop being a sandwich and start being you? At what point does it stop being a sandwich, stop being you, and start being waste matter? Is it a sandwich while a bite of it is in your mouth? What about the baker who made the bread and the oven the bread came from? Isn't even the heavy industrial oven a part of the sandwich? Isn't the baker, who sweats and labors over your bread part of the sandwich? What about the peanuts and the earth from which the peanuts came?

The experience of enlightenment cannot be conceptualized or expressed through language. If you are to understand the true nature of reality, you must experience that reality directly. So read away, but then put down the book and practice. It is the only way you will experience your true self and see the world's true nature.

We tend to view things as if they are completely separate from all other things. We try to view each part of our world as individual, frozen pieces of matter. But this is an incomplete view of reality. Everything is interconnected.

Experience versus Conceptualization

When we describe things we are conceptualizing them. We are not experiencing them. The experience of the sandwich is much different from the conceptualization of the sandwich, just as the experience of enlightenment is much different from the conceptualization of enlightenment. When we eat a sandwich, our minds create a self who eats and a sandwich that gets eaten. However, the experience of eating the sandwich is completely different. Where does the sandwich begin, and where do you end? It is easy to see that once the sandwich enters your mouth, the division gets blurred. But this division is entirely created by our duality-perceiving minds. Try this exercise. When you start to perceive things as dualistic, say to yourself, "Not two. One."

In *One Bird, One Stone,* Sean Murphy tells this enlightenment story.

> *Maezumi Roshi sits on the porch of the Los Angeles Zen Center when a disheveled, drunk, and depressed man staggers up.*
> *"Wharrsh . . . it like to be enlightened?" the drunk man asks.*
> *Maezumi looked at him before answering:*
> *"Depressing," he said.*

Now, after saying all that, there is one description of enlightenment that we liked very much. In *Journey to the Center,* Matthew Flickstein says the following: "At the moment of enlightenment, the concept of an experiencer who is having an experience totally dissolves. It is analogous to what would happen to a salt doll who jumped into the ocean to see what it was like; the doll would become one with the ocean that it was experiencing." Wonderful!

"Enlightenment has to do with relationship—not with any one individual's attainments—and in particular with the kinds of relationship in which everything is at stake and nothing is in principle excluded as impossible. In short . . . enlightenment should not be seen as private and experiential in nature, but as irreducibly and intimately social." —Peter Hershock

Sitting as Enlightenment

The purpose of Zen is to see things as they really are. As Bodhidharma said, Zen is "a special transmission outside the scriptures, not based on words or letters, a direct pointing to the heart of reality so that we might see into our own nature and wake up." When we see things exactly as they are, we are truly awake. And so when we sit, we let go of our old ways of thinking. Seeing the world, we enter the moment. As we enter the moment, we see things as they really are and we are awake, perhaps for the first time. In Zen, we see things as they truly are and we let them go as it is. We observe our thoughts and we let them go. We observe our breath and we let it go. We hear a bird sing, and we let it go. If you always keep your mind on your breath and your breathing, you will experience the freedom of Zen.

Controlling Our Thoughts

In *Zen Mind, Beginner's Mind,* Shunryu Suzuki tells us that the way to control your cattle is to give them a large meadow to roam in. In the same way, he tells us, we can control our thoughts. Do not try to stop your thoughts or wrestle them to the ground. Let them run their way through your mind. Let them come in, let them go out. It is when we try to control something that we find we have no control at all. Suzuki tells us that if we try to control our thinking it means we are bothered by it. Do not be bothered by anything. Everything is perfect exactly as it is.

Shikantaza

So when you are sitting, just sit. This is called *shikantaza*—just sitting. In *shikantaza* there is no goal—in the way there is a striving for enlightenment in other Zen practices. Enlightenment is realized with sitting. Sitting is the practice in and of itself. Remember, we already have what we need. As we sit, we realize our Buddha-nature. Therefore, sitting is enlightenment itself.

FACT

When we just sit, there is no other. There is no I, there is no you, there is no room that we sit in, no time that we sit. Everything is as one. We are just awareness as we sit, breathing in, breathing out.

In nearly everything we do, we have goals. The goals might be very clear, or they might be subtle. We might go to school to get a good job, we might eat to curb our appetite. We diet to lose weight. We exercise to stay fit or train for a marathon. We garden to keep the weeds from taking over, and we care for our children so they will be safe. But in *shikantaza* we have no goal. We sit and rest in awareness. There is no goal except to be aware of the moment. Even if we sit to become enlightened, we are creating a situation in which we want to be somewhere else: Where we are isn't where we want to be. But when we sit *shikantaza,* we accept that this moment is exactly as it is meant to be. It is perfect, and so is everything in the moment, including ourselves.

I'm Awake: Now What?

Once you achieve enlightenment, then what? You keep practicing. Even the Dalai Lama meditates every day. Sitting is enlightenment itself, and it is through sitting that you realize that everyone is one, everything is of the same thing. Does the wave know it is part of the ocean? The wave starts far off the shore and crests as it comes in. It reaches its peak then crashes on the beach, flowing back into the water until it is no longer discernible. We are much like that wave—a part of the huge ocean of the universe.

"Enlightenment, for a wave in the ocean, is the moment the wave realizes it is water. When we realize we are not separate, but a part of the huge ocean of everything, we become enlightened. We realize this through practice, and we remain awake and aware of this through more practice." —Thich Nhat Hanh

Some people who realize enlightenment go on to serve others by teaching or doing some kind of helpful work. Others don't change much, but they experience their lives differently than they did before. What you do once you realize enlightenment is up to you. While everything changes on the inside, you might decide not to change much on the outside.

The Bodhisattva Path

As mentioned earlier, one of the choices you can make as an enlightened being is to spend your life in service to others. This is the bodhisattva path. A bodhisattva is a person who either has already attained enlightenment or is ready to attain the final enlightenment but puts it off in order to re-enter the cycle of *samsara* and save all sentient beings. A bodhisattva is the embodiment of compassion.

A bodhisattva willingly strives to be born once again into the endless cycles of *samsara* in order to constantly help others toward enlightenment. More simply, a bodhisattva is someone who dedicates his or her life to helping others. Wisdom is necessary for the bodhisattva so that he or she can realize how to help others attain nirvana. This elevated degree of compassion—loving all beings and all states completely and helping them toward enlightenment—is known as *skillful means*. Wisdom is part of the skillful means the bodhisattva must have in order to help others. This wisdom heart is also called *bodhicitta*. All bodhisattvas generate *bodhicitta*. Here are some modern-day bodhisattvas.

FACT

You may be familiar with one of the bodhisattvas who is often represented in Buddhist artwork. Manjushri, the bodhisattva of wisdom, symbolizes the wisdom one needs in order to seek the truth. He is often seen with one hand holding a sword and the sacred text of wisdom—the *Prajna-paramita Sutra*. The sword symbolizes the need to cut through illusion to the heart of wisdom.

Thich Nhat Hanh

Thich Nhat Hanh is a modern-day bodhisattva whose efforts at worldwide peace have inspired people all over the world. In 1967 he was nominated for the Nobel Peace Prize by Martin Luther King, Jr. Perhaps one of the most beloved Buddhist teachers in the West, Thich Nhat Hanh's teachings on mindfulness, peace, and religious tolerance have touched the hearts of millions. Thich Nhat Hanh was Chairman of the Vietnamese Peace Brigade during the Vietnam War. He has tirelessly strived to promote peace and interreligious tolerance, gaining a loyal following the world over.

He has brought the similarities between Christianity and Buddhism to the attention of many and has opened eyes and hearts wherever he teaches. He continues to show us that we are all connected and all the same, and his teachings are a great bridge for any who choose to cross. Thich Nhat Hanh teaches the essence of Zen, but he also imparts the essence of all religions. At the heart of every religion is the desire for love and true connection with something greater than ourselves— whether we call it the Truth, God, or Allah—and with each other.

Joan Halifax

Another bodhisattva in our midst is Joan Halifax, founder and roshi of the Upaya Zen Center in Santa Fe, New Mexico. She started the program Being with the Dying, which is aimed at helping caregivers work with dying people and at changing our relationship to both the dying and living. The program focuses on training health-care professionals who can then take their work with the dying back to their own institutions. They can then teach these practices to other health-care professionals. The center opens its doors to the public with retreats aimed at caregivers and the terminally or seriously ill, helping them to practice mindfulness, compassion, and honesty.

These are just two examples of modern-day bodhisattvas, but there are many to be found living among us.

ALERT!

The goal of a bodhisattva is to achieve the highest level of being. The bodhisattva strives to help you find your Buddha-nature and strives to help all sentient beings find their Buddha-natures. The Buddha is the ultimate bodhisattva.

Engaging the World

The spirit of service and giving is at the heart of Zen practice. Zen aims to open the heart, and when the heart is open, we live for others. When we live our life for others, we are engaged with the world, helping the world to be a better place. Service is an integral part of practice. Practice Zen by getting out there and making the world a better place. Volunteer your time, and connect with others. Be a part of your community. It is by giving away that we get so much back.

If you are awake, you see clearly that nothing is independent, that everything is connected. It then becomes difficult to sit back and do nothing. Everyone is a mirror. If you see someone hurting, then you will hurt as well. Helping others starts to seem selfish as so much is gotten back in return.

How to Help?

There are so many ways to give, large and small. Practice both in your daily life. Small ways to give include simple things like these: smiling at a stranger, making dinner for an elderly neighbor, cleaning up garbage in your neighborhood, or taking in a stray animal. Here are a few larger ways to help: volunteering at a hospice program or at your local hospital, or working at a homeless shelter or animal shelter. Driving for Meals on Wheels is a wonderful way to help out the sick and needy in your own backyard. Whatever you do, you will quickly realize that you feel better in this world when you are helping others. It is the best way to help yourself.

When you realize enlightenment, you will become the essence of compassion. As such, you might be driven to dedicate your life in service to others.

Chapter 10

Zen and Troubled Times

S ometimes our biggest stumbling blocks to Zen practice are hard times. When tragedy strikes, it can be very difficult to continue a strong practice. We are unprepared, and we are caught off-guard. Our Zen practice probably doesn't count for much if it can't be there with us when we need it most. So let's take a look at how you can handle tough times with a Zen approach.

Suffering

According to Zen, life is filled with suffering. But the kind of suffering you experience when you lose a family member is quite different from the kind of suffering you experience when you are longing for a new car. Maintaining a Zen attitude to life is much easier when things are going your way! Tragedy puts everyone to the test, and tragedy, sadly, often wins. But when tough times hit you—and they will, as no one is exempt from life's pains as well as pleasures—you can rely on your practice to help pull you through.

Accept Adversity

We *can* accept what is happening to us. Acceptance is an enormously powerful tool in life at the heart of Zen practice. When bad things happen, it is human nature to try to worm out of the way. Denial is a very powerful force in many people's lives. If a person finds out she has cancer, one of the first things she will do is deny it. Elizabeth Kübler-Ross, in her powerful book *On Death and Dying,* relates the five stages that a dying person goes through when they are told they have a terminal illness: denial, anger, bargaining, depression, and acceptance. Our first reaction is often to say, "No!" when something terrible is happening to us. But as many of us have found out in life, often the greatest tragedies make way for the greatest gifts. Through a newfound knowledge of terminal illness, many people have remarked that they truly woke up and felt more alive than they ever had in their life to date.

"It is often thought that the Buddha's doctrine teaches us that suffering will disappear if one has meditated long enough, or if one sees everything differently. It isn't that at all. Suffering isn't going to go away; the one who suffers is going to go away." —Ayya Khema

Live in the Day

One way to use your practice when suffering hits is to look for the silver lining in the very dark cloud. The dharma is everywhere, and lessons abound. Do not live in the future but live in the present instead. If you are dying, die when you die and not today. You probably still have so much life left in you that to die before your time would really be the most horrible tragedy. Even if you have one day, there is so much beauty and life in that one day. Don't waste it worrying about tomorrow.

Practice Sitting

When tragedy hits, sit no matter what. Sit if you are in pain, sit if you are weeping, sit if you are too tired to hold up your head. Sit if you are due at a funeral, if your family needs you, if you have a week's worth of food to make in two hours for your suffering neighbors. If you sit, you will improve your chances of weathering the storm. If you can weather the storm, you can be of help to others who might need you very much.

Turn to Others

Turn your mind to the others in your life who need comfort, assistance, and peace. Of course, staying tuned to the moment is very hard work. We want nothing more than to run away. But stay with whatever is happening in your life, and accept reality with open arms.

FACT

Remember that awakening means realizing what is really happening—living in the here and now. So when you feel yourself getting caught up in present circumstances, stop and ask yourself, "What is happening right now?" Be mindful of your situation.

Worrying

How much time in your life have you spent worrying? Worrying must be one of the greatest wastes of time known to man. When we worry, we are living in a constant "What if . . . ?" Live now; do not live in the future what-ifs. What are you worried about right now? Maybe your car payment is coming up and you don't have the money to pay it. Maybe you are afraid that you might be laid off at work. Maybe your mother is sick and you are waiting for test results. Maybe you are worried your dog may dig a hole under your new fence and run away while you're at work. Maybe you are worried that the lump in your breast is cancer. You could be worried about ten thousand things.

Unnecessary Stress?

Life can be filled with things to worry over. However, many of these same things we worry about can have a golden opportunity within their center. If you get laid off, perhaps it will free you up to get that dream job you had been afraid to pursue. Perhaps your mother's illness is an opportunity for the two of you to get closer and share a more intimate bond than has been possible thus far. Even something as frightening as cancer can completely transform you into a happier and more peaceful, satisfied person.

Sometimes those things we worry over never come to be. Sometimes they come to be, but the results birth opportunities we never dreamed possible.

Your Zen practice can be very useful in times of great stress. If you feel anxious, just go back to your breath. Breathe in deeply, breathe out. Concentrate on your breath, and it will help to keep you calm. Use your breath meditation to help you cope with difficult emotions.

Other times, the very thing we are afraid of turns out to be, in the end, the thing we would wish for if we only knew to do so. A woman was waiting for test results to find out if she had multiple sclerosis. Her husband worried and worried that she would have it, all the while praying for something else. The doctor eventually said it might not be multiple sclerosis but could be something much worse. Before he knew it, the husband was praying his wife had multiple sclerosis after all! We always think we know the answers and we know what is best, but we rarely, if ever, do.

Stressed Out and Sick

It is awful to be sick and filled with stress. Sickness can wear us down, making us feel tired, depleted, and useless. Sometimes, however, our emotions surrounding our sickness are worse than the sickness itself. We can worry that we will never feel better, that we will be useless forever. We worry that we are missing work and will be fired or reprimanded. Let the worries go. Watch them, and let them pass through you. Concentrate on being well.

Zen Master Seung Sahn tells us, "Don't be afraid of your sickness. At times everybody is afraid of what will happen to their body. However, the only difference between human beings when it comes to death is: go early, go late. So again, what is a human being? You must find this! Then when you die, your direction will be clear." He tells us that our mission in life is to find our true nature. Your true nature is not your physical body. Getting sick can be helpful to us. When we are sick, we do not want a new car, a new dress, a new house. We are filled with our sickness. Be sick, and ask yourself who your true self is. Your body is sick, but your true self is not sick.

There are no promises in life, and life is not always fair. However, there are always lessons we can learn, even within the darkest clouds. Pay attention to everything that happens, and look for the lessons within the darkness.

Dealing with Sick Family and Friends

When those we love are ill, under the weather, or otherwise in need, we roll up our sleeves and do what we can. If you know how to cook, you can make meals for those who cannot do it for themselves. You can read to a sick friend or family member, or you can sit and hold someone's hand. Sitting in silence with a friend during hard times can be enormously comforting. A friend told us she remembered the moment when she fell in love with the man who was to become her husband.

She had just found out that her mother had cancer and was stunned and distraught. Her boyfriend just sat with her in silence, holding her hand and offering her the comfort of his presence. He had just lost his own mother and knew there were no words to comfort, but with his body and his very being he offered what solace he could.

Acknowledge, Connect, and Act

What about the sick and suffering on an even greater scale? What can we do? It is our job to look suffering in the face and acknowledge it. We need to see the suffering in the world. We look at the starving families in Third World countries, the war-ravaged countries in the Middle East, the broken bodies of soldiers, of women and children blown apart by mines. We look squarely in the face of suffering and see its true nature. We see that at the heart of the suffering is greed, fear, and hatred. We see that at the heart of starvation is greed, fear, and hatred. We see that the heart of suffering is the illusion of separation. Yet many of us turn our backs to suffering on a daily basis and ignore its existence.

Everyone we know will die. This seems like a ridiculous statement of fact, but few people really absorb their own impermanence while they are alive. No one you know will escape death. Be mindful of death around you as part of your practice. It is essential to come face to face with impermanence.

To practice Zen is to look into the heart of the world, to see things as they are. There is no separation between you and the starving children of the world. We see the world in terms of us and them, but there is no us and them. If you see parts of the world as separate from yourself, then you do not see the true nature of reality. You must see into the suffering, acknowledge the suffering, and drop the illusion of separation. The illusion of separation has not solved the world's problems; it has increased them. We have had the answers for thousands of years, but if we do not put the answers into practice they are as useless as a bucket with a hole in it.

You can feed someone today. You can acknowledge suffering and open your heart. Then you will have taken a real step toward helping.

Facing Death

Of course, sometimes we cannot roll up our sleeves and help. Sometimes those we love die, and we live with the knowledge we will no longer see them on this earth. The first thing you can do is to stay with your feelings.

Release Emotions

Accept the grief that will descend upon you. Your grief is real and true, and it is important to grieve for our friends on this earth. Sometimes our losses can be so overwhelming that we are fearful of our feelings. We are afraid to feel the grief in case it annihilates us.

Feelings never killed anyone, however, no matter how much it seems your feeling might consume you. If you do not let yourself feel your emotions, you will repress them, and repressing your feelings puts great stress on your body and mind. Meditate during your grief. It may take a very long time to get through the pain to the other side where peacefulness will be waiting once again, but eventually it will happen.

QUESTION?

What can you do to get through a loss?
Stay in the moment. Attend to all the little details of life that still need attending to. Prepare food, do the laundry, pay your bills, go grocery shopping. All these little things make up your life moments. Stay in the moment and you will survive.

Confront the Fear

All living beings die. This is a truth that is impossible to deny. Even if you never wanted to be born, you will still die. No one yet has escaped death. As they say, "No one here gets out alive." The Buddha started his search for the truth after having an encounter with death. As he saw the sick and dying outside his childhood home and the body of a dead man being carried through the streets, he realized that all that was beautiful in life comes to an end. The realization of impermanence compelled Siddhartha to leave his home in search of an end to the suffering he perceived.

If we live face-to-face with a clear awareness of our inevitable death, every moment we are alive becomes precious—each day is filled with wonder. If you spend time with the very sick or the terminally ill, this truth will be brought home to you every day. It is a good practice to confront that which frightens you, and death frightens most of us.

Accept the Inevitable

The more we watch death as entertainment, the further away we seem to get from it as a realized inevitability. We try to escape death at all costs—sometimes even at the cost of our personal human dignity. Through our Zen practice we can learn, perhaps, how to die gracefully. We can learn how to help one another die with dignity and peace. We do not have to prolong life beyond reason and grace.

Buddha used to encourage his disciples to sit with the dead, with the rotting and decomposing corpses, so that the nature of impermanence would be understood and experienced.

When a friend lost her father recently, she thought she'd never be able to sit on the cushion again. The idea of sitting still was so frightening to her that she tried to avoid it altogether. But, fortunately, she was part of a practice group, and she showed up at the zendo for her regular weekly sit shortly after her father's death.

She managed to sit still through the entire sit, though she said she sobbed the entire time. She kept sitting, and soon she found that it was during her sit that she was closest to her father and derived the most comfort. Sitting connects us to everything around us, even those who are no longer in our presence.

Impermanence

An old Zen story tells of a very clever Zen student who eventually went on to become a great Zen master. One day the student broke his teacher's most prized teacup, a rare and precious object. Suddenly, he heard the sound of his teacher's footsteps approaching, and quickly he hid the broken teacup behind his back.

When his teacher entered the room, the student said, "Master, why do people die?"

The Zen master replied, "It is natural to die. Everything has to die, as it only has so long to live."

The student quickly produced the broken teacup. "Master," he said, "it was time for your teacup to die."

The Nature of Change

Impermanence is the nature of the world. Zen teaches us that we die every day, moment by moment. Things come up and they pass away. The moment is here, and then it is gone. The flower blooms and then dies. A delicious meal is in front of us, then we eat it, and it is gone. The wedding you were waiting for with such anticipation comes, and then it passes. Your child grows right before your very eyes—one day he is an infant and then suddenly a college graduate. Your cute little kitten is a mangy old tom before you know it. Fall turns into winter. Winter gives way to spring. The seeds give way to melons. We face change every day. All this change is transformation.

We rise in the morning, we go through the day, and everything changes every minute. We are not the same person at the end of the day that we were at the beginning. Sleep transforms us, food transforms us, a shower transforms us. We want more than anything to freeze time, to stop change, but we cannot. There is nothing in our bodies that is exactly the same as it was when we were children. We have completely changed from the inside out. The only thing tying us to that child inside is our memory. And our memory is not very reliable. Deep inside us, we are desperately afraid that we won't survive facing the nature of impermanence, but we will.

Take a look around you at all the people you know who have survived a terrible tragedy. Look at the neighbor who lost her husband, the woman at work who lost her child. You can see around you families who have lost their primary income through layoffs or firings. You can find people surviving cancer, the loss of a limb, or blindness. Perhaps the reason we refer to these as "losses" is that eventually these losses can be found again. You can find something within the loss that makes it a gain in some way after all.

"Cancer—it stops you in your tracks. Where did you think you were going? Sometimes it takes a really extreme circumstance—like facing our own mortality— before we're willing to look at, and really drop, our own stuff." —Katharine Thanas

Understanding Impermanence

We live in a society and a world that likes to believe we have stakes on this earth. We convince ourselves we own people, animals, land, and stuff. We don't "own" anything, however. Anything we have today can be gone tomorrow. Many people became supremely aware of this in the declines of the stock market in recent years. Millionaires one day were struggling the next. Here today, gone tomorrow. You just can't take it with you, wherever it is you think you are going. Here's a story of a man who truly wanted to take it all with him.

An elderly woman lost her husband to cancer and was left to face her golden years alone with no mate. Before he died, however, her husband—an affluent man who loved his money above all else—made her promise to bury him with his fortune.

"Promise me, love, you will let me take it with me. I can't bear to go into eternity without everything I've worked so hard for."

The poor woman could not imagine how she would survive, but she granted her husband his dying wish. After the funeral, her son overheard her telling her friend of her husband's last request. The son was horrified, thinking of his poor destitute mother.

"Mother, you didn't bury him with his money, did you?" he asked with dread.

"Yes, honey, I always keep my promises," she said. "I wrote him a check."

The poor man could not face leaving earth without all he had worked so hard to achieve. Fortunately, his wife had a good sense of humor.

Having a Positive Outlook

Impermanence is not a negative of the universe. In fact, impermanence is often our good friend. When you are in extreme pain or discomfort, you can take comfort in the knowledge that the pain will pass. Women in labor can count on the fact that the baby is eventually going to come out. The pain will end. Bitter winter gives way to the warming of spring. A bad mood gives way to a good one. The bulb gives way to the flower. The batter gives way to the cake. Change is a wonderful thing.

FACT

If we go back to the Four Noble Truths, we see another way of looking at suffering (*duhkha*) is impermanence. Therefore, instead of saying, "Life is suffering," we can say that "Life is impermanence." Our suffering comes from our inability to accept that impermanence.

If we can live with impermanence, if we can accept the nature of impermanence, we will be free. We can say "yes" to change. We can celebrate change. Without change, our blood wouldn't flow, our breath wouldn't move, our hearts wouldn't beat. Without change, the wonder of the world would not be ours. Everything would be frozen, stopped, dead. Change is life itself. It is the essence of energy and all that exists.

Living Through Zen

The practice of Zen gives us the tools with which we can understand the nature of impermanence. Our Zen practice is a door through which we can move into another world, a world of acceptance and truth. We can see things as they are, as they really are *right now*. We do not live in the future or the past. We do not cling to things and try to freeze time. We do not wish things were different or strive to change that which cannot be changed. We live in the wisdom of *what is*.

If we are living Zen, we live this inscription from a Zen gong:

> Birth and death is a grave event;
> How transient is life!
> Every minute is to be grasped.
> Time waits for nobody.

Through our Zen practice, we learn how to live every minute of our lives. We are fully present for everything that changes. It is a beautiful way to live. Whether we meet death, sickness, joy, or fear, we just show up. We do not live in denial of anything, and we do not try to escape. We accept the world just as it is, and through this acceptance, we find great peace and happiness. Ⓔ

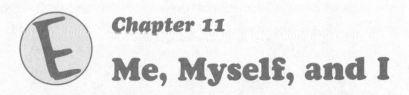

Chapter 11

Me, Myself, and I

The question "Who am I?" is one that drives many people out on a spiritual quest. As we get older, we wonder who we truly are. We try to build ourselves anew. Many people who turn to Zen are motivated by a quest for self and start the adventure often thinking that somewhere along the way a well-defined "me" will form.

Who Am I?

This is the essential question that drives us to the cushion in the first place. It is the cause of the wonderful doubt that gets us to finally sit down, quiet our minds, and begin seeking answers to that age-old question with fierce determination and longing. At the heart of those three essentials of Zen practice—doubt, determination, and faith—is the question "Who am I?" We doubt who we are. We are determined to find the real "me," and we have great faith that we can find an answer. We might even believe that once we find the answer, we will be happy for the rest of our lives.

Doubtful Mind

When you hit the cushion, it will not be too long before it becomes evident that the elusive "me" you have been searching for is a ghost. What happens then? The question of "Who am I?" is one of our koans in life. And if we have enough doubt to ask the question we are in a wonderful place not only to *begin* our Zen practice, but also to *continue* our Zen practice. Doubt fuels our practice. If we do not doubt, our practice stagnates—we are stuck.

FACT

Zen monk Chong Hae Sunim says, in the Winter 2002 issue of *Buddhadharma* magazine, "If you are correctly working on your [koan], then you aren't in the realm of like or dislike . . . Don't-know mind is before like and dislike . . . before opposites at all, even life and death."

If you are doubtful, you do not know what you like or what you dislike, and so you are not in a judging state of mind. You do not judge yourself, others, the quality of your sit, or the way that you feel. If you are in don't-know mind, you are asking, "Who am I?" and "What is this?" Your heart is filled with the effort of keeping an open mind. In essence, you are a wide-open heart when you are filled with doubt.

Discovering the Self

To ask the question "Who am I?" is to open your heart to discovery. When we sit, we sit with a question, and we start to realize that we have no idea who we are. What does it mean to be a woman? What does it mean to be tall? What does it mean to be an accountant? Does a tall, female accountant capture the essence of who you are? What if you added other characteristics of who you are?

Take a moment to write down ten characteristics that describe who you are:

1. I am . . .   6. I am . . .
2. I am . . .   7. I am . . .
3. I am . . .   8. I am . . .
4. I am . . .   9. I am . . .
5. I am . . .   10. I am . . .

Now take a look at the entire list. Do these adjectives capture you? For instance, you might have written down the following: male, short, thin, beard, funny, hiker, graphic artist, dog owner, food-lover, and atheist. Is that all you are? Are you more or less than these words? Do these words, in fact, capture anything at all about you? I am sure the answer is an emphatic "No!" There is some "other-essence" about you that you cannot capture with words. This otherness is something elusive that you cannot put your finger on. The search for this otherness is what keeps you probing for an answer to that old question, "Who am I?"

"There is no you to say 'I.' What we call 'I' is just a swinging door which moves when we inhale and when we exhale. It just moves; that is all. When your mind is pure and calm enough to follow this movement, there is nothing: no 'I', no world, no mind nor body; just a swinging door." —Shunryu Suzuki, Zen Mind, Beginner's Mind

Where Did I Go?

You are not a string of words, a group of adjectives and nouns. Even if you were a group of adjectives and nouns today, those adjectives and nouns might be different tomorrow. We are always changing, never the same from one moment to the next. On a simple level, even if you are a graphic artist today, you might not be a graphic artist tomorrow. Perhaps today your hair is brown, but tomorrow it will be blond. Scientific research shows that seven years from now, not one cell in our body will be the same as it is today. Tomorrow you won't even physically be the same "you" as you are right at this moment. Your skin, hair, your very *cells* will be different.

The Aggregates

The Buddha described the self as a group of "aggregates." The aggregates are parts of your mind and body, and they come together to create an impression of what is "me." Each of these aggregates is interdependent with the others. We might look in the mirror and see with our eyes a reflection in the mirror that we perceive as "me." Without our eyes, our vision, our perception of ourselves, and our physical appearance, we wouldn't have that moment where we think, "I look terrible today." The aggregates together make up the moment.

FACT

We are all like a river. The river is made up of tiny drops of water that are made up of elements such as hydrogen and oxygen. Does one drop of water make a river? Does one hundred thousand drops of water make a river? What makes a river a river? A river is just an idea that we have formed and agree upon, an idea that is made up of a collection of aggregates.

The Buddha realized that there was no definitive "I," no fixed "I" that never changed and remained reliable from one minute to the next. You cannot be sure that tomorrow you will wake up and look in the mirror and see the same reflection that you see today. In fact, you can be sure that you *will not* see the same reflection tomorrow that you see today. Your skin will be different, your hair will be different, your mood will be different, even the mirror will be different. Maybe tomorrow you will look in the mirror and say, "I look marvelous!" Each of us is a series of experiences, elements, phenomena, and perceptions that move from one moment to another.

Think of a cow. What is it that makes the cow a cow? Is it the black-and-white spots? Is it the "moo" sound she makes? Is it the milk that comes from her body? Is it the long lashes and the big cow eyes? Is it the hooves and udder? Is it all of these things together? It is certainly not all of these things taken separately. A "moo" sound is not a cow, an udder is not a cow, long lashes and hooves are not a cow. Each of these aggregates comes together to form a collection of aggregates that we know as "cow."

Self-Illusion

You cannot see one part of a river—one handful of water—and stop it to examine it. You would just have a handful of water. The handful of water would not be the river. We are much the same. We are ever-changing, just like a river is ever-changing. The cow is the same as well—it, too, is ever-changing. We are all a series of thoughts, impressions, perceptions, actions, and sensory reactions that change from moment to moment. Yet we define ourselves by these aggregates that cannot be anchored.

"We go outside after a rainstorm and are delighted if a rainbow appears in the sky. But when we look more deeply, it becomes clear that there is no 'thing' called 'rainbow' apart from the particular conditions of air and moisture and light. Each of us is like that rainbow—an appearance, a magical display, arising out of our various elements of mind and body."
—Joseph Goldstein

At the heart of our practice lies a great fear of this knowledge. We run from the idea of not being an anchored self in the world. It is a frightening thought to consider that we are ever-changing energy. Once we find the willingness to sit despite our fear, we find the willingness to accept our fear—then, suddenly, our fear disappears.

When you start to see that you are ever-changing and cannot be fixed in time and space, and that the nature of the entire world is ever-changing and cannot be fixed in time and space, you might ask the question: Then where did I go? You didn't go anywhere. The idea of self is an illusion. As you practice Zen, you will start to see, in very small glimpses, that the separation of you and the cow and the river and the world is *all* an illusion.

If There Is No Me, What about You?

If the illusion of self is realized, ego disappears. Once there is no "self," a great compassion arises in its place. All boundaries between you and the rest of the world disappear. You no longer have a self to protect. No longer will you feel inclined to defensiveness. You see everything as interdependent, and you realize that to harm another is to harm yourself.

Through Practice to Compassion

The best you can do on any day of your life is to practice. When you practice you have the hope of waking up to this wonderful, infinite compassion. You have the hope of giving to the world what it needs the most: love. So if there is no me, there is a capacity for tremendous care and love, and this is what the world needs most. That is why in Zen, we say we sit for all sentient beings. People who practice Zen are like an army fighting for the life of the world. They are sitting so that compassion can manifest in the world, and life can be lived with care for another.

If there is no self, there is an amazing capacity for helping. Many Zen masters dedicate their lives to the bodhisattva way—helping others to awaken to this wonderful compassion. Many of the great religions and spiritual practices tell us the same thing: True happiness lies in getting outside of ourselves and helping others. To be locked inside oneself, obsessed with one's own thoughts and needs, is to truly suffer. It is to suffer the bondage of self. Real freedom exists when you cease thinking of yourself all day long. Have you ever done any volunteer work or helped out a friend in need? It's a wonderfully invigorating experience, and you probably noticed at the end of the day that your mood was buoyant and your energy level was high. Try it out for yourself in the near future. Volunteer your time somewhere, or help out someone in need.

FACT

It is easy to start to question your practice and to wonder why you are striving to discover a self that really does not exist. But we hear a voice calling to us and telling us to keep asking, to keep searching for the truth. It is the voice that brought us to the cushion. And it takes us from asking about ourselves to asking about others.

We live in a time in which we are often coddled and told, "Take care of yourself." We are admonished to take time for ourselves and pamper ourselves. We deserve time off, long baths, new clothes, and a dinner out. We overindulge, overspend, and overeat. And we are not happy! Clearly, the way to a peaceful life is not through spending more money, eating more food, and paying more attention to your own needs. If you are fed, housed, clothed, and healthy, then you are in good shape to help someone else. But the compassionate spirit that arises through your practice will lead you naturally down this path. If you don't want to invest the time now to get out of yourself, you will find it happening more naturally as your practice deepens.

Giving It Up: Acceptance

We have a very strong desire to control our own lives. We want to know that we are in charge and can change anything, and we live in a society that encourages this belief. Often, it is very hard for us to realize that we're not really in control. We're unwilling to accept circumstances or events that make us feel vulnerable and powerless.

Acceptance does not mean that we roll over and play dead. It doesn't mean we admit defeat every time something happens to us. But it does mean that we can know the difference between when we can change something and when we cannot.

If I sit every day, will I definitely reach enlightenment someday?
It is not guaranteed that you will live long enough to reach enlightenment. But if you are sitting, you are practicing Zen meditation, and this is a wonderful way to live. You will reap the rewards of Zen whether you realize enlightenment or not.

Learning Acceptance

We learn acceptance by sitting on the cushion. We sit still, as our practice asks us to be absolutely still so that we can watch the breath, watch our thoughts, and still our minds. And as we sit, unmoving, we start to learn the meaning of acceptance. We *accept* the pain in our bodies. We accept the thoughts that are rolling through our minds. We accept the time that we must sit through until the buzzer rings. And this acceptance means we let go of the desire to move, perhaps over and over again, twenty times a minute.

We then learn to apply this newfound skill to our lives. We think if we just work out, we will have a perfect body. We think if we work enough overtime, we will get a raise. We think if we look perfect, we will find a beautiful mate, or if we are good enough, our parents will be proud. But we cannot control what other people think of us, and we cannot change the structure of our bodies. We learn to accept ourselves just as we are.

ALERT!

Do not go through your life thinking you will love yourself someday in the future when you are rich enough, fit enough, or handsome enough. Acceptance means we can learn to live in the day, in the moment, with what is right in front of us.

We have been conditioned to believe that the answer to our happiness question is out there somewhere. Maybe we believe it is at the gym, in our parents' eyes, in a rabbi's approval, a boss's handshake. However, if we are looking for our higher power outside of ourselves, we are looking for something separate from ourselves. We experience ourselves as being separate from our higher power: alone and outside.

Looking Inside Oneself

Once we turn inside for the answers, we start to hear the real truth. Our teacher can be the finger pointing at the moon—she can show us the path to happiness. But she cannot take us there or make it happen for us. Acceptance is a path toward our happiness. We can accept ourselves just as we are. Accept the moment just as it is. We are perfect right at this minute. If you sit, you will find love—not just love for others, but a deep and abiding love for yourself. This is perhaps the most surprising result of Zen practice.

There is a wonderful little book called *There Is Nothing Wrong with You* by Zen teacher Cheri Huber. Cheri tells us that the way to self-love is Zen practice. She says, "In our sitting practice, we go to that place of inherent goodness, we find that deep sense of well-being within ourselves, and we become friends with that. We go there, and we see that being there is wonderful. For the period of time that we're there, all the problems fall away, everything falls into place. And then we leave and get caught up in something. And we come back. That's why rather than taking our spiritual practice into daily life, we bring our daily life into our spiritual practice. We're creating a circle of compassion and we keep bringing the events of our life into it."

Grant me the serenity to accept the things I cannot change. The courage to change the things I can. And the wisdom to know the difference. —The Serenity Prayer

When we go to that "place of inherent goodness," we are accepting that everything is exactly as it should be, and everything in that moment is perfect *no matter what is going on*. We rarely stay there as we have to engage in the world at large, but we can return to that acceptance, that "place of inherent goodness," whenever we want to. Magic.

Where Do I Go After Death?

The Buddha didn't address questions such as "What happens to me after death?" as he thought they were a waste of time. We cannot possibly know what happens in the future, not until that time arrives.

Unnecessary Worry

You are going to die. No one yet has managed to escape death. There is absolutely nothing you can do about this fact of life. But you can spend your time on earth living your life, instead of worrying about what is going to happen after you move on. It might be entertaining to sit around with your friends discussing the possibilities of life after death. But concerning yourself with such matters is not the path to enlightenment. Remember, you cannot know the answer to the question of life after death. The way to a peaceful life does not lie in wondering what will happen next. It is in accepting what is happening now.

Reincarnation

During the Buddha's lifetime, it was a common belief in India that life followed life until enlightenment broke the circle. Depending on your karma, you could be reborn as a human, a hungry ghost, a denizen of hell, or another form of life.

FACT

Many Buddhists believe that there are six different life forms into which you can be reborn. They are gods, humans, titans, animals, hungry ghosts, and denizens of hell. An action we take in this lifetime corresponds with the life we end up in the next. In that sense, we are heir to our actions.

Karma

We all have karma. Our karma is a result of our intentions when we perform any given act. If we steal something, it is not necessarily the act of stealing that leaves us with negative karma but the intent we have when we steal. If we steal to feed our starving baby, we might not incur any negative karma. However, if we steal from someone because we dislike that person and want him or her to suffer, then we will incur bad karma.

Our karma is carried from one life to another, and it affects the life form we take in lives to come. For instance, if you commit murder with hatred in your heart, you might be reborn as a denizen of hell in your next life. If you are a denizen of hell, it might take many more lifetimes to work your way upward toward a more desirable life form, such as the life of a god. However, it is only in the human life form that we can realize enlightenment.

The Human Life

The realization of enlightenment is the only way to break the endless circle of rebirth: *samsara*. Therefore, it is a great opportunity to be born into human life. You have a chance to work toward enlightenment, and it has most likely taken you thousands of lifetimes to reach this point. You have the chance, here and now, to take advantage of this opportunity. Life is too precious to waste one moment.

Reincarnation can also be understood to mean that we have many opportunities for true life in this one lifetime we are living now. We die many deaths every day. Every minute that passes is a mini-death. We are ever-changing, ever-dying, and ever being reborn. We have the opportunity over and again to do it right.

Do not put off what you can do right now. Do not sit around thinking about what it is like after you die, or what it would be like to be enlightened. Do not wonder what it is like to be peaceful and to find that "place of inherent peace." Find it.

Answering the Call

Zen practice, whether you believe in reincarnation or not, is an opportunity to wake up to your Buddha-nature and fill the hole that has been sitting inside you all this time. You can stop and listen to yourself and hear the voice that is calling out to you to find your true self. You know, somewhere in your body, inside yourself, in your own true heart, that there is something calling to you, and you want to answer it. Take the time to answer the call. You have the opportunity every day to begin your practice and to continue your practice. You have the opportunity to wake up to your nature, to see the truth.

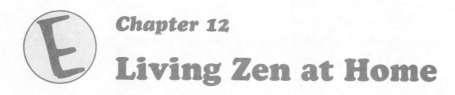

Chapter 12

Living Zen at Home

The first thing you can do to bring Zen into your home is to start a meditation practice. Set up a space for meditation, and make sure you are comfortable with it. You can bring harmony and peace into your home and make your home a place of rest. Your home should be a refuge for you from the pressures of the outside world.

Setting Up a Peaceful Space

Look around your home for an area that you can change into a permanent meditation space. Perhaps you have a room that is not used frequently. If you don't have an entire room, look for a part of a room you can claim as your own. Is there a corner of the bedroom you can turn into a meditation space?

For specifics on setting up your zendo, see Chapter 13. Here, we are concerned with actually locating a space that will, day in and day out, be ready when you need it.

Family Schedule

Finding a part of the house or apartment that isn't in use is usually not an easy task. But your meditation practice is something that should rank very high on your list of things to do each day—along with eating and dressing. If necessary, negotiate with other family members to get the space you need. Perhaps you can work out a time schedule. For instance, if you decide to take a small corner of your living room as a meditation space, then offer to get up before everyone else is awake so they don't have to worry about disturbing you by walking through the living room on their way out to work. Don't expect people to adjust their schedules for you, necessarily, but work around what is currently in place. See if you can secure a time of day when no one will disturb you.

It is very important that you secure a space in your home for meditation where you will not be disturbed. Sitting while listening to someone watch television, talk on the phone, or listen to music is not a good idea, especially for a beginning Zen student. It will discourage you unnecessarily.

Pet Interference

Pets can interfere with your practice, but there are two schools of thought on this. One says to live with the distraction, and your practice will be stronger for it. The other is more easily dealt with. Lock the pets up while you do your meditation. Put them in another room or let them outside if possible. Cats and dogs have a way of knowing instinctively when you least want them to sit on your lap. Dogs can get very excited when you get down to their level. You don't want to have to concentrate on your breathing while a dog is getting friendly with your leg!

So the first order of business is setting up your meditation space. Once this space is secured, you can move on to the rest of the house. As mentioned earlier, your home is a sanctuary. If it looks and smells like a sanctuary, you'll be more inclined to experience it as a sanctuary.

Cleaning, Organizing, Simplifying

While you are starting out in your practice, you can nurture a Zen attitude toward the rest of your home as well. We tend to get very attached to our possessions in life. We have certain objects that mean much to us, and we gather more all the time. However, if we are not surrounded by objects of desire, we can have an easier time letting go of our wants. If our house is a cluttered mess, it is harder for our brains not to follow suit. So let's start with two objectives: clean up and simplify.

Cleanup Crew

The first thing you can do to bring your home in line with your practice is to clean it up. Start with one room at a time. Clean each one thoroughly and with great attention to detail. This is a Zen exercise in and of itself. Focus on each task at hand, and throw yourself into it, living in the moment as you clean and straighten from top to bottom. Depending on your home, this may take some time, so make sure you allow yourself enough time to get it done.

Scrub down your kitchen and your bathrooms, vacuum, and dust the entire house. Find a home for all the miscellaneous items you have collected and put them away. As you clean, focus your attention on your hands and your senses. Stay in the moment, and you can actually enjoy the process of cleaning. Each room should contribute to a feeling of peacefulness and inner serenity. If your home is clean, your mind will feel much more at ease, and it won't be distracted by thoughts of cleanup.

If you get ahead of yourself, you will start to feel overwhelmed and tired. You might have months' worth of magazines and newspapers sitting on your living room floor. Perhaps you have CDs scattered all around, or books falling out of the bookshelves. You might have art supplies or bills covering the kitchen table. Perhaps the children's toys are all over the hallway, and the bathroom is regurgitating beauty supplies and discarded clothing.

"Zen is not some kind of excitement, but concentration on our usual everyday routine . . . When you do something, you should burn yourself up completely, like a good bonfire, leaving no trace of yourself."
—Shunryu Suzuki

Everything should have a home base, and that home base should be somewhere tucked out of the direct line of sight. Perhaps you can get a toy box for the toys, a basket for the newspapers and magazines, a cabinet for the art supplies, and a file cabinet for the bills. Better yet, pay the bills immediately, recycle the newspapers and magazines right after reading them, and pass on the toys as soon as the children grow out of them. Ask yourself this: How often do you go back and reread an old magazine? Is it time to get rid of that huge pile of old *Outside* magazines? Once the house is clean, you can focus on the next step: simplifying.

Simple Spaces

The goal when we simplify is not to throw out all of our worldly goods. We merely want to simplify as much as possible so that our minds are not as cluttered as our homes. You have electronic devices galore: computers, fax machines, cell phones, home phones, televisions, DVDs, stereos, hair dryers, clocks, kitchen appliances, and more, all with their incumbent wiring and plugs. This jumble adds up to a lot of clutter and confusion. What is absolutely necessary for your life? Can you put anything away? Can you live without something? Live by this rule: If an item complicates your life more than simplifies it, get rid of it.

Manifest plainness,
Embrace simplicity,
Reduce selfishness,
Have few desires.
—Lao-Tzu, *Tao Te Ching*

Look at the surfaces in your home. Is every inch of your kitchen counter covered in stuff? Do you have knickknacks and photographs everywhere? Does your mind jump from item to item all the time? Clean off as many surfaces as you can so that you create a sense of spaciousness in your home. Your mind will flow from room to room and over the surfaces instead of getting trapped in the clutter everywhere you look. If the room you are looking at is focused on showing off rather than creating peace, it's time to change the room.

Also, honestly consider all the things you will never use. Do you have a box of dishes you will never use but are saving in case your child needs them in college someday? Are you saving your Barbie dolls or your old electric guitar just because it feels good to have them in your attic? Do you have records you haven't listened to in years? Old letters and ticket stubs? Is your garage filled with tools you won't use in a hundred years? Perhaps it's time for some spring cleaning. We can often feel overwhelmed by the clutter in our homes. Simplify and free up your mind and your spirit. Make your life as easy as you can. What is most important? Keep asking that question until you have simplified things considerably. Then simplify some more.

Time Management

A response that might come readily to your lips when you read about simplifying your home is, "I don't have time for that. I don't have time for anything! My plate is too full." The only thing all of us have in equal measure is time. No one has any more or less time than you do. What you do with your time is completely up to you. If you feel that your time is not your own, you are being controlled by it.

Take a careful look at your timetable for the day and week. Write down what you are doing in your time out of work. Are you wasting time in a million different ways? Time that you could use to a much greater end? You probably have plenty of time to worry each day. Even if you can't finish a task today, start one. You can do a little bit each day. It's like the old adage: How do you eat an elephant? A bite at a time!

FACT

Remember that all of your possessions are only stuff. They are not important. Your scrapbook from high school is not your memory of high school. Your memory of high school is not high school either. Why not live in the present instead of the past?

Eco-Friendly Environment

In addition to simplifying space and organizing time, you might also want to consider adopting policies at home that reflect an eco-friendly home life. A life, the Zen way, is to practice compassion toward all living beings, including our Earth. Things to consider in the long-term might be alternative methods of transportation whenever possible, solar power, conserving water and heat, eco-friendly detergents and cleaners, and growing organic food in your garden. It's just as the German astronomer Johannes Kepler once said: "Nature uses as little as possible of anything." You can, too.

Living Peacefully

Zen is a program of action, though it doesn't appear to be as you spend so much of your time sitting on a pillow. But you can take actions to make your life more peaceful, and sitting is absolutely one action that will create a life of serenity and peace, even if before you might not have had much of either.

We can be peaceful by learning when to speak and when to be quiet. Often we start or further an argument by indulging in a hasty retort, a badly thought-out response. Sometimes it is better to hold your tongue and keep the quiet. If your spouse or roommate is in a bad mood and takes it out on you, is it necessary to respond in kind? Can you be peaceful and let him or her be? How important is it to have your say? Every time you "have your say," you are indulging your ego and moving away from your practice. That does not mean that to practice Zen is to be a doormat. Sometimes the right thing to do is nothing at all. And sometimes the greatest strength is seen in silence.

"People say 'I want peace.' If you remove I (ego), and your want (desire), you are left with peace."
—Satya Sai Baba

The Greatest Challenge

There is an old Zen story about what to do when challenged by another. It goes like this.

> *Once there lived a powerful warrior, who was growing old but could still beat any challenger he met. He was known throughout the land, and many students sought him out so they could study under him and learn his powerful warrior ways.*
>
> *One day, a much younger and aspiring warrior arrived at the older warrior's village. The young warrior was determined to be the first to succeed in defeating the old master. He was not only a powerful, strong young man, but he had a discerning eye and could spot the weakness in another that would prove to be the key to victory. He always waited for his opponent to strike first so he could detect whatever weakness the other man had. Then he would strike fast and hard. He always won his battles this way.*
>
> *The old master's students were worried. They did not want their great teacher to take up the challenge of the stranger who had entered their village. But the old master was firm in his decision and prepared to fight the younger man.*

The fight started with the young man hurling one insult after another at the old man. He whipped dirt into the old man's eyes and spit in his face. For long hours he verbally abused the old man, calling him names, insulting his family, and yelling every curse and terrible thing imaginable to stir the old teacher into action. But the old warrior was wise and stood his ground, waiting still and calm for the storm to stop. At long last, the young warrior wore himself out and fell down in exhaustion. He was shamed and defeated.

While his students were greatly relieved that their master was not harmed, they were somewhat disappointed that he had not taken up arms against the annoying and rude young warrior. They asked him, "How could you put up with so much indignity? How did you defeat him?"

The master replied with a question of his own. "If someone comes to give you a gift and you do not receive it, to whom does the gift belong?"

FACT

Sometimes the best response to another is silence. It might feel wrong to hold silence when provoked by another but, as the saying goes, would you rather be right or happy?

Keeping the Peace

We do not have to engage in arguments and respond when insulted or provoked. We can sit in silence and breathe, one breath at a time. This is very difficult practice at first. It feels wrong not to respond when we are threatened or aggravated by another. You can always say to yourself, "How important is it?" If the answer is "Pretty darned important," then still hold your tongue and wait until your initial response has passed. Then ask yourself again. If the answer is still the same, find a peaceful and appropriate way to respond. You don't have to be unpleasant, insulting, or rude to communicate your feelings effectively. Remember who is holding the gift to begin with.

Here are some practical ways to maintain peace in your life and with the others in your life:

"We can never obtain peace in the world if we neglect the inner world and don't make peace with ourselves. World Peace must develop out of inner peace."
— The Dalai Lama

- Be quiet when doubtful if your response will be a compassionate one.
- Strive to do for others, and do not expect anything in return.
- Be gentle with others whenever possible.
- Listen carefully at all times.
- If someone is upset with you, listen and remain silent unless your words will comfort or alleviate pain.
- If you need to say something that might be hard for another to hear, say it with compassion.
- Be quiet and careful around the home whenever possible.
- Be considerate of others at all times.
- Respect privacy.
- Be the person whom you would like to live with yourself.

House Chores Are Practice

You can also practice Zen at home with work practice every day. Every household chore you do can be an opportunity for mindfulness. Stay in the moment, and be thankful for the task at hand. Pay attention to your hands and the rest of your body as you move through the house. Be mindful of the noises you hear and the scents that greet you. Focus on what you are doing, and every time your thoughts start to wander, bring them back to the task at hand.

Doing Laundry

Doing laundry is an opportunity to be thankful, to be in the moment, and to realize the connection we have with all things. When you put the bag of laundry down by the washing machine, say a mindfulness prayer before you begin. Be thankful for the clothes that protect you from the elements and that keep you warm, dry, and protected from the sun. Say aloud, "I am thankful for these clothes. These clothes protect me and keep me safe and help me maintain my well-being. I am thankful for the fabric from which these clothes were made, and for the hands that worked the machines that stitched the seams together."

FACT

We take so much for granted in our lives. We have so much in our lives, so much to do and so much to follow up on, that we end up ignoring a great deal of it. We mindlessly do a simple task, such as laundry, with no consideration for the abundance that fills our lives.

Be mindful of your greater connection to the world as you touch the clothing that covered your body this week. Be grateful for the means to keep your clothing clean and fresh. As you separate the clothing, be mindful of the colors, the variety, and the feeling of the fabrics in your hands. Fill the machines, and marvel at the abundance of water you have at your fingertips. Be careful not to waste water by using a larger cycle than is necessary.

Cooking

Another household task, cooking, is also a wonderful opportunity for Zen practice. There are many small details to attend to while cooking, and we can focus in on every one of them. We connect with the earth in a wonderful way as we handle the produce that comes to us from the soil we walk upon. We feel the life around us and give thanks for the food that sustains us so we can continue to practice each day.

We can say a mindfulness prayer as we start our preparations for a home-cooked meal. We can say thanks for the earth that feeds us, the sun that supports us, the seeds that provide for us. We can eat everything that we prepare and waste nothing at all. We can become more economical in our cooking—so waste is a word of the past—and we learn to value every morsel that we are fortunate enough to create. Our hearts can be filled with gratitude as we make our meals and eat them, focusing our full attention on each and every task.

Sometimes, however, we can feel resentful that we are the ones cooking, cleaning, and taking care of the home while others watch television, work, or play around outside. According to Bernard Glassman and Rick Fields in *Instructions to the Cook: A Zen Master's Lessons in Living a Life That Matters,* when Dogen asked the monastery cook why he didn't have the assistants do the hard work of drying mushrooms in the sun, he replied, "I am not other people." What does he mean by that? This is the only life you have to lead. Lead it now. Don't let others do what is yours to do right now at this moment.

"When we cook—and live—with this kind of attention [when washing the dishes, just wash the dishes] the most ordinary acts and the humblest ingredients are revealed as they truly are." —Glassman and Fields, Instructions to the Cook: A Zen Master's Lessons in Living a Life That Matters

The Stink of Enlightenment

Don't get too attached to your spirituality, at home or anywhere else. People who get too attached to Zen are said to have the "stink of enlightenment." The stink of Zen can be understood as "a holier than thou" attitude of self-congratulation. Sometimes people who follow a spiritual path can get very caught up in their own spirituality. They can get attached to their "spiritual glow," and the result can be an attitude that falls short.

You might start to feel the world is a wonderful place. You might see the spiritual light of life everywhere and feel in love with the world all over again. That is a truly wonderful way to experience life, and we are extremely pleased for you. However, don't ever lose sight of the nature of impermanence. A loss can bring you up short, no matter where you are. When we lose friends, family, pets, and jobs, we can feel intense sorrow and loss, but this loss is also a part of life. Acknowledge your feelings. Don't expect that you will ever rise above loss and never feel pain.

Finding the Buddha Within

Every task you do at home should be done with great focus and awareness. Simple things like dusting, vacuuming, and making the bed are all moments in which you can find the Buddha within. What is the Buddha within? It is making the bed, eating the toast, dusting the floors, petting the cat, doing the laundry, feeding the family.

You are human, and you will be human for the rest of your life. You will feel pain, sorrow, anger, and probably fear. But with your Zen practice you will learn what to do with those feelings. You will know you can return to your pillow and connect with something bigger than your small self. Eventually, you will see the Buddha everywhere, but only if you are paying attention. The Buddha is in your home, in the details.

Engage in life. Don't use your spirituality to keep you separate from others or from life's events. Life can be painful, messy, and disorderly, and you should accept the true nature of your life.

Make your home a place where you are free from the cluttered mind and life of today's chaotic world. Find a sanctuary in your kitchen, in your bedroom, in your bathroom, and next to the washing machine. Keep your home orderly and simple, and your mind will follow thereafter. This is the wonder of life: each moment lived. Don't let it pass you by.

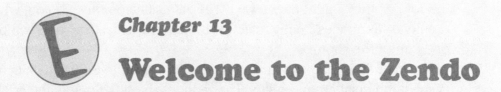

Chapter 13

Welcome to the Zendo

In Chapter 12, we suggested you set up a space at home so that you have a place to do your daily sit. Whether you sit at home, a local meditation center, or a monastery, the room in which you will sit is known as the zendo. If you only have a corner to call your own, this is fine as well. One wonderful aspect of Zen is that you can take it anywhere you go!

Introduction to the Zendo

If you were to enter a monastery or a meditation center, the zendo would most likely be a large basically empty room. Most likely there will be zabutons (meditation mats) and zafus (meditation cushions) throughout the room, lined up in orderly rows. They might face each other across the row, or they might face a wall. The zafu sits atop the zabuton, which cushions your knees from contact with the hard floor. The altar will be at one end of the room.

The zendo is akin to a chapel you might enter in a Christian church. Respect and quiet are necessary. The zendo is the heart of the center where you will be practicing. It is where zazen takes place, where the teacher gives his talk, and where you might have tea and sometimes *oryoki*.

QUESTION?

What is *oryoki*?
Oryoki is the collection of utensils, linens, and bowls used for formal, ritualized eating in the zendo. Traditionally, when nuns and monks were ordained, they would be given an *oryoki* set tied in the napkin. Today, *oryoki* is a ceremony, and not every meal will be eaten in the zendo this way.

You should learn the rules of the zendo in which you are meditating. Some larger centers and monasteries provide introductory programs for new members. You might be asked if it is your first time sitting zazen. If you answer in the affirmative, you will be pulled out of the group and taken into a smaller room where instruction on beginning zazen will be given. If you are not sure of what to do, don't worry about it. Just be aware, and follow the person next to you to the best of your ability. Most centers are geared toward helping the newcomer, and the atmosphere will be helpful and respectful.

The Altar

The altar can usually be found at the far side of the zendo, away from the entrance. The teacher, or *roshi,* will sit closest to the altar. Altars are usually associated with worship, so you might wonder why an altar appears in a zendo as no one is worshipping a god. An altar is used for several different reasons. The primary reason is that repetition, ceremony, and habit play a large part in any meditation practice. The altar is usually the one structure in the zendo. It is a visual reminder of the importance of practice. It signifies faith in practice.

An altar also paves the way for an awakening of the senses. On the altar you might find a Buddha statue, burning incense, a gong of some kind, and a fresh flower arrangement. You can gaze at the Buddha, smell the incense and the flowers, hear the bell as it rings, and bow to the altar, engaging your senses and awakening your awareness of the moment. Either on the altar or nearby, you will find the altar supplies, including a good supply of additional incense, candles, and matches or a lighter to light the candle.

The Buddha Statue and Incense

The Buddha statue usually has a base, or holder, so that the Buddha is slightly elevated above the other pieces on the altar. The statue is placed toward the back of the altar, and is present so that your attention can be focused on the Buddha and his teachings. The incense holder is often placed in front of the Buddha, in the center of the altar or slightly to the side. In order to ensure that the incense sticks remain upright, the incense holder contains ashes from the burning of many incense sticks. These ashes keep the new sticks standing, so that they don't list to one side.

FACT

If you are starting a new incense bowl at home and do not yet have ashes from the incense used during many meditations, you can always place rice in the bottom of the incense holder. A cupful of rice works just as well to ensure the stability of the incense stick.

The Flowers and the Candle

Flowers symbolize the nature of impermanence. A vase full of flowers is usually placed to one side of the altar. The teacher or a senior-ranking member of the *sangha* will make the flower arrangement. The flower arrangements are usually very simple and beautiful.

The candle can also be placed to one side. The candle symbolizes the light of truth shining through the darkness of delusion.

The Offering

Sometimes an offering to the Buddha will also be left on the altar. Tea is a common offering, and a cup of tea is placed in front of the Buddha statue to honor the Buddha. Some zendos will also have side altars that might have statues on them as well, such as a statue of one of the bodhisattvas.

Zendo's Headmaster

Some of the people in the zendo are assigned jobs other than the job of sitting zazen. There are also rules and rituals in a zendo that must be followed. It is the *jikijitsu's* (also known as the *jikido*) job to enforce these rules. These rules are in place so that the zendo is orderly, and practice continues with a minimum of distractions. But being in the moment is the aim of everyone in the zendo, and it is the *jikijitsu's* job to respond in the moment to anything that arises, enforcing the quiet and respect of the zendo.

The Role of *Jikijitsu*

The *jikijitsu* will make sure all doors are shut and windows are either shut or open. He or she is also the person who walks around the zendo with the *kyosaku,* the wooden mallet used to strike people across the back on request. The *jikijitsu* keeps time, ringing the bell when zazen is to start, and ringing it again to signify when a period of zazen is over. The *jikijitsu* also corrects posture, reprimands when people make noise or distract others, and often inspires other members of the *sangha.* The *jikijitsu* is the person you are most likely to feel great animosity toward as your legs start to hurt and your back screams out in pain while he or she seems to sadistically refrain from ringing the ending bell.

There is, of course, also the *roshi,* or meditation teacher. The *roshi* holds *dokusan* and gives *teisho* talks. There are many other roles for people in the monastery, but the *jikijitsu* is the head of the zendo.

One of the roles of the *jikijitsu* is to keep a cool comfortable temperature inside the zendo. If the temperature is not to your liking, please sit in another spot, either closer to or further from open windows, or simply change your clothes. However, don't try to change them inside the zendo!

Zendo Attire

It is important to make sure your personal appearance reflects the simplicity and the respect of the zendo. In Chapter 5, we briefly mentioned what kind of clothes you should wear in a zendo.

Clothing

Do not wear anything too bright, as bright colors are unnecessarily distracting. This does not mean that people who practice Zen are somber, dark people running around dressed in black all the time. However, wearing a dark color in the zendo is appropriate.

Wear something very comfortable. Some people find yoga clothes work well while sitting. Loose trousers and long skirts for women also work well. Just make sure the skirt is long enough to cover your legs if you choose to wear one. Robes are acceptable wear in the zendo as well.

It is not recommended that you wear your favorite pair of jeans. What might seem comfortable all day long will suddenly be extremely uncomfortable if you sit still for prolonged periods of time. Jeans will cut off your circulation, and before you know it, your entire attention will be focused on the pins and needles in your legs!

Plain T-shirts in a dark color are acceptable to wear, but stay away from white T-shirts and those with slogans on them. The zendo might be somewhat chilly, so make sure you have a sweater or covering in case you get cold. You can wear long underwear under your clothing if the temperature warrants it.

Accessories

Refrain from wearing eye-catching jewelry, such as many necklaces, bracelets, or very large earrings. Do not wear belts with flashy buckles. Zen is not for the flashy, and the zendo is not a place to show off your fashion sense. Wear moderate and discreet clothing and only accessorize if you must—wedding rings and simple chain necklaces will be fine. Makeup should also be kept to a minimum. When you are sitting, you are trying to still the ego mind, and makeup, perfume, and flashy jewelry are usually not conducive to shrinking the ego. If your look says, "I'm HERE!" then you will probably want to think about changing your attire.

The Hair

Although your hair might be your crowning glory, if it is long you might want to tie it back from your face in a neat ponytail. If your hair constantly falls into your face, you might want to think of a way to keep it back so you do not get distracted. Otherwise, you might spend your entire sit fending off the desire to toss your hair back quickly.

Socks or bare feet? You might want to wear socks if your feet get cold, but bare feet are most welcome in the zendo. However, do make sure your feet are in relatively good form. If they're not, cover up the toes with socks and take care of the feet for next time if you care to go barefoot.

No Shoes

What about the shoes? You never wear shoes into the zendo. It is considered bad form and is not respectful. At the door to the zendo there will be a place for your shoes. There will either be little cubbyholes set up for you to place your shoes within, or you can just line them up after the last person's shoes. There will most likely be many pairs of shoes lined up outside the zendo walls. Note where yours are so that when you leave the zendo, you can retrieve them easily.

Zendo Behavior

Before you enter the zendo, take off your shoes—and your socks if desired. When you pass through the entryway to the zendo, you will perform a bow—called a *gassho*—to the altar. To *gassho*, put both palms together and bow from the waist. Your fingers should be extended, and your hands should be only a few inches from the tip of your nose. After you bow, place your hands just below your chest, against your upper abdomen. Make a fist with your left hand and place your left thumb within the fist so that it is covered and not sticking up. Place your right hand over your left hand, covering your fist. This is the proper posture for moving about the zendo.

Find your seat in the zendo. If it is your first visit, find a zafu that looks unattended. If there is a name by the zafu, or a personal object on the pillow, someone has already claimed it as a place to sit. Do not cross in front of the altar or move behind it. Follow the lines of the zafus as you move through the zendo, moving up the rows and not crossing over in the middle of the zendo. Do not step over or on the zabutons or zafus.

When you reach your zafu, *gassho* and bow to the zafu, turn and *gassho,* bow to the opposite side, and take your seat, either facing the wall or the others, depending on the style of the zendo. Wait for the bell to ring three times, signaling the beginning of zazen.

The Rules

Let's take a look at some of the rules you should follow to avoid being reprimanded by the *jikijitsu.*

First of all, do not stare at others. If you need to watch someone to see what you should do next, do so modestly and quietly out of the corner of your eye. Keep your head down and focus your attention on the floor in front of you. Do not strike up a conversation with the person next to you. This is not a time for talking. If you absolutely must ask a question, do so as quietly as humanly possible. Be aware that you are distracting your neighbor. Of course, if the zazen period is in session, you should never speak short of earthquake, fire, or personal emergency.

Once the *jikijitsu* rings the bell signaling the beginning of zazen, do not speak or move, and do not leave your seated position. If you have a personal emergency, you should leave if staying will cause more disturbance. If you are going to re-enter the zendo, you should wait until the current zazen period is finished and the bell has been rung three times once again. The time to squirm around to ensure a comfortable seated position is before the bell rings three times for the beginning of the sit. If you are uncomfortable, sit it out, and your practice will get better. Everyone who begins Zen practice experiences great pain during zazen, so don't think you are unique. If others can sit through it, you can as well. It is only pain, and it will not kill you.

Breathe as quietly as you can. Do not take deep, loud breaths. If you can hear yourself breathing, you can be certain that others can hear you breathing as well. You can hear a pin drop in a zendo during zazen, so imagine what a loud, raspy breathing routine sounds like. Be mindful of those around you and respectful of others' meditation time.

QUESTION?

Is the Zen custom of *kyosaku* safe?
The *kyosaku*, a light strike on the back with a stick, is given by *jikijitsu* during meditation when one becomes drowsy or has difficulty concentrating. It is given only to those who request it, is not painful or harmful, and is very beneficial in clearing the mind and in making the meditation more meaningful.

When the zazen session is over, you are free to shake out your legs, gently and quietly of course. And you might want to shrug your shoulders, stretch your neck, and engage in otherwise discreet stretches. Don't stand until the teacher stands, as a show of respect. The teacher will walk out of the zendo, and you can follow the person in front you. When you exit, you may once again put on your shoes.

There are activities other than zazen that take place in the zendo.

There is tea service, walking meditation, dharma talks, and more. Please see Chapter 17 for more information on sesshin and going on retreats.

Gassho and Bowing

Newcomers to Zen often ask about *gassho* and bowing. *Gassho* means, literally, "to place the two palms together." A *gassho* then, is placing the hands in a prayer-like position. The bow comes from the waist. The two gestures are performed together, so you *gassho* and bow.

Gesture of Enlightenment

When we bring both hands together, we are expressing symbolically the joining of two into one. Therefore, the *gassho* is a gesture of enlightenment. It is a sign of respect that dates back to the enlightenment of the Buddha.

Both *gassho* and bowing are common to all schools of Buddhism and are not limited to Zen practice.

It is said that when the Buddha arose from his position under the bodhi tree, he had realized enlightenment. He went on his way and eventually ran into the ascetics whom he had previously been practicing with. Upon seeing their old friend Shakyamuni, they realized instantly that he had become a Buddha and had realized enlightenment. They each simultaneously put their hands together and bowed in respect to the Buddha, and *gassho* and bowing have been a tradition in Buddhism ever since.

Sign of Respect

Bowing is also a sign of deep respect and should be done with mindfulness. When you bow from the waist, be mindful of your bowing. Do not bow too fast or too slow, but bow humbly and moderately. If you bow too fast, your bow will appear to be casual and lacking in reverence. If you bow too slowly, you will give the appearance of the "stink of Zen," as discussed in the last chapter. You will get the feel for the appropriate way to bow if you spend time in a zendo with others.

"As long as there is true bowing, the Buddha Way shall not deteriorate." —Dogen

There are two kinds of bow you will encounter in daily practice. There is the standing bow, which we have discussed so far, and then there is the prostration bow. The full prostration is performed like this:

1. Start from a standing position with your hands in *gassho*.
2. Bend from the waist, get down on your knees, using your hands if necessary, and place your forehead on the floor. Your hands should be on either side of your head, palms up to the ceiling. Your body is touching the floor only at elbows, knees, hands, and forehead.
3. When your forehead touches the ground, raise your hands up slightly in a gesture of respect.
4. Raise yourself back to your feet and repeat.

Bowing should be done with great respect and mindfulness of every movement. When you bow, you are showing your respect for your Buddha-nature and the true nature of the world.

Setting Up Your Zendo at Home

You can set up a zendo at home if you have an extra room in your home that doesn't get much use. If you are sitting alone, you might only have your one zafu and zabuton, but you can always get a local sitting group together one day a week at your home and add cushions as necessary.

The Supplies

You can decorate the room with Zen art, such as calligraphy or Japanese paintings. Tibetan Buddhist art is also appropriate. You can find some beautiful *thangkas* or mandalas online or at a Tibetan or Asian art gallery. You may also have statues of Buddhas or bodhisattvas that you can use for your main altar and side altars, if you choose to have them.

Check back to the list of altar supplies given in this chapter (see the section titled "The Altar") and set up an altar at one end of the room, making sure to include incense and holder, Buddha statue, candle, and flowers. You can find altar supplies online at many of the meditation supply stores. You can even buy beautiful handmade altars online that affix easily to a wall. For instance, the Zen Mountain Monastery in Mount Tremper, New York, has a wonderful online store that can meet your needs for an at-home zendo.

Thangkas are paintings, often done on canvas, that are turned into scrolls, framed in silk, and hung from a dowel. Many *thangkas* are also mandalas. They depict images of deities, such as Avalokiteshvara—the bodhisattva of compassion—or any of the numerous Tibetan deities. They are often used as meditative devices and are hung by the altar.

At-Home Sitting Group

Starting a local sitting group is a wonderful way to keep your practice alive and ensure that you sit regularly. Sometimes a Zen center or monastery might be within commuting distance but too far away to allow you to visit more than once a week or so. If you have a sitting group that meets at your house for a morning, evening, or weekend sit, it can motivate you to sit more frequently.

We know of sitting groups that meet at a member's house once a week in a room set up as a zendo. They do three sits of twenty-five minutes each, with breaks for walking meditation in between the sits to stretch out the legs. The sits take place every Sunday at 7:00 A.M. This leaves plenty of time in the day for the members of this *sangha* to do whatever they choose with their rest of their Sunday morning and afternoon.

After the last sit, they do a short tea service on the cushions and then congregate in the kitchen for a social half hour. This *sangha* has been gathering this way for several years, and Sunday mornings have become a highlight of the week for participants as they share their spirituality and reinforce their commitment to practice.

Bringing your Zen practice into your home by creating a zendo and perhaps inviting others to join you is a wonderful blessing. Today, the world is a fast-paced, chaotic, and stressful place a great deal of the time. We run from place to place, feel overworked, and often feel there is not enough time in life to get everything done we'd like to get done. Making your home a peaceful, simple haven, with a room where you can drop your small self completely is a great gift to give yourself.

Simplify your life, simplify your home, and make it a place free of anxiety, greed, and chaos, a little at a time. Add a zendo to your simplified home, and you will have a sanctuary to go when you are stressed, tired, angry, or upset. And that place will beckon to you every day to continue your beautiful practice. Ⓔ

Chapter 14

Working Zen: Practice in the Office

Don't leave your practice at home! It's portable. Take your practice everywhere with you, even to the office or wherever you may work. Zen practice is not limited to the twenty-five minutes we may spend sitting on a zafu. It infiltrates our life and guides our actions and minds from dawn until we close our eyes at night. And this includes, of course, our lives at work.

Wherever You Go, There You Are

If you are serious about your Zen practice, the question will probably cross your mind at some point whether you should enter a monastery and devote your life completely to practice. Family, friends, work, and the world at large can interfere with your wonderful sense of peace and challenge your equanimity.

Is it a good idea for you to throw down your life, renounce all of your belongings, perhaps shave your head, and enter the monastic life? It depends. Monastery life is a wonderful path for some people. However, many more consider entering a monastery as a means of escaping the day-to-day life with which they have difficulty coping. Just remember, wherever you go, there you are. In other words, *you* will be at the monastery. You cannot escape yourself, and you cannot escape your problems for long.

After a time, you might discover that your problems have, in fact, followed you to the monastery. For example, if you had trouble dealing with others at your work, outside the monastery, you will find that you have to deal with others in the monastery as well. You might, for a time, feel that you have escaped certain issues, and they might even have gone to the back burner. But, often, these parts of ourselves that we need to contend with are blessings in disguise. In the world outside the monastery, we confront these issues, and we learn to grow and change. Our practice is harder because of them and, therefore, our practice grows stronger.

It is an individual choice whether or not you will pick the monastic or layperson's life. But if you lean toward a monastic life, make sure it is because you are going *toward* the monastic life and not because you are *running away* from the world at large.

If you really want to practice Zen, you might want to come down from the mountaintop, and enter the marketplace. Don't keep it to yourself. Share your Zen life with others. Take your Zen practice out of seclusion and into the modern-day market—work.

Taking Zen to Work

Work is a big part of our lives. Whether you love your job, hate your job, or are indifferent to it, you spend quite a bit of time working. Some of us, the lucky ones, absolutely love our work and look forward to showing up every day. Others would gladly throw their jobs over in a millisecond if they thought they could find one that suited them better. A great majority of people, however, fall somewhere in the middle, sometimes liking and sometimes disliking their work. Your Zen practice can contribute to your ability to deal more effectively with the conflicts you encounter in the office.

Making Distinctions

Whatever we do and wherever we do it, we tend to set up likes and dislikes at work, or we might rank things we do according to our own value system. How many times have you heard someone complaining about a task at work, preferring to do one task over another? One of our friends, who is the boss at his job, always says to his employees when they complain about a certain task, "You get paid from nine o'clock to five o'clock if you are working, so why does it matter what you do in that time?" It matters to us because all day long we make distinctions.

Our distinctions range from, "I like the coffee, but I hate that creamer they put out" to "I like writing my monthly status report, but I hate filing the paperwork." If you listen to your thoughts all day, you will recognize a constant parade of distinctions. "She's nice, he's an idiot; Mondays suck, but Fridays are great; the bathroom on the second floor beats the bathroom on the third floor; Andy has an ugly shirt on today, but the one Susan wears is great; this pen is awful, where's my favorite pen?" And on and on and on.

Making distinctions is the same as having preferences. Having preferences can often lead to a kind of suffering as we elevate one thing over another. If you are thinking, "This pen is awful, where is my favorite pen?" you are certainly not living in the moment. You are living in the future moment when you envision having the pen that will make you feel better. Feel fine with the pen you have now. This is the road to happiness. As the Sixth Patriarch of Zen, Hui-neng, once said, "While we may say that humans mark distinctions of north and south, in terms of Buddha-nature south and north do not exist."

FACT

One way to practice Zen at work is to become aware of the distinctions you are making. Then focus your acceptance on what is going on right in front of you. You do not necessarily have to *love* what you are doing but just to do it. Put your attention on the task itself, not on how you feel about the task.

What did he mean by this? How could north and south not exist? Think about it this way. If you were to head north and keep on going, you would eventually be walking south. There is no distinction between north and south, east and west. These distinctions are created by us to facilitate communication. Directions such as these are useful, but they are not the *truth*.

Forming Opinions

We make distinctions not only within our jobs but also about our jobs. We form instant opinions about people based on the work they do. "What do you do?" is a question we are often greeted with when introduced to new people. The answer we give can often create a strong impression on someone else without our saying anything other than naming our occupation.

Think about your own impressions of the people who work in other professions. What would you think if you were introduced to someone who said he was a judge? A beauty queen? A mechanic? A lawyer? A priest? A rabbi? A television producer? A writer of novels?

Take a moment to consider your first thoughts upon hearing someone else's profession. If someone were to say that he or she was a politician, what would your immediate impression be of that person?

More distinctions most likely. Lawyers are bad, doctors are good, producers are greedy, politicians are liars and so on. We form judgments about other people merely from knowing what work they do. We may even feel less inclined to talk to someone just because we have formed judgments about their profession! Don't define yourself by your own job, and don't define another by his or her job. Your job is not who you are, and that applies to all people. Drop the distinctions and judgments, and try to stay open at work.

Overheard: A man told his date that he was dissatisfied with his profession of counselor and was looking for new work. "What do you want to do?" she asked him.

"I want to snowboard, run, and go camping," he said, seriously, "but no one will pay me for it!"

Don't trap yourself in small mind by defining yourself by what you do. Big mind!

Right Livelihood

As you continuously practice Zen, you might eventually consider that the work you are doing is not conducive to following Right Livelihood. Right Livelihood first requires that you look at your choices for work, and then that you decide if what you are doing to put food on the table is causing harm to anyone or anything else. Then, you should take it one step further and find work that not only is free from harming others but is actually *helpful* to others. We should live an honorable life, one in which we do service in our communities, large or small. There are certainly occupations that you will avoid if you are practicing Zen. Some of the more obvious occupations to avoid might include:

- The creation or sale of weapons
- Animal testing
- Executioner
- Worker in a slaughterhouse
- Furrier
- Drug dealer
- Dealer in a casino
- Prostitute

Choosing a Career

With so many career opportunities available to us, it is often difficult to make the decision about what Right Livelihood is when choosing a career. As a Zen practitioner, you are probably looking for a job that promotes peace and doesn't cause injury to others.

"The most important step in building support for Right Livelihood is giving back more than you get. It's not really a matter of keeping track in some kind of ledger book. It's more a function of the attitude that you adopt in caring for yourself and those around you. If you show an interest in helping and sharing, those around you will start helping you and sharing more with you."
—Claude Whitmyer

It is hard to know if the company you are working for, which might be extremely large, is performing harmful acts in some area, somewhere. Perhaps your company is exploiting workers in a developing country, or perhaps byproducts of your company's manufacturing process are polluting the environment. Sylvia Boorstein addresses this concern in her book, *It's Easier Than You Think:* "It's hard to know the wholesomeness of all the products of any corporation, corporate mergers being what they are. Who knows what else is being manufactured by my detergent company's subsidiaries? . . . For me, a complete picture of wholesome Right Livelihood is even larger than the proscriptions that reflect *external choices.* Wholesome internal choices—healthy attitudes about one's work—also contribute to mental happiness and peace of mind. Everyone's livelihood is an opportunity for self-esteem."

Ultimately you must decide for yourself if your occupation is one in which you are comfortable. If your attitude at work is good, perhaps what you do doesn't matter as much as how you do it.

As a practicing Buddhist, you are hoping to realize enlightenment by working toward a serene existence throughout the world. Any negative energy you extend, whether at home, on the job, or while shopping at the mall, will take away from your serenity and the serenity of others. It will cause unrest in the environment. When choosing a job, it's important to consider harmlessness and your serenity. Can you practice harmlessness while working in a nuclear weapons plant? Can you clear-cut a forest and maintain serenity for yourself and others? Can you test cosmetics on animals? In order to have Right Livelihood, we must examine everything we do in life, including our occupations, and spend our work time practicing peacefulness and kindness in the world.

FACT

There is actually an award for Right Livelihood given every year by the Right Livelihood Foundation in Stockholm, Sweden. The award was established in 1980 to honor and support people or organizations who have "performed outstanding work on behalf of our planet and its people." There are now more than 100 laureates from forty-eight countries around the world.

Zen and the Military Career

According to the Buddha, no war is a just war. There is no reason on earth worthy of picking up arms against another person. There is no justification for striking out at another. To commit any violent act is clearly against the Buddha's teaching and not in the spirit of your Zen practice and training.

Therefore you might ask: What about a career in the military—is that Right Livelihood? Fighting is not living a compassionate and loving life. Fighting, even if in self-defense, has at its goal the harm of another. But sometimes military forces are on peacekeeping missions. Is this then a focus on Right Livelihood? The Buddha lived in a time where Right Livelihood was, perhaps, more easily defined. Today, things seem to fall into a gray area more readily.

Empty Mind

In Zen, we speak of empty mind, of emptying the mind of the self. In most occupations today, it would seem to be extremely difficult to go through the day with empty mind. Tasks call to us, and we interact with others throughout the work hours. However, living in empty mind at work can be a wonderful way to spend your time.

"This does not mean a closed mind, but actually an empty mind and a ready mind. If your mind is empty, it is always ready for anything; it is open to everything. In the beginner's mind there are many possibilities; in the expert's mind there are few."
—Shunryu Suzuki, <u>Zen Mind, Beginner's Mind</u>

Just think. If you are free from the ego constantly inserting itself at work, you can focus wholly on the task at hand, and you can *do* what you need to do instead of *thinking* about what you need to do, meanwhile judging yourself or others the entire time you do it.

Losing Yourself in Work

How much time do you spend actually thinking about doing the tasks you dislike doing, instead of doing them? This is procrastination. In other words, become the task that you are undertaking on any given day. Throw yourself into it, mindful of every aspect of the work you tackle. For instance, you can be mindful of typing, focusing completely on the document in front of you rather than thinking about the Internet site you want to check before you leave for lunch.

Losing yourself in your work is of course easier with some tasks than others. You will probably find it easier to become your work if you are doing physical work, rather than if you are working with numbers or managing a crowded roomful of people. When you are doing physical work, you will first strive for mindfulness and then, as Philip Kapleau says in *The Three Pillars of Zen,* "mindlessness." He says, "These are simply two different degrees of absorption. Mindfulness is a state wherein one is totally aware in any situation and so always able to respond appropriately. Yet one is *aware* that one is aware. Mindlessness, on the other hand, or 'no-mindedness' as it has been called, is a condition of such complete absorption that there is no vestige of self-awareness."

You will find that if you can work in a state of mindfulness (or mindlessness), you will perform the tasks at exactly the level they need to be performed. You will neither move too slow or too fast; everything will be exactly as it should be.

We often do tasks with half our mind. Some of us multitask all day long. We speak on the phone while typing reports; we file while speaking to coworkers. Do one thing at a time and throw yourself completely into what is right in front of you. Empty your mind of all other matters.

There is a wonderful freedom in entering fully into the moment. All of your preconceptions disappear. Your mind opens up and you have more energy. Your thoughts are not draining the life force from you as you struggle to focus on work when you'd rather be thinking about dinner. As your mind opens, your concentration expands, and you find your work gets done at a higher level, a level that you had been unable to reach.

Stressing Out on the Job

You can use your Zen practice to keep the stress level down at work as well. Take a few moments to meditate every day, several times a day if you can. You will find the break refreshing and calming.

The Zazen Break Remedy

Even if you work in a cubicle, you can practice zazen right at your desk. Just sit up straight and focus on your breathing. If you are uncomfortable closing your eyes, keep them open and focus on the floor or down at your desk.

You can take zazen breaks in any profession. If you have a five-minute break, do some breathing exercises to rejuvenate your flagging spirit and release some tension. As you breathe in, watch the breath as it comes into your nose, down your throat, and into your lungs, expanding them. Imagine the breath going down through your stomach into your *hora.* Then imagine the breath coming back up your stomach, out your throat and nose, and into the world. Follow the breath all the way to the end, and you will find a blankness there. The stress will seep out of you if you do these exercises for several minutes.

FACT

It is sometimes helpful to keep some reading material nearby while you are at work. Reading a passage from a book on Zen or a few quotations from others who practice can help you get back to center. There are some wonderful meditation books on the shelves these days—daily wisdom quotation collections that can serve as a resting place in a stressful environment.

Try to continue the exercise until you feel the stress abate somewhat and until your thinking slows down. Sometimes our thoughts can start to race at work as we get caught up in the drama of the day. Learn to space breaks so that you interrupt this cycle of thinking and avoid becoming wholly ego-driven. At the end of the day, it is not our work that exhausts us—it is our incessant thinking. It drains us and wears us out.

It's All in the Attitude

Taking Zen to work means approaching work with an attitude of compassion and service. What can you do to make your workplace a more compassionate environment? Practicing the steps of the Eightfold Path at work will help you actualize a worthy attitude every day.

If we are practicing Right Speech at work, we hold back any inappropriate or harsh words and try to make our criticism compassionate and helpful. When we find ourselves in disagreement with a coworker over a work issue, we speak honestly and clearly, maintaining a calm demeanor. We put forth Right Effort at work, not overworking or slacking off, but doing the work necessary to get our job done well. We make an effort to understand what others need to accomplish and be helpful whenever we can.

With Right Mindfulness and Right Concentration, we practice the focus necessary to actually do our work, instead of playing around or procrastinating. We avoid wasting company assets, whether they be time, money, or office supplies. We use our powers of concentration to be efficient workers, using our time well. We strive at all times for a humble outlook and for the willingness to work hard. If we are managers, we act as leaders and live up to our responsibility. Although sometimes we want to be a friend instead of a boss, we must look at our job responsibilities and perform them to the best of our ability.

Being mindful at work and avoiding making distinctions does not mean that you should force yourself to stay in a job you dislike. If you have the choice to move to another job that might make your life a little easier or more pleasant, don't stop yourself from doing it. You are human.

We give respect to our coworkers and understand the interconnectedness of work. We know that our part of a job does not stand alone. It is affected by everyone else at work and, in turn, affects everyone else at work. We clearly see our place in the bigger picture and are able to remain humble because of it. If we practice the steps of the Eightfold Path at work and in every aspect of our lives, we are honing our Zen practice every day.

Bringing compassion and kindness into the office can be difficult for some people. There are probably people at the office you might not like very much, people who make you feel crazy, short-tempered, or judgmental. But practicing Zen is practicing loving-kindness to all sentient beings. As writer Natalie Goldberg was told when she asked her teacher, Dainin Katagiri, what all sentient beings are, "We have to be kind even to the chair, the air, the paper, and the street. That's how big and accepting our minds have to become." So start with the coworkers who drive you crazy. It's good practice for the chairs.

When a student asked Thich Nhat Hanh how she could be more mindful at work, he replied, "I try to find the way to do things that is most pleasurable. There may be many different ways to perform a given task— but the one that holds my attention best is the one that is most pleasant."

Successful Relationships at Work

Successful relationships at work are the same as successful relationships at home. If you'd like to improve your relationship with other people, take the focus off yourself and put it on what you can do for others. This does not mean buying people presents and bribing them at work. Instead, do what needs to be done to complete the tasks at hand.

Do not do other people's jobs for them. If we are capable people, we often pick up other people's slack. However, while it is wonderful to help others, sometimes doing someone else's job for them is not helpful at all. Doing service in any situation is a gift to yourself. If you complete other people's tasks for them, you could be taking away an opportunity that person might have to find the joy in forgetting oneself and doing service for another.

If we practice Zen in every aspect of our lives, we will find that we get along with those around us much better than we have before. We will have an inner peace that allows us to practice compassion and tolerance with our families as well as our coworkers. We will have a better ability to focus on our jobs and, therefore, we will become better employees. We will be helpful and concerned with the welfare of those who share our lives.And if we are ill-tempered or feel unhappy, if we are in pain or if we make mistakes, we will know that we can return to the basics of our practice and regain our perspective. We can always go back to the cushion and start our day again. (E)

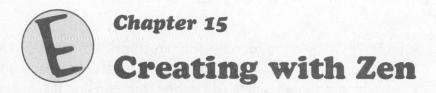

Chapter 15

Creating with Zen

Since the time of the Buddha, art and Zen practice have walked hand in hand. Indeed, to many Zen teachers, art practice is an essential part of Zen training. Our creativity is a wonderful expression of our true nature and our interconnectedness with all things. In Zen, art is engaged the same way everything else is engaged— with entire mind and spirit.

Art as Practice

Art is a form of Zen practice. When one picks up a paintbrush, gardening shears, a pen, or any other artistic tool, the possibility arises of dropping the ego and fully engaging with the art. We can lose our discerning mind and become that which we create, so that it is impossible to tell where the art begins and the artist ends.

FACT

John Daido Loori is the founder and director of the Mountain and Rivers Order of Zen Buddhism, in the United States and abroad. The training program practiced by the Mountain and Rivers order is known as the Eight Gates of Zen. Art practice is one of the Eight Gates of Zen practice, as well as zazen, Zen study, academic study, liturgy, Right Action, body practice, and work practice.

Discover Your Creative Side

Many of us might immediately think to ourselves that we have absolutely no creative side whatsoever. The thought of trying to draw fills us with dread. We think of the immature, childlike drawings we have produced. We think back to efforts at painting, sewing, carpentry, gardening, or cooking, and cringe at the thought of sharing our results with anyone.

However, if you think you do not have a creative side, think again. We are creative every day of our lives. We decorate our homes, schedule the day's activities, cook our meals, dress ourselves, doodle, write e-mails or letters, sing made-up songs in the car, and make hundreds of other creative acts every single day.

Our very existence is an act of creation. The world itself is bursting with creativity, birthing energy in one form or another every second, over and over again, all the time. Butterflies, earthworms, maggots, water, air, thunder, rainfall, people, viruses, clowns, electricity . . . everything around us is a manifestation of the energy of creativity. Does the flower think it cannot bloom a bud? Does a sun think it cannot light the sky?

Somewhere inside you is a creative force. Learn to express your inner creativity. Try different mediums, and you will be sure to find that which works for you. Traditional Zen art forms include calligraphy, painting, archery, gardening, flower-arranging, the tea ceremony, swordsmanship, poetry (such as haiku) photography, and more. However, do not be limited by tradition. There are thousands of ways to express yourself creatively, and you can find one that works for you if you give yourself the willingness to let go and drop the critical, self-centered mind.

I celebrate myself, and sing myself:
And what I assume you shall assume,
For every atom belonging in me
as good as belongs to you.
—Walt Whitman, "Song of Myself"

Mindfulness Training

Art practice is mindfulness training. The art we create first comes out of technical training we receive in group classes, on our own, or through individual instruction. The technical training—once it is mastered—is then eventually expressed in spontaneous practice. The artist strives to free himself from the bondage of small self and create art from the Big Mind that is accessible to us all. Zen art tends to be simple, sometimes stark, and lovely. Just as we discussed simplicity at home in earlier chapters, we find we strive for simplicity in our art as well.

When you approach a creative act in Zen, don't worry about what you are doing. Don't judge yourself or allow your inner critic to run wild. Art practice is not about the result, it is about the process. Anyone can arrange some flowers. But doing so mindfully, expressing the creativity of your Buddha-nature, turns flower-arranging into a Zen practice. Just quiet your mind, and let yourself go.

Zen Gardening

You have probably seen a Zen garden somewhere. If you haven't seen a full-scale, real-life Zen garden, then you might have noticed the little Zen rock gardening kits in your local bookstore. What might strike you about these miniature rock gardens is their simplicity. Zen gardens are not filled to capacity with flowers, shrubbery, statuary, and garden ornaments. They are simple, stark, and lovely.

Some of our city parks house beautiful Zen and Japanese gardens. These are some of the most exquisite gardens to be found anywhere. The stark beauty inspires serenity and peace.

QUESTION?

Why is sand used in Zen gardens?
Japanese Zen masters traditionally created gardens out of rocks and sand. The sand was raked into patterns that could be destroyed quickly, emphasizing the impermanence of all things.

Garden Equipment

You can try to create a Zen garden at home, a wonderful way to express creativity. Here are some supplies you will find useful:

- Sand, gravel, or stone
- Rocks
- Plants, such as evergreens or other shrubbery
- A rake
- Tools for tamping down the earth

This is a task that can be done by anyone, whether you own acres of land or rent a small one-room apartment. Start by creating a space where you can lay some sand. For some, it might be a large ten-foot by ten-foot area in the backyard. Others might simply use an old shoebox or cake pan. In place of sand, you can also use gravel or small rocks, though if you're looking to create the "movement" effect achieved with sand, we highly recommend it over gravel. For those building a full-scale garden, you might want to create a box using railroad ties, bricks, stone, or some other creative and complementary border to define the garden. We've even seen some people use old dinner plates collected at garage sales.

If you prefer to leave your borders open, you can simply lay your sand down in one area, allowing the garden to flow into the rest of the landscape.

Landscaping

Before beginning, it's important to prepare the ground for the sand or gravel. Remove any existing foliage. If you leave grass down, it will grow up through the sand, so prepare the earth for whatever you plan to lay on top of it. Tamp the ground down to ensure that it is level and the soil does not shift. Consult with a local gardening store on ground preparation.

The sand you will use for your Zen garden is not beach sand. You will need some crushed granite, which comes in a variety of shades.

Meanwhile, you can collect the rocks you will use for your garden. In Zen gardens, the sand is usually symbolic of water, which is where the effect of movement applies. The rocks symbolize mountains or islands. You can use the rake to move the sand around, creating different types of movement around your mountains. Gravel or stone do not possess the same ability for manipulation that sand has, but you can nevertheless create the illusion of movement by sweeping the path of the gravel or stone around the rocks, creating an image of a moving river.

Place your rocks in the garden, and plant any shrubbery you choose, arranging the foliage around the garden. There are many wonderful books on Zen gardening that might inspire ideas for arrangements.

These types of Zen gardens are known as dry gardens, or *karesansui*. One of the most famous dry gardens, Ryoanji, can be found in Japan and is more than 650 years old. As final touches, you can add bridges and lanterns to your garden as well.

If you live in an apartment, you can add foliage to your garden by planting small plants or a miniature bonsai garden.

Spiritual Experience

The actual creation of your garden is a wonderful spiritual experience, but you can continue to use your garden for meditation once it is completed. You can use it for zazen and walking meditation. Mindfully maintain your Zen garden; clean it of debris that might get blown into it, such as leaves and branches. When you rake the sand into different patterns, focus your mind on the breath and enter a deep meditative state, where you can let go of the thinking mind and become the rake, the sand, the garden.

When we garden, we connect with our environment in a powerful way. We become intimate with the cycle of life. With our hands immersed in the earth itself, it is easy to drop our sense of self and feel the deep connection we have with the energy of the planet.

Your garden does not, of course, have to be solely made up of rocks and sand. It does not have to be stark either. Express yourself through your gardening, and celebrate the abundance of life you encounter. It doesn't matter what kind of garden you create, gardening in any form is a wonderful way to try out your Zen art practice.

Symbol of Impermanence

Our garden is a meditation on impermanence. If we spend time in our garden, we see the change of the seasons. We might start to notice that the passage from one season to the next is not as clear-cut as we once imagined. During the depths of winter, buds start to appear on the trees—harbingers of spring. During the height of summer, some of the trees might start dropping their leaves, telling us that fall is around the corner. We don't wake up on the morning of the winter equinox and say: Winter is here. Perhaps it has snowed in November. Perhaps there is a heat wave in February. Change is constant, and impermanence can be noticed everywhere.

As we garden, we find ourselves completely connected to the laws of impermanence as we see the buds fall from the stems of our flowers. We see the lilac bush bloom in early May and the blossoms fall two weeks later. We see the sunflowers in late summer and the chrysanthemums in the fall. We see everything arise and fall, and we can find great comfort in the parade of life. We meditate on the impermanence around us.

FACT

Zen gardens in monasteries were used for contemplation. They were often designed to actively aid the monk in meditation.

Whether you've created a Zen garden out of sand, or already have a favorite flower garden, this little place can be used for wonderful meditation sessions. Take the time to sit in your garden, or any garden of your choosing, and practice breath meditation. Lose yourself in the smell of the flowers and freshly cut grass. Listen to the sound of the birds or the ringing of nearby wind chimes. Hear the rustle of a tree's leaves and the swish of a gentle breeze.

By focusing on your garden and the earth around you, moments of enlightenment will come to you as you drop away from yourself and meld with the environment and your garden. If we lose our connection to the world or our environment, we lose an integral part of ourselves and an opportunity to connect with life in a powerful way. Anyone with an appreciation for the environment knows and feels the connection we have with every living thing on earth, from the soil to the trees to the birds in the sky.

Calligraphy

One of the most popular Zen art forms is Japanese calligraphy, which is also referred to as *zenga*. Through this spiritual expression, the artist must be in touch with Buddha-nature in order to fully create an expression of enlightenment. A proper brushstroke only comes from a union with the world. To practice calligraphy to the utmost, the artist becomes one with the brush. There is no "I" and no pen, only the act itself.

The Roots of *Zenga*

Since the seventh century, Zen monks have been using Japanese calligraphy as part of art practice and meditation. It was not uncommon for Japanese calligraphy and painting to be a koan. One of the most common examples of *zenga* is the very simplistic open circle, called *enso* (think of a capital "O" made with a brushstroke). A very popular *zenga* during the Edo period of Japan in the eighteenth century, the *enso* symbolized enlightenment, emptiness, and life itself.

The Art of Precision and Unity

Calligraphy is a very precise and concentrated craft, making it perfect for Zen practice. During the creation of each letter, word, or picture, the artist must be careful to not have even the slightest hesitation. A moment of pause can cause the ink to blot on the thin rice paper, ruining the calligraphy or painting. Because of the precision it takes to create calligraphy, the technique is learned, practiced, and perfected over many years.

A calligraphy artist has to be one with his art, and much like Zen meditation, his craftsmanship must be honed by practicing and training for many years.

One way to look at the connection between a calligraphy artist and her art is to ask yourself some seemingly simple questions. Where is the beginning and end of the self? Is the tear falling from your eye part of you, or part of the tissue you wipe it away with? Is the sweat on your forehead part of you, or your hat? Once your tears dry on your handkerchief, where do they go? Where are the lines that define what is us and what is not us? The same questions apply to Zen art practice, including calligraphy. The boundary between artist and art is impossible to define. There is, in fact, no boundary—just as there is no boundary between the air, the earth, and ourselves. Everything is dependent on each other. Once the boundary between art supplies, art, and self are gone, the art can be fully executed. It is an illusion that we are separate from anything, and once we truly see that there is no separation, we are truly ready to create and see that which arises out of us.

Trying Your Hand at *Zenga*

If you are interested in the practice of calligraphy, check out your local art supply store or bookstore. There are many wonderful beginner books on calligraphy if you'd like to try it at home. You can also find a teacher or take a class to learn the technical skills necessary to free yourself up for some wonderful art practice. It's important to keep in mind that no matter what Zen art you choose to practice, the key word, as with your meditation, is practice. No artist is going to pick up a brush and find perfection with the first stroke. It takes many years before you can become one with your supplies and, eventually, your art.

"Seeing forms with the whole body and mind, hearing sounds with the whole body and mind, one understands them intimately." —Dogen

Flower-Arranging

Flower-arranging is one of many Zen art forms. Called ikebana, Japanese flower-arranging evolved in Japan over many centuries, and like art everywhere, is continuing to develop throughout the world. While it is suspected that ikebana has been around even longer, the first written proof of this art can be traced back to the fifteenth century, to the first ikebana school. Like calligraphy and music, many years of training and practice are required before an artist achieves the technical skills necessary to perform the art well. This is an amazing concept to most. After all, it's just arranging flowers. How hard can it be?

The truth is that ikebana is more than just the simple flower-arranging you and I do with the flowers from our garden. In ikebana, there are many different techniques involved in fastening the flowers into an arrangement. In addition, contrary to many Western arrangements, the essence of ikebana is simplicity. Artists use very few flowers, since leaves and stems are equally important to the arrangement. This technique uses the flowers, the container, and the space around the flower arrangement as part of the artistic impression.

FACT

The experience of ikebana is contemplative, respectful, and disciplined. When you arrange flowers, you try to express the form, beauty, and life of the flowers. Ikebana and calligraphy are moving meditations, in which we follow the movement of our hands as we respond in the moment to our craft.

Like any craft or art, there are many different styles of ikebana. Some styles use low containers and pile flowers on the top. Other styles involve placing flowers in tall, narrow vases and presenting them in a more relaxed, tossed-in look. Like Zen practice as a whole, ikebana strives to stay in touch with the environment around us, and this means using seasonal flowers and foliage in a natural presentation. When we practice the art of flower-arranging, we enter into the moment as we do with all of our art practices. We engage with the organic matter, the flowers, and the plants of the earth. We use the flower, the empty space around the flower, the container, and the setting. We are mindful of the materials we use as well as the environment in which we use them. We strive for harmony with all.

Poetry

When we were children, we made up poems and silly rhymes all the time. But as we get older, we become more self-conscious and the silly songs and rhymes of childhood fall away. And so does much of our spontaneity. Perhaps we are playful like children with our spouses or very close friends, but for the most part we hide these lovely, natural, and fun impulses from others. We lose the wonder we had as a child when we saw the infinite everywhere.

Children have the wonderful ability to spend hours doing nothing at all. An entire afternoon can be spent playing with sticks or bowls of water. A creek bed can provide an entire summer's entertainment, and a few trees can become an entire world in and of themselves. Because of its spontaneity and playfulness, children love haiku. It is a form of poetry that they can engage in with much enthusiasm, as haiku is written in a moment of inspiration that arises out of spontaneity, as all Zen art does.

The Haiku

Unlike much Western poetry, the Japanese haiku doesn't need to rhyme. Haiku traditionally follows a 5-7-5 pattern. The first line has five syllables, the second line seven syllables, and the last line five syllables. Because the rules of haiku are more lenient than other poetry, it is easier and more fun for beginners to participate in. The 5-7-5 rule is especially easy to follow, although it is not a requirement. The really important thing to remember when creating a haiku is that the practice only uses necessary words. No spare words or symbols are allowed. Like all Zen art, haikus are written when the small self drops and the artist (or poet in this case) is in touch with the unity of all things. Like calligraphy and ikebana, haiku is a mindfulness meditation. In order to create haiku, one must be mindful of everything around oneself—and, of course, ready to write things down. Most commonly, haikus speak of everyday life and nature.

In most haiku, you'll find that one of the lines subtly (usually with one word) indicates to the reader the season the haiku refers to, thereby giving it a sense of time and place. Wild plums, for instance, would indicate summer, while fallen leaves would signify autumn.

Like Zen, there is no self in haiku, and the poems usually do not include a participant. Rarely will you find an adjective in haiku, since adjectives present an opinion and therefore suggest a participant to supply that opinion. For example, you would never say "beautiful" wild plums or "crisply" fallen leaves.

Basho

Basho is largely regarded as one of the masters of haiku. He was born in seventeenth-century Japan and given the name Matsuo Munefusa. As a young man, Basho was a samurai warrior, but eventually he put down his sword and picked up the pen for poetry. The word "basho" means "banana leaves," and Basho came by this name as he spent many years living in a hut made of banana leaves. Here is an example of Basho's haiku.

old pond . . .
A frog leaps in
water's sound

This haiku does not follow the traditional rules of 5-7-5, but it is wonderfully evocative and reveals the sanctity of the small things, such as the sound of water as a frog jumps in his pond. These are the indescribably beautiful elements of life: the movement of frogs, the sounds of water, a body of water. Haikus capture a reverence for the simple things in life. These are the things we often take for granted but which have the capacity to move us to tears if we would just wake up.

FACT

Haiku happens all the time, wherever there are people who are "in touch" with the world of their senses and with their own feeling response to it.

Unlimited Creativity

You are not, of course, limited to trying a more traditional form of Zen art practice. You do not have to choose to express yourself through calligraphy, ikebana, gardening, or poetry. There are a multitude of ways to express your creativity. Here are a few ideas for you to try to free up your creative spirit and indulge in some art practice:

- Refinishing furniture
- Woodworking
- Music
- Painting, such as watercolors or acrylics
- Knitting
- Crocheting or cross-stitch
- Basket making
- Pottery
- Cooking
- Creative writing

Check out classes at a local high school or university, and enroll in something that interests you. You can become efficient in the technical mastery of your art, but do not confuse this with art practice. When you bring your Zen practice to your art, the boundary between you and your art will disappear. Art practice emphasizes our interconnectedness with all things. The more you exercise your creative side, the more you will understand about yourself, about others, and about the world around you.

Open Your Dharma Eye

When you know something with your whole body, mind, and spirit, the lines between you and others disappear. The judging mind vanishes. You become the act itself—the brush, the rake, the flower, the poem, the sound, the art—and the reference system you use to interpret the universe no longer exists.

If this makes no sense to us, we continue to practice. John Daido Loori, in the *Eight Gates of Zen*, tells us that Dogen asks, "How do you paint Spring?" If we paint flowers, fruit, and trees do we paint spring? No, says Dogen. "When you paint Spring, do not paint willows, plums, peaches, or apricots, but just paint Spring." If we cannot yet paint spring, we must go back to our practice and endeavor to open our dharma eye, so we can see things as they truly are. Through our Zen practice, we might find the way to experience the world as it really is and open our hearts, our minds, and our spirits.

Chapter 16

Zen and Your Body: The Zen Athlete

Athletic pursuit and Zen might not seem like a good match. After all, you might wonder why you want to be in shape for all that sitting around. However, zazen takes a great deal of energy, and it generates a healthy amount of energy, too. Zen and athletic activity have a long shared history. As long as Zen has been around, it has been paired with physical pursuits as well.

Respect Your Body

In the lovely little book *What Would Buddha Do?* by Franz Metcalf, Metcalf poses this question: What would the Buddha do to be happy? In answer, he quotes from the *Jataka Tales,* a collection of stories used by the Buddha and descendants of the Buddha to help Buddhists develop character.

> *Seek health, the greatest blessing; follow virtue. Listen to people, read good books and learn.*
> *Be truthful; break the chain of sad attachment. These six paths lead to the greatest good.*

We notice that health comes first in the list. Maintaining good health is important to the Zen practitioner. We must respect the small self we carry around every day. It is our body that gets us on the cushion and gives us the opportunity to practice.

Do not get caught up in the idea that the small self is not important. Without this body and this mind, we would not be able to continue our practice. We strive to keep our body in good shape and should treat it at least as well as we treat our cars.

Unfortunately, in today's world we often treat our cars better than we treat our bodies. We buy the best gas money can buy and schedule regular service appointments for our automobiles. We check the oil and the air in the tires more often than we check out our own health. We service the car more than we ever consider going to the doctor.

Take Care of Your Body

Take care of this body you have. Feed it well, just as you feed your car well. That means eating real food, not food laden with chemicals, preservatives, and artificial sweeteners. So much of the food we eat today is treated with chemicals and preservatives. We eat on the run and grab a bag of potato chips, a candy bar, or any other food that we consider convenient. Fast food can be found on nearly every corner, and neon lights scream at us to eat unhealthy food that is convenient, quick, and inexpensive. However, as the saying goes, we are what we eat, and we cannot maintain good health if we eat food that is not nourishing for us.

Do not mistreat your body with drugs and alcohol. Exercise your body regularly so it doesn't age before its time. You don't have to be a master athlete to be in shape, but you can walk every day, spend ten minutes stretching, or do a peaceful exercise program such as yoga. Honor the body that gives you such opportunity every day.

If you prepare your own meals at home, you will know that the ingredients you are using are healthy and fresh. You will also be connected to the earth if you handle the fruits and vegetables that go into your meals. Be mindful of the fuel you give your body. You probably wouldn't put a second-rate oil or gasoline into your car, so give your body the same care and consideration.

The Zen Athlete

How can Zen help you if you are an athlete? First, we need to define the word "athlete." When many of us think of athletes, we think of the sports heroes who make millions of dollars each year or those Olympic athletes with their strong, lithe bodies and hours of training. In truth, each and every one of us, no matter our skill level, can be an athlete. Consider yourself an athlete if you spend two days a week in spin class, three days lifting weights, or regular participation on the yoga mat. Whether you're a pro or an amateur just looking to get into shape, Zen practice and exercise can only benefit your athletic training.

Focusing Your Mind

In Zen practice we learn how to focus our minds. We start by focusing on our breath, and then we might move on to koan practice, where we throw our entire mind and body into our koan. We learn what to do with obsessive, persistent thought patterns, and we hone the ability to stay focused for long periods of time. We live in the moment, remaining undistracted by noises and enticements to focus on the past or the present.

Phil Jackson, the Chicago Bulls basketball coach who led the Bulls to six world championships and the Los Angeles Lakers to one, wrote a book about Zen and basketball called *Sacred Hoops: Spiritual Lessons of a Hard Wood Warrior*. Jackson was determined to bring the practices of Zen into the realm of professional sports and taught his players some basic Zen precepts.

"I've learned that the most effective way to forge a winning team is to call on the players' need to connect with something larger than themselves. Even for those who don't consider themselves 'spiritual' in a conventional sense, creating a successful team . . . is essentially a spiritual act." —Phil Jackson, *Sacred Hoops*

Jackson introduced the ideas of selfless team playing, moment-to-moment awareness, and compassion toward others into the game of basketball. He taught his players—including such stars as Michael Jordan, Scottie Pippen, and Dennis Rodman—how to leave the ego-focus behind and turn the "me into a we." He showed them how to stay in the moment, not thinking but doing. And his players learned in the midst of chaos how to keep the focus on the game and therefore how to win. Jackson brought a spiritual element into his coaching and led his teams to victory over and over again.

Wrestler O-nami

In the compilation *Zen Flesh, Zen Bones*, by Paul Reps and Nyogen Senzaki, there is the Zen story about the great wrestler O-nami, which means Great Waves. Great Waves was a very strong wrestler, but he was painfully shy and hated competing in public. He could throw anyone to the mat in private, but in public he always lost. One day Great Waves went to a Zen master for advice.

"Great Waves is your name," the Zen master told him. "So stay in this temple tonight." The Zen master told him to become the huge waves "sweeping everything before them, swallowing all in their path."

Then he would no longer be a wrestler afraid. Great Waves sat in the temple all night. At first he tried to imagine the waves, then he thought of different things. Eventually he turned toward feeling more and more like the waves. By the end of the night the waves had become so big that the room was filled with the waves like a giant sea.

The Zen master entered and found Great Waves smiling. "You are the waves now," he said. "Nothing can disturb you."

Great Waves went on to be an undefeated wrestler in Japan.

FACT

Zen practice can help your performance whether you play on a team or you run by yourself, whether you are playing against an opponent or are trying to beat your own personal best.

The Zone

Most athletes dream about hitting the "zone." If you have ever been a runner or played serious sports, you might have hit the zone at some point yourself. The zone is also familiar to those who have practiced Zen for some time. The zone is when you *become* whatever it is you are doing and lose yourself entirely. For athletes, the zone signifies ultimate athletic performance.

Reaching the Athletic Climax

The zone is the height of athletic performance where everything comes together: years of training, natural ability, confidence, energy, and concentration. For the athlete, it is the most sought-after moment in the pursuit of excellence in sports. To hit the zone is to achieve moments that are truly wondrous and exceptional.

Athletes surpass their own personal best in the zone. They reach goals they had only dreamed of making and become one with their sport and bodies. The zone is a spiritual experience much sought after by many athletes. According to Andrew Cooper in his article "In the Zone: The Zen of Sports" *(Shambhala Sun Online),* "For many of today's athletes, psychological preparation has become as necessary a part of training as physical conditioning, perfecting one's skills, and learning strategy." Today, athletes are increasingly aware of the impact that psychological preparation has on their performance. Training, practice, and physical condition are not the only necessities for peak performance.

Dropping of the Self

Zen practice can help athletes focus better, become less self-conscious, and push themselves into the zone. The zone is essentially the dropping of the small self, the moment when *you are the running, you are the pass, you are the shot.* You become the ball, the toss, the air streaking toward the finish line. There is great freedom in dropping the small self and losing that consciousness that we drag around like a two-ton anchor all day long. If self-consciousness returns, we are thrust out of the zone and back into our normal state of mind, conscious of everyone around us, including all the chaos and distraction. We lose the focus of the moment and return to our normal performance abilities.

You don't have to hire a sports psychologist to help you reach this kind of performance. It is possible that your Zen practice can help you reach your peak in sports, in all facets of your life. Just as we drop our small self in our art practice in Zen, we can also drop our self in sports ranging from basketball to golf, from archery to track.

The concept of the zone is perhaps where many people unfamiliar with Zen practices can understand Zen most clearly. The zone is a familiar idea to many Westerners who spend a great deal of time around sports, either as players or spectators. If you are not an athletic person yourself, perhaps the concept of the zone, or practicing Zen around athletic pursuits, will entice you to enter a new world and put on a pair of sneakers. We don't recommend that you practice Zen solely to increase your sports performance, but if it gets anyone on the cushion, that's okay with us.

If you are skeptical about the uses of Zen in sports, just take a look at the spirituality shelves at your local bookstore. You will see such titles as these, and more: *Zen in the Art of Golf; The Zen of Tennis; Moving Zen: One Man's Journey to the Heart of Karate; Beginner's Guide to Zen and the Art of Windsurfing;* and *Hoops Zen.*

Zen and Competition

Competition seems decidedly anti-Zen. Zen is a peaceful practice aimed at the dropping of ego. Competitive sports seem to glorify ego and promote an "us and them" mentality, which is certainly antithetical to a Zen way of life. However, when you engage in any athletic activity, whether you are in a team sport playing against another team, a solo sport playing against another player, or a solo activity competing against your own personal best, the key is in your approach to the activity rather than the activity itself.

If you take into sports what you have learned in your Zen practice, you will try to become one with whatever you are doing. As seen in the example of Phil Jackson and the Chicago Bulls, that can mean acting in perfect harmony with your teammates or acting in harmony when you are throwing the ball, releasing the bow, delivering a kick, running, and so on. When we practice Zen in a *sangha,* we see the *sangha* as our own Zen team. We do work practice together, cleaning up the Zen center and grounds, with each person taking on one small role. Each role separately is small, but when they're all put together, the Zen center remains clean and efficient.

In team sports, you play your role on your team much the way you would clean up your area of the Zen center. You do it with awareness and focus, entering the moment and directing your whole mind and body into the task. If you are the shortstop, you do not play pitcher. Your goal is the team goal, not your own personal goal. Instead of glorifying the ego, team sports have the potential to create an environment for wonderful Zen practice. You do not focus on winning but on doing what it is you are doing at any given time. To focus on winning is to leave the moment and lose your concentration.

> *"When you do something, if you fix your mind on the activity with some confidence, the quality of your state of mind is the activity itself. When you are concentrated on the quality of your being, you are prepared for the activity."*
> —Shunryu Suzuki,
> Zen Mind, Beginner's Mind

Once the idea of winning enters your mind, self-consciousness arrives, and focus is weakened.

Zen and Martial Arts

Martial arts and Zen seem like diametrically opposed practices. The martial arts seem to promote a warrior mentality while Zen encapsulates a peacekeeping one. When we think of martial arts, we think of kickboxing, karate, Jackie Chan movies, Hong Kong films, and Bruce Lee. We think of breaking things, hurting people, and the samurai spirit. So what do Zen and the martial arts have in common? And how did the two ever meet?

The Legend versus the Truth

It is said that the monks of Shaolin monastery were in feeble condition. They were not eating well and were in terrible physical shape. The monks were sitting without engaging in any physical activity and they had become languid, sluggish, and stupefied. But Bodhidharma arrived, took stock of the situation, and immediately set out to invigorate the practice of the stultified monks. He soon had them practicing kung fu and shortly turned them around into invigorated, aware, and energized practitioners.

FACT

While martial arts seems to be most commonly related to warriors and kung fu films, the art actually places a greater emphasis on discipline, awareness, and unity than it does on fighting. If you have ever seen one of the *Karate Kid* movies, you have seen a very simple portrayal of the ethics of martial arts fighting.

Mental Training

When you practice any of the martial arts, you try to become the movement. The real connection with Zen and the martial arts is in the mental training. In karate, tae kwon do, tai chi chuan, and other martial arts, the mind must become as disciplined as the body. Although much time is spent on physical training, such as kicking, sit-ups, push-ups, arm thrusts, punching, and so on, martial arts are also a form of moving meditation. It is equally important (if not more so) to get the mind trained so the movements can become natural and your mind, body, and spirit can find union in the movement.

Amazing things can happen in martial arts studios. We went to a kung fu exhibition to see a friend, a petite, lightweight woman, break a brick with her hand. We knew she was no Incredible Hulk (no magic involved), and we also knew they were not holding her baby hostage at knifepoint (no incredible surge of adrenaline was likely). Her mental training—along with the momentum of her movement— gave her the ability to slice through the bricks with what looked to us like great ease (though we are sure the bruises didn't feel very good afterward).

Awareness

People who practice the martial arts know that the awareness they train for is about unity and flow.

Most of us imagine "focus" to mean narrowing in on one thing and losing the ability to notice anything else. For instance, if you were playing the piano and were totally focused, you might not hear the phone ring. This is not what we mean when we speak of awareness in Zen or the martial arts. If you were fighting an opponent in martial arts and you were completely focused on the arms of your opponent as he came quickly toward you, you might miss the kick that swept your feet out from under you.

Similarly, when we practice zazen, we do not lose awareness of our environment just because we are focused on our breath or our koan. We are, in fact, completely aware of our environment and have reached a mental focus that allows us to be present with the unity of all things. We are aware that everything is fluid—all things change.

To focus on one thing—such as the hands of your opponent in a karate match—is to ignore the fluidity of things. If you ignore the fluidity of something, the flow of it, you freeze it. And if you freeze something in an effort to capture it, it is lost to you forever.

The Samurai

An essential part of martial arts training, therefore, is the meditation practice necessary to develop the concentration to become a good fighter. Although we might think of the martial arts as attracting a warrior class of people who indulge in a lust for violence, the ethics a samurai lives with are not what one might think. An ideal samurai practices both mental and physical discipline, staying away from pollutants such as alcohol. A samurai practices meditation and compassion, striving to be of service to his community. Samurais are open-minded, resourceful, and nonviolent, using violence only when absolutely necessary.

Zen was intricately associated with the life of the samurai class in Japan. The mental discipline that can be found in Zen practice was of great use to the samurai class. If you think of a soldier in battle, you realize that a soldier has to act immediately. He cannot plan his every next move but must move from action to action in order to stay alive.

Zen can help the soldier as he comes aware of the flowing nature of things and moves without thought, one with his actions and his environment. If a soldier stops to weigh the consequences of his actions, he can find himself on his back on the ground in seconds. So while our immediate thought is that the peaceful ways of the Zen practitioner and the warring ways of the samurai are diametrically opposed to one another, there are places where the two meet in harmony.

For a student of the martial arts today, Zen practice is an invaluable tool for becoming proficient in any of the arts, from karate to kung fu, to tai chi, to aikido.

Yoga

Yoga is an exercise system designed to promote mental, spiritual, and physical health. Yoga has been around for thousands of years. The practice is believed to have come from the Himalayan region of Nepal, Tibet, and the Indian subcontinent—the same region that gave birth to Buddhism 2,500 years ago. Developing out of the spiritual practices of Hinduism, yoga quickly spread to encompass other prevalent Eastern spiritual practices such as Taoism and Buddhism. It has been closely tied to Buddhist practices ever since.

If you are interested in taking up yoga, there are many different styles from which you can choose, such as bhakti yoga, karma yoga, ashtanga yoga, jnana yoga, kundalini yoga, hatha yoga, power yoga, and more. Hatha yoga is probably the form of yoga most familiar to Western practitioners.

Different styles of yoga emphasize different aspects of exercise. Some forms of yoga emphasize holding each exercise in form perfectly, others emphasize the chakra points of energy in the body, and still others focus on relaxation and the power of gravity to assist in each movement.

Movement and Flexibility

Yoga is a wonderful complement to Zen practice. Just like zazen is a seated meditation, yoga is a moving meditation. Awareness is a central part of all yoga exercises. As you move into each new position, you are completely aware and focused on your body and your breath. You try to become one with the movement. Yoga is not just a series of stretching or warm-up exercises. It is a total health program aimed at balance and connection. Zen meditation can help you develop your focus so that your yoga practice intensifies.

"With loving reverence, we bow to the divine inner sun, the most splendid light in all the worlds. Please illumine our minds!" —Rig Veda

Yoga exercises were originally used by ascetics to maintain flexibility and strength, ensuring that they could sit meditating for long periods of time in the lotus position, helping them to maintain health so they could live long lives pursuing their spiritual goals. Today, many people practice yoga to remain toned, fit, and flexible. But many also turn to yoga to help them decompress from stressful, over-busy, and hectic lifestyles. Yoga slows you down, and, like Zen, it stresses awareness of the moment.

Focus on Breathing

In yoga, the breath is essential to practice, just as it is in Zen. You breathe through your nose, maintaining awareness of the breath, slowly and regularly. You do not force your breath, making it too long, loud, or unnatural. When we are beginners, sometimes when we concentrate on the breath, it suddenly seems difficult to breathe, and we wonder how we manage when we aren't paying attention. Just relax, and soon your breathing will return to a more normal rhythm.

Both Zen practice and yoga practice realize the healing potential of the breath. We can heal our minds, our bodies, and our spirits by focusing our attention directly on the breath and holding it there as we take air in, breathe air out, over and again.

When we slow down, our breathing slows down with us. If we learn to breathe more deeply and slowly, but naturally, we can prolong our lives as the oxygen helps to keep our blood purified and our minds and bodies are freed from excess stress and tension. When we breathe freely and deeply, our bodies relax, saving us from the hunched-over, tightly held posture we assume much of the day if we are not conscious of our breathing.

FACT

The breath not only supplies our minds and our bodies with the oxygen we need to maintain life, but our breath also releases toxins from our bodies. It cleanses our blood as the oxygen floods through our vessels, detoxifying us and keeping us healthy

Yoga Benefits

According to the Web site ✑*www.holisticonline.com*, healthy breathing, such as the breathing one learns through Zen practice and yoga practice, can have the following beneficial effects on your health:

- Your skin will glow and relax, reducing lines and wrinkles.
- You burn fat more efficiently.
- You will have better digestion.
- You will have increased health of the nervous system.
- You will decrease the workload for your heart.

And there are many benefits beyond those. Many people find it a natural progression to go from their yoga practice into Zen practice as yoga opens them to the benefits of meditation. Yoga can then help your Zen practice by helping you maintain flexibility. It's a wonderful complement to Zen as they share many of the same basic beliefs, including awareness, breath meditation, daily practice, healthy lifestyle choices, and discipline.

As we practice Zen, we come to realize that our body houses our mind and spirit. We need to show great respect to our old sack of bones. If we are not in good health, our Zen practice will suffer, and so will we.

We learn to take good care of our bodies with exercise, good food, and rest. We enter our sports and our exercise with vigor, dedication, and mindfulness. And soon we also find that our athletic activities improve greatly with our improved concentration and mental acuity. Whether you are a great athlete, a daily yoga practitioner, a weekend athlete, or an armchair athlete, Zen practice can give you the mental discipline to approach your athletic life in an entirely new way. Ⓔ

Chapter 17

Going on Retreats: Sesshin

Today there are many different kinds of spiritual retreats available to the person searching for a break from the chaos of modern life. There are spa retreats, religious retreats, silent retreats, eco retreats, adventure retreats, yoga retreats, and so on. The person looking for a week of spirituality and meditation would probably be quite surprised if he or she ended up at sesshin!

Retreats

A Zen meditation retreat is called a sesshin. Sesshin can vary in length from a weekend sesshin—which is two days—to a prolonged sesshin of a week or more. However, an average time for a sesshin is five to seven days. A Zen retreat is a unique experience. During a sesshin, you have prolonged periods of concentrated zazen. Most of your time in sesshin is spent sitting—you can sit ten to twelve hours a day. If this sounds extreme, well, that's because it is. And it's designed that way for a reason, which we will discuss in the pages to come.

If you are working on a koan, you probably will not make much "progress" on it until you go to sesshin. The effort you put forth in sesshin will help you move into your koan and call it with your whole heart and body, as you are free from any other distractions but living with your koan. It is in sesshin that we get the opportunity to truly open our hearts like a flower and become free of our daily self. As our ego becomes smaller and smaller through the efforts of repeated concentrated zazen practice, we start to unfold. Perception changes. We become open to new experiences, and it is with this open heart that we start to discover a world we have somehow forgotten.

Closed-Doors Policy

Sesshin is a safe place. Your teacher will have created a wonderfully safe environment in which you can sit, undisturbed by the outside world for hours and days on end.

It is an unusual gift to have the opportunity to practice in sesshin. It is very difficult practice that challenges everyone to the depths of their being, but it is an opportunity you will never forget once you've participated. A sesshin won't necessarily take place in a monastery, though many do. It can be held in a private home, a Zen center, a spiritual retreat house, or any area that the teacher has found to be a practical, safe, and useful lodging.

Once the doors close on a sesshin, no one from the outside world will intrude on your time. The environment will be closed to the sesshin participants to ensure that your practice can remain focused and undisturbed. Meals, beds, and bathrooms are provided so you do not have to think of preparations of any kind, unless of course you volunteer to participate in such preparations. Once the doors close and sesshin begins, you will find that you are free to enter into your practice with a whole heart, mind, and body for the length of time you have signed on.

When you work with your koan in sesshin, take it with you everywhere you go. When you wake up in the morning call to your koan as soon as you are aware. As you eat and walk, become your koan, throw your entire being into it and call to it with your whole heart.

It is such a rare and precious gift to be given a stretch of time that you can dedicate to your practice. Take advantage of it, and know that you are in a wonderfully safe place, where you can completely let go and immerse yourself.

Preparing for Sesshin

You should always check with your Zen teacher before leaving for sesshin to see if there is anything you need to bring. Depending on the sesshin, you might need your own bedding and towels, but other than necessities, you should bring along a minimum of belongings.

Maintaining quiet the entire time is an important part of sesshin. Please—no Walkmans or music of any kind.

Sesshin is a time during which you will strive to leave small mind behind and enter a new mind. Therefore, you should avoid bringing along items that enforce your ego and keep bringing you back to awareness of self. It is helpful to leave makeup, curling irons, colognes, perfumes, and beauty aids at home. You will have no need for lipstick, mousse, aftershave, jewelry, or fashion accessories, though a hair dryer can be useful if you dislike a wet head after a shower. We recommend leaving reading materials at home as well, although a diary is a nice addition if you want to take time to journal your experience.

Bring with you only the essentials you will need for a few days away from home. Your clothing should be comfortable and casual, the same clothes you wear for daily zazen practice. However, a few items of warm clothing will be helpful as the Zen centers, monasteries, and retreat houses are often quite chilly inside. Also bring along a pair of shoes that are easy to slip in and out of. As you walk from zendo to dormitory, you will want to have a pair of shoes, but since you will be taking them on and off all day it is nice if you can easily slip out of them. Clogs, sandals, or slip-ons are good choices for footwear.

FACT

Remember: Before you enter the zendo, take off your shoes. It is not appropriate to have footwear in the zendo.

Check with your sesshin leader, but you will most likely need to bring along toiletries such as shampoo, soap, toothpaste, toothbrush, and so on. Shaving is optional, and showering can be taken advantage of daily or less frequently, if you choose. It is helpful to bring along a bottle of water that you can refill so you can assure you are adequately hydrated.

Daily Schedule

The daily schedule for a sesshin is intimidating to the uninitiated (and often to the initiated as well). The idea of sitting zazen for hours on end is quite overwhelming. But you do it a moment at a time, and if you approach it this way, it will be easier to manage.

The frequency of sesshin is up to your teacher or center. You may find your center holds sesshin frequently. Many monasteries and centers hold seven-day sesshins once a month. You can attend sesshin as often as you like, but as many people need to fit retreats in around their families, work schedules, and vacations, the frequency of sesshin is an individual choice. We recommend going as frequently as you can. But once you start going, you just might find you want to go back as soon as possible!

A typical day in sesshin might look like this:

4:30 A.M.: Wake-up

5:00–7:30: Sutra practice, tea, morning zazen (with bathroom breaks)

7:30–8:00: Breakfast

8:30–10:00: Cleanup, work practice, and break

10:00 A.M.–12:30 P.M.: Zazen and lecture

12:30–1:00: Lunch

1:00–1:30: Cleanup

1:30–2:30: Rest period

2:30–3:30: Zazen

3:30–4:30: Shower and rest

4:30–5:30: Zazen and afternoon sutras

5:30–6:00: Dinner

6:00–6:30: Cleanup

6:30–8:00: Rest period

8:00–11:00: Zazen, *kinhin,* and *dokusan*

11:00: Bed

Sesshin Behavior

There are numerous opportunities for bathroom breaks and water stops. The teacher will let you know when it is all right to leave the zendo. Everyone leaves at once, so don't ever just stand up and take off. During the sesshin, everyone acts together as a whole. Individuality is not stressed during sesshin!

It is advised that you not take to active exercise during the brief breaks between sits. You will want to rest as much as possible. Also remember that if you make any noises, you are distracting others from deep practice. Even the sound of anything other than light breathing can be enough to disturb the precious moments of zazen. Be as quiet as you can. Refrain from moving with every fiber of your being. Sit as still as you can and realize that no one in the room is getting away with no pain. Others are in pain just as you are.

Sesshin can be a very painful experience, both emotionally and physically. But there are moments of incredible wonder as well. A whole lifetime is lived during sesshin, one moment at a time. Just follow what others are doing and sit your heart out.

"Be gentle with yourself. Be kind to yourself. You may not be perfect, but you are all you've got to work with. The process of becoming who you will be begins first with the total acceptance of who you are."
—Bhante Henepola Gunaratna
Mindfulness in Plain English

Exhaustion

You probably feel exhausted just reading the sesshin schedule. Maybe you have trouble with sleepiness when sitting as is, and you cannot imagine how you will get through a week of intensive zazen. You are wondering how you can deal with the inevitable exhaustion of sesshin.

Use Your Breaks

The first few days of sesshin are, indeed, exhausting. But you might notice that there are many breaks built into the day. Take advantage of these breaks. Go back to your room, lie down on your bed, and go to sleep. You might be surprised to find that you fall immediately into a deep sleep and awake with your alarm a short while later quite refreshed. Don't bring work along to sesshin or a great book you have been dying to read, expecting to get a few chapters in after morning sutras and zazen. *Go to sleep.*

As the days fall into one another, you will notice something strange, however. As you continue to dive into your bed during breaks, you might find suddenly that you cannot go to sleep. At first you might panic and think there is something wrong. But you will be fine, so don't worry yourself about it.

As we practice zazen, we tap into the energy source that is present all the time, but we are too distracted in our small minds to appreciate it. We are being fed by that energy, and as the days go on, we realize we are buzzing with it. We then lie in bed at midnight, eyes wide open, wondering why we cannot sleep.

In our daily lives, we think we are exhausted from hard work, such as cooking, cleaning, mowing the lawn, and so on. We think we are exhausted in our bodies. But in truth, we are exhausted by our minds' efforts to constantly keep busy. When we stop thinking for a while, we realize what a drain thinking really is!

Dokusan

During sesshin, we meet with our teacher in a private one-on-one called *dokusan*. *Dokusan* is a wonderful opportunity for you to share your practice with your teacher. During zazen practice, students go into a private room, away from the zendo, to meet with the teacher. This usually happens in one of two ways. *Dokusan* might be announced by the *jikijitsu* during zazen. All students who want to take part in *dokusan* will hurry over to the *dokusan* room and take a seat in line, each awaiting his or her turn for a private meeting. In some Zen centers and monasteries, the students run full-out to beat each other to the front of the line.

In other situations, the beginning of *dokusan* is signaled by the *jikijitsu*, or perhaps by the teacher leaving the zendo, and each person goes one at a time, in order of their seating in the zendo. It is highly recommended that you attend *dokusan*, as the teacher can guide you in your practice. *Dokusan* is a rare and precious opportunity, and many students try as hard as they can to ensure they have the time to meet with the teacher.

Each Zen center, monastery, or sitting group might have small differences in the way they practice, including rules for *dokusan*. Don't be afraid to ask any questions of your teacher or other group members. Differences can be expected between procedures as each *sangha* is unique.

Dokusan Etiquette

When you enter the *dokusan* room, bow to the teacher and to the altar before sitting on the cushion that will be waiting for you in front of the teacher, who will also be sitting on a zafu. Tell the teacher what koan you are working with, as he might have hundreds of students and may not be able to remember each and every person's koan. Then try to answer your koan in whatever way you feel compelled to do so. Koans are not answered with your rational mind, so you might refrain from having a dialogue with your teacher about your koan.

FACT

Dokusan time is precious to all students. Respect your fellow students' right to equal time as well. Do not dally on your way back to your cushion, but hurry so that others can also make it to *dokusan.*

A successful answer will not begin, "I think . . ." If you find yourself headed in this direction, you can be quite sure you are going the wrong way. Strange noises have been known to ensue from the *dokusan* room. If you are self-conscious and inhibited, you are not entering big mind, so don't be discouraged. Return to your pillow, and resume practice. If you give an unsatisfactory answer, the teacher might ring a bell, signaling your time in *dokusan* is over. When it is time to leave, bow and walk quickly out of the room, respecting others' needs to meet with the teacher as well.

The Questions

When you are new to practice, your questions for the teacher will be straightforward. This is completely acceptable and expected. Many students want to know what kind of questions they can ask their teacher. Whatever question you want to ask, you can be assured it will be kept in strict confidence, as the relationship between Zen student and teacher is private and unique. Similarly, you should not talk with others about your time in *dokusan,* as it is privileged and confidential information. You might ask your teacher some of the burning issues of your life, or your questions might be of a more mellow variety, such as if your posture is correct. You might also want to tell your teacher what is happening in zazen, reporting updates as you go. Your teacher will let you know when it is time to move into more mature practice.

As we have mentioned earlier, your teacher might at first seem wonderfully supportive and accommodating, only later to change to a strict and disapproving demeanor. Your teacher is there to be a mirror for you: Try to see yourself

QUESTION?

How long does *dokusan* last?

Dokusan time is short. You can expect to spend just a few minutes alone with the teacher. Your time might be as short as thirty seconds, or it might be as long as several minutes. Ten minutes is a long time for *dokusan.*

Kinhin

During zazen practice in sesshin you will have breaks from sitting practice. Some of these breaks will be walking meditations, called *kinhin.* *Kinhin* is designed to give the legs a break as they tend to get very sore and stiff during sustained zazen sessions. As you walk around the room, your legs will loosen up a little bit, and you will get a break from any pressure on your legs during zazen.

How to Practice *Kinhin*

When it is time for *kinhin,* all members of the *sangha* will rise to their feet, *gassho* to their zafus, and follow one another in a walking meditation around the zendo. When you rise, make sure you are careful as your legs may be stiff or may have fallen asleep. If your feet and legs are tingling, make sure you take it easy when you stand. Take your time— you might fall over if you stand quickly.

Walking meditation is taken at an extremely slow pace, usually one step per breath. Your body should retain the same posture as you practice during zazen: back straight, chin slightly down, neck straight, eyes on the floor. Your breath and awareness should be the same as during sitting meditation as well. You hand can be held at chest level, with one hand covering the other, the bottom hand balled into a fist. For instance, place your right hand over your left hand, with your right thumb covering the top of the fisted left hand.

If you are working on a koan, work on it in *kinhin* as well. If you are calling Mu, continue to call Mu. If you are practicing breath meditation, count your breaths, starting over as soon as you lose your concentration. *Kinhin* is not a rest period, and you should not deliberately start thinking of holiday shopping or redecorating your living room.

The duration of *kinhin* varies, but is usually anywhere from five to fifteen minutes. If you are walking with a group, as you will be during sesshin, keep pace with the group and walk as though you are one entity. The leader will signal when *kinhin* is over. At that time, return to your cushion, bow to the cushion, turn and bow to the room, then take your seat once again.

Meal Practice

Meals during sesshin are taken as a group, and practice continues throughout the meal. Follow the lead of others in your *sangha* and be respectful of your food, your companions, and the quiet. You will most likely have three meals a day during sesshin, and during breakfast and lunch sutras will be recited. A sutra book containing verses will usually be provided for you, so if you do not have the sutras memorized, you can follow along with everyone else.

Here is a sample of a sutra recited at mealtime—

Verse of the Midday Meal
The gifts of the Three Merits (thoroughness, cleanliness, honesty) and the Six Tastes (hot, salty, bitter, sour, sweet, bland), we give to all beings: the Buddha, the priests, all people, animals, and plants of this world . . . To all of them we offer praise.

Eating Manners

It is traditional to eat with chopsticks, so if you are unable to do so, let someone know beforehand. Many groups will be accommodating, though some may not be. Try to eat at the same pace as everyone else. You do not want to find yourself with a full bowl of food while everyone else waits for you to finish. *Sangha* members sit together and rise together. Eating is a group activity, and no one will leave until you are finished.

Meals will be hearty vegetarian fare and will be balanced. Caffeine and sugar will not be served as they will interfere with your practice. A typical breakfast might consist of oatmeal, toast, and fruit. Lunch might be a few vegetables and brown rice. Eat enough to sustain yourself. We eat so that we can sit. Do not overindulge, and do not underindulge. Remember, we are walking the middle path and strive for moderation at all times. Cleanup and rest period usually follow a meal so that you have adequate time to digest and don't get after-meal sleepiness during zazen.

Work Practice

During each day of sesshin, you will also take part in work practice. The *sangha* must clean the zendo, take care of the altar, clean the bathrooms, the halls, the dorms, and the kitchen. Perhaps you will be assigned garden work or will be asked to sweep the steps or wash windows. Whatever your task, do it mindfully, staying focused on the task at hand.

Plunging into Work

When you are working, do not focus on the end of your work. Try to immerse yourself completely in what you are doing instead of thinking of the coming rest period or the end of the job. We always try to stay in the moment, but during sesshin we have the opportunity to truly lose ourselves in our work so that work stretches out in front of us, behind us, and is all we know. We are scrubbing the floor, washing the windows, and wiping the tables, all completely and thoroughly. When we are performing what we might consider menial tasks, we are often focused on finishing them.

"If we can reach the understanding of what we actually are, there is no better remedy for eliminating all suffering. This is the heart of all spiritual practices."
—Kalu Rinpoche
Luminous Mind

In Zen practice, we make no such distinctions and judgments. The moment is all there is, and we enter the moment with our entire being, grateful for the moment we have. The past and future slip away until all that exists lives in the moment right at hand. The entire world rests in the moment of washing the window. The moment of our hand, the cloth, the glass . . . that is all that is. If we do this practice successfully at sesshin, we can learn—perhaps—to take it home with us into our houses, where we learn to be alive as we wash our clothes, cook our meals, and tend to our families.

Sesshin Benefits

Sesshin has been used for hundreds of years by Zen practitioners. It is a privilege to have the opportunity to attend a sesshin, and while it might be a daunting prospect for a newcomer, it is soon something you might look forward to with anticipation and willingness.

Sangha Unity

During sesshin, follow what others are doing. If the *sangha* is sitting zazen, sit zazen. If the *sangha* is resting, rest. During rest periods, do not clean or eat. During zazen, be present in the zendo, and do not stay in bed for rest. Be present with the *sangha,* and act as a group. This is not a time to exercise your individuality.

The safety of the world during sesshin is a rare and wonderful time. We are in a setting where we are safe from distraction and we can focus wholly on our practice. The world drops away as we are left free to discover ourselves, to search for the answers to the deepest questions our entire beings cry out to answer. We sit in union with a group and feel compassion for every member of the *sangha*. How brave each and every member is to be willing to sit—to bravely look into your own heart and ask the meaning of life's deepest questions.

Sesshin is a wonderful opportunity, and though it is a very difficult endeavor that tests you to the roots of who you are, you will not be sorry you took the opportunity to embark on its adventure. Ⓔ

Chapter 18

 **Zen Lives Today:
Western Zen Masters**

Since Zen showed up on Western shores, we have had the fortune to see some wonderful Zen teachers in the United States. Each of the teachers profiled here has made important contributions to the world through his or her face-to-face teaching and often also through the written word. Their impact has been felt around the world, as well as in the small towns of mainstream America. There is only room to profile a few of these wonderful teachers, but there are many more.

Philip Kapleau

Philip Kapleau founded the Zen Center in Rochester, New York. He is a prolific author and beloved teacher who played a key role in bringing Zen to the attention of the American public. The Zen Center in Rochester, established in 1966, has grown to include affiliated Zen centers across the world, including the United States, Canada, and Europe.

Kapleau is perhaps best-known for writing *The Three Pillars of Zen,* a book that introduced Zen to many Westerners and encouraged them to get out of their chairs, where they sat reading about Zen, and onto their zafus where they could actually experience it.

The Court Reporter

As a young man, Kapleau studied law and became a court reporter for state and federal courts in Connecticut. However, during World War II, he was appointed by the International Military Tribunal to cover the war crimes trials in Nuremberg, Germany. There he noticed that the Germans seemed unrepentant for their crimes, and this left a strong impression on him. He was then sent over to Tokyo, Japan, to report on the aftermath of the war there, and was struck by the difference in the responses he saw in Japan from the ones he had seen in Germany. The Japanese were repentant for their crimes and believed they were suffering the consequences of the atrocious acts committed during war. The Japanese believed in karma, and karma was catching up with them. This made a deep impression on Kapleau, and he left Japan with a curiosity about Buddhism that was to flower in the coming years.

FACT

Philip Kapleau has written several excellent books on Zen. He is the author of many books, including *The Three Pillars of Zen, Zen: Merging of East and West, To Cherish All Life, Awakening to Zen,* and *The Zen of Living and Dying: A Practical and Spiritual Guide.*

Once back in the States, Kapleau continued to think about both the Germans and the Japanese and about their different attitudes in dealing with their war crimes. Despite starting a successful business, Kapleau was depressed, anxious, and dissatisfied. No amount of material success could satisfy him.

Zen Training

In a search for peace and happiness, Kapleau eventually sought out D. T. Suzuki, whom he had met while in Japan. Simply studying Buddhism did not seem to be helping Kapleau in the ways he needed, and he came to believe he needed to experience Zen instead of just studying it. He decided to leave his business and head over to Japan to pursue Zen training. Kapleau subsequently completed thirteen years of formal Zen training, finishing his studies under Zen master Yasutani, before returning to the United States in 1966.

Yasutani and Kapleau had differences of opinion over teaching, and they had a falling out after Kapleau returned home. Kapleau has received permission to teach others from Roshi Yasutani, but he never received full dharma transmission. Yet he was eager to bring Zen to American hearts. He met with disapproval from his teacher over some of the choices he was making, such as translating the Heart Sutra into English for sutra practice. Their relationship came to an end.

The Rochester Zen Center

The Rochester Zen Center, therefore, does not have any lineage with Japanese Zen. Some people might view the Zen Center as lacking, due to the broken lineage. Since Kapleau never formally finished receiving dharma transmission from his Zen master, some have questioned his authenticity.

However, the Rochester Zen Center is a thriving home to more than 600 Zen practitioners. It is one of the largest and most respected Zen centers in North America, with sitting groups and sister centers in Mexico, Germany, and throughout the United States. The Rochester Zen Center offers daily meditation services, residential training programs, and introductory workshops. Through Kapleau and his dharma heir, Bodhin Kjolhede, the center has introduced Zen practice to middle America and helped form the face of Western Zen today.

Bernie Glassman

Bernard Tetsugen Glassman is one of America's most provocative Zen teachers. He was born in Brighton Beach, Brooklyn, to Eastern European parents, and was raised in the Jewish faith with strong socialist proclivities. Glassman grew up to be an aeronautical engineer, and received a Ph.D. in applied mathematics. He didn't start Zen practice until 1967, when he began studying under Taizan Maezumi Roshi, founder of the Zen Center of Los Angeles. Nine years later, he received dharma transmission.

"When I was in Vietnam, so many of our villages were being bombed. Along with my monastic brothers and sisters, I had to decide what to do. Should we continue to practice in our monasteries or should we leave the meditation halls in order to help the people who were suffering under the bombs? After careful reflection, we decided to do both—to go out and help people and to do so in mindfulness. We called it engaged Buddhism. Mindfulness must be engaged. Once there is seeing, there must be acting." —Thich Nhat Hanh

Engaged Buddhism

A promoter of Engaged Buddhism, Bernie Glassman founded the Greyston Bakery in New York City in 1982. He had a dream—to start a business that would employ the members of his *sangha* so they could concentrate more fully on their practice and contribute to the practice of Engaged Buddhism. He didn't want his *sangha* to have to work their day jobs—he wanted them to be able to engage in practice completely, giving back to the communities that needed it. Still operating today, the bakery employs more than sixty-five people and generates an annual income of more than $3.5 million.

Because of his great success with the bakery, Glassman was able to expand his work by starting a nonprofit corporation in 1993. The major goals of the Greyston Foundation are to support programs that can provide social improvement and economic empowerment to those in the most need. The foundation takes the original ideas behind the bakery and brings them to a much grander scale. By using the profits from the bakery, the foundation is able to provide housing for the homeless, child care, jobs for the unemployed, job training, and residential and outpatient care for victims of HIV/AIDS. Most people are probably most familiar with Greyston through its partnership with Ben & Jerry's ice cream.

FACT

Greyston provides over 2 million pounds of brownies a year for such Ben & Jerry's flavors as Chocolate Fudge Brownie Ice Cream and Half Baked. The common concern these two companies have for social issues make them wonderful complements to one another.

The Peacemaker Order

Once Greyston was established and able to operate fully on its own, Roshi Glassman (with Roshi Sandra Holmes) continued his work by creating an order of Zen practitioners devoted to the cause of peace. The Peacemaker Order is an international peacemaking group with members all over the world from all religious and spiritual backgrounds. Members of the order include people and organizations from all of the world's five major religions. Just some of the organizations involved in the order include Greyston Mandala, Prison Dharma Network, and Upaya Study Center in Santa Fe, California; StadtRaum in Germany; Mexico City Village, Mexico; La Rete d'Indra in Italy; and Shanti Relief Committee in Japan.

Robert Aitken

Robert Aitken was born in Pennsylvania, but he moved to Hawaii when he was a young boy and remains there to this day. In the fall of 1935, he entered the University of Hawaii and eventually earned his degree in English literature. While at the university, his interest was piqued by peace activists, an interest that would grow over the coming years.

In 1940, Aitken took a job at Pacific Naval Air Base Contractors, where he was sent to Midway to work for a year, followed by five months in Guam. World War II began soon thereafter, and when Guam fell, he was captured by the Japanese. He was soon transported back to Japan and interned in a camp for the remainder of the war. While at the camp, Aitken was introduced to Buddhism and the possibility of Zen practice.

The war confirmed Aitken's pacifist leanings as he watched the bombings and the displacement of people from their homes. When he returned to the States, Aitken continued his education in Japanese studies and eventually went on to get his master's degree in Japanese studies in 1950. He left for Japan once again, this time voluntarily, and spent a year studying and sitting zazen with Nakagawa Soen Roshi, a teacher, poet, and peacemaker. In 1974, he was given approval to teach Zen, and then in 1985, received full dharma transmission from Yamada Ko'un Roshi, Abbot of the Sanbo Kyodan in Kamakura, Japan.

In 1959, Robert Aitken and his late wife, Anne Hopkins Aitken, founded the Diamond Sangha, a Zen Buddhist Center in Honolulu, Hawaii. Today, the Diamond Sangha is a collection of Zen centers and sister associations in Argentina, Australia, New Zealand, and the United States. In 1978, Aitken went on to cofound the Buddhist Peace fellowship, an organization that serves as an agent for Engaged Buddhism.

The aim of the Buddhist Peace Fellowship is to bring peace and freedom to institutions, social systems, individuals, and groups by teaching the wisdom of compassion.

Aitken has had a long-standing interest in haiku poetry as well. His written work includes the books *A Zen Wave: Basho's Haiku & Zen; Taking the Path of Zen,* and *The Mind of Clover: Essays in Zen Buddhist Ethics.*

Richard Baker

In December 1971, shortly before his death, Shunryu Suzuki Roshi, one of the most beloved Zen teachers in the United States, named Richard Baker as his dharma heir. Baker was also set to take over official leadership of the San Francisco Zen Center—the first Buddhist monastery in the United States. Suzuki had been the founder of the Zen Center, which made Richard Baker only the second abbot to lead the institution. Baker would eventually become one of the more controversial figures in Western Zen history.

The Influential Abbot

Richard Baker, a Harvard graduate, served the center from 1971 until 1983. He studied Zen in Japan at Antaiji, Eiheiji, and Daitokuji Zen monasteries from 1968 to 1971. He accomplished many wonderful things as abbot. He was instrumental in the purchase of Tassajara Zen Mountain Center and the purchase of Green Gulch Farm. The center is an important part of the larger community, with a prison outreach program, a homeless aid program, organic farming, and more. Baker was also the force behind the organization of the center's financial foundation, which included, among other assets, Greens Restaurant at Fort Mason and Tassajara Bakery in San Francisco. He helped take the center from its grass roots, bare-bones beginnings to a multifaceted, multimillion-dollar, financially stable organization with a membership in the hundreds and a public image to maintain.

The Scandal and the Aftermath

The end of Baker's San Francisco Zen Center life came at the 1983 Peace Conference at Tassajara. It was here that he was forced to step down, as the members of his center could no longer stand for his ongoing sexual indiscretions and the center's more recent financial difficulties. Baker stepped down and moved on. The monastery changed its direction, cut back its operation to eliminate financial bloat, and redirected its leadership. No longer would a single abbot run the center, but a group of abbots would lead, and the group itself would be monitored by a council of its peers.

Richard Baker had done much for the San Francisco Zen Center and had contributed greatly to the practice of many Zen students. He had been a proponent of yogic teachings and the relation between Zen and current social issues. It is interesting to note that when he stepped down, many of his students and followers turned their backs on him, but still others helped him regain his feet elsewhere and create a new life for himself.

> It is important to note that people who practice Zen, including Zen masters, abbots, and teachers of all kinds, are still people practicing Zen. Sexual and financial scandals have hit Zen centers just as they have hit many churches and other institutions. It is possible to be enlightened and flawed, but it doesn't necessarily mean the master is a fake if such flaws are encountered in him or her.

Today, Richard Baker is founder and leader of the Dharma Sangha centers in the United States and Germany. In the United States, he lives at Dharma Sangha's Crestone Mountain Zen Center in Crestone, Colorado, and in Germany at Dharma Sangha's Buddhist Study Center in the Black Forest.

Charlotte Joko Beck

In the 1960s, Charlotte Joko Beck undertook Zen training with Hakuun Yasutani Roshi and Soen Nakagawa Roshi. In 1983, she became the third Dharma heir of Hakuyu Maezumi Roshi of the Zen Center of Los Angeles. She is currently the lead teacher at the San Diego Zen Center in San Diego, California, where she teaches alongside Elizabeth Hamilton.

Ordinary Mind School of Zen

Charlotte Joko Beck and her dharma followers and successors have established the Ordinary Mind School of Zen. She is warmly spoken of by such Zen masters as Robert Aitken ("I trust her and learn from her").

The Ordinary Mind Zen School issues the following statement: "The Ordinary Mind School intends to manifest and support practice of the Awakened Way, as expressed in the teaching of Charlotte Joko Beck. There is no affiliation with other Zen groups or religious denominations; however, membership in this school does not preclude individual affiliation with other groups. Within the school there is no hierarchy of Dharma Successors."

According to the Ordinary Mind School of Zen, "The Awakened Way is universal; the medium and methods of realization vary according to circumstances. Each Dharma Successor in the School may apply diverse practice approaches and determine the structure of any organization that s/he may develop to facilitate practice.

The Successors acknowledge that they are ongoing students, and that the quality of their teaching derives from the quality of their practice. As ongoing students, teachers are committed to the openness and fluidity of practice, wherein the wisdom of the absolute may be manifested in/as our life. An important function of this school is the ongoing examination and development of effective teaching approaches to insure comprehensive practice in all aspects of living." The Ordinary Mind School has satellite branches across the United States—from California to New York—and in Europe.

Other Accomplishments

Charlotte Joko Beck is also an author of two books *(Everyday Zen: Love and Work* and *Nothing Special: Living Zen)* and several short articles. She is a much-loved Zen teacher who has brought her own personal approach into the zendo and created a school of Zen arising from her own experiences practicing Zen. She has contributed much to the American Zen life and is a widely respected Zen master.

Joan Halifax

Joan Halifax, Ph.D., is a founder and roshi of the Upaya Zen Center in Santa Fe, New Mexico. She is a Buddhist teacher, anthropologist, and author. In addition, she has served on the faculties of Columbia University, the University of Miami School of Medicine, the New School for Social Research in New York City, the Naropa Institute, and the California Institute for Integral Studies.

FACT

Joan Halifax's books include *The Human Encounter with Death* (with Stanislav Grof), *The Fruitful Darkness, Shamanic Voices, Shaman: The Wounded Healer, Simplicity in the Complex: A Buddhist Life in America,* and *Being with Dying.*

Halifax has practiced Buddhism since the late 1960s. Zen Master Seung Sahn, founding teacher of the Dharma Zen Center in Los Angeles, formally ordained her in 1976. In 1990, she received the Lamp Transmission from Zen Master Thich Nhat Hanh. She is a founding teacher in the Zen Peacemaker Order of Roshi Bernie Glassman and the late Sensei Jishu Holmes. Halifax is greatly known for her work with the dying. The programs at the Upaya Center include Being with the Dying, the Partners Program, the Prison Project, and the Kailash Education Fund.

The Being with the Dying Program

One of the center's best known programs, Being with the Dying, was developed to help caregivers work with those who are dying. It is an effort to change the relationship between the living and the dying.

Through the program, health-care professionals are trained to better assist patients who are facing the end of life by learning new perspectives on death and dying, grief counseling, community development, cultural perspectives on death, grief, bereavement, and the psychological and spiritual issues related to death and dying. Rather than just learning how to deal with the medical or physical aspects of dying, health-care workers are better prepared to deal with the spiritual and emotional aspects of life's final stage.

After going through the program, these workers can then take their new practices back to their own institutions and teach others what they have learned. These remarkable retreats are not just meant for members of the center. The public is welcome and invited to attend to learn how to practice mindfulness, compassion, and honesty. The center offers retreats for caregivers as well as the terminally or seriously ill.

The Partners and Prison Programs

The Partners Program works to match dying people with caregivers most suited to their needs. The program complements the help with both hospice workers and medical professionals. Based in Mexico, another program, the Prison Project, offers mindfulness training to inmates. Its aim is to reduce stress in prison. In addition, the Kailish Education Fund provides educational opportunities to some of the poorest children in Nepal.

John Daido Loori

John Daido Loori Roshi is dharma heir of Hakuyu Taizan Maezumi Roshi of the White Plum lineage—see the next section on Rev. Madeline Ko-i Bastis—and is the current abbot of Zen Mountain Monastery in Mount Tremper, New York, located in the scenic Catskill Mountains. He is president of Dharma Communications, has been instrumental in bringing Zen to cyberspace, and is the founder and director of the Mountains and Rivers Order of associated Zen Buddhist practice centers and sitting groups. He is also the author of many books, including *The Eight Gates of Zen, Two Arrows Meeting in Mid-Air: The Zen Koan, Invoking Reality, Celebrating Everyday Life,* and *Making Love with Light.*

The Eight Gates of Zen

John Daido Loori Roshi teaches the practices of the Eight Gates of Zen. As he says in his book *The Eight Gates of Zen,* "The Eight Gates and the Ten Stages are the ceaseless practice of Dogen Zenji's *Mountains and Rivers*—practice that engages the whole body and mind, that encompasses and fills all space and time." The Eight Gates of Zen practiced at Zen Mountain Monastery are as follows:

1. Zazen
2. Zen study
3. Academic study
4. Liturgy

5. Right Action
6. Art practice
7. Body practice
8. Work practice

QUESTION?

What is the White Plum lineage?

The White Plum lineage is made up of Zen teachers who received transmission from Hakuyu Taizen Maezumi, one of the most influential modern Zen teachers. Taizen Maezumi was a dharma successor to three different lineages of the Soto as well as the Rinzai school of Zen. John Loori, Joan Halifax, and Bernie Glassman are all teachers in the White Plum lineage.

The Cybermonk

John Daido Loori has a background in science and has been interested in computers since the 1950s. He has been instrumental in bringing Zen into the world of cyberspace, and the Zen Mountain Monastery Web site (*www.zen-mtn.org*) offers access to senior monastics as well as online training for those who cannot make it to a Zen center or monastery. If you access the Web site, you can e-mail the "Cybermonk" and get answers to your dharma questions. Dharma Communications, the outreach arm of Zen Mountain Monastery, reaches out to the community through different media means. Inmates, isolated practitioners, and those who are homebound can access Zen training through journals, catalogs, videos, audiotapes, books, and interactive multimedia formats. The monastery has an online store that sells Zen supplies, artwork, and more.

Rev. Madeline Ko-i Bastis

The Rev. Madeline Ko-i Bastis is a Zen priest in the White Plum lineage. She received dharma transmission from Peter Muryo Matthiessen Roshi in 1993. Madeline Ko-i Bastis was the first Zen Buddhist to be board-certified as a hospital chaplain, and she works tirelessly to help those who are sick and in need of care.

The Peaceful Dwelling Project

Rev. Madeline Ko-i Bastis is the founding director of the Peaceful Dwelling Project, also known as the "Retreat Without Walls." The Peaceful Dwelling Project is an educational organization that promotes the use of meditation for spiritual, emotional, and physical healing. The project offers spiritual retreats for those with serious, life-changing illnesses and those who care for them. Being a caregiver is a tireless job, and many caregivers often find themselves neglecting their own personal care—both spiritually and physically. The Peaceful Dwelling Project aims to help these caregivers stay healthy through workshops and healing retreats. The project also trains clergy and health-care professionals. Meditation is offered as an alternative healing source.

The Caregiver

Rev. Madeline Ko-i Bastis works out of New York, home of the Peaceful Dwelling Project. She has offered help to people with illnesses ranging from cancer to AIDS. She has helped battered women, people with psychiatric illnesses, substance abusers, teens in need, people in detox, Alzheimer's patients, and more. She is an author of two books (*Peaceful Dwelling: Meditations for Healing and Living* and *Heart of Forgiveness: A Practical Path to Healing*), has published several articles, and speaks at conferences in the United States and abroad. Ⓔ

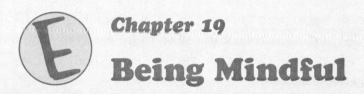

Chapter 19

Being Mindful

To live with Zen is to practice mindfulness all day long. When we practice mindfulness, we make an effort to be aware all the time. We think, we feel, but we try not to attach to our thoughts and our feelings. When we are mindful, we are aware of what is going on externally as well as what is going on inside of ourselves. When you are mindful, you are not judging. You are simply aware.

Mindfulness

When you start to practice Zen, you start with the breath. You become aware of each breath you take. You are aware of the in-breath, then you are aware of the out-breath. You breathe in. You breathe out. Over and over again. You stay with each breath and remain mindful of each intake and each exhalation.

As you continue to practice, you can move mindfulness into your daily life and your daily activities. You strive to be aware of each moment and each action you take. When you eat, you eat. When you clean, you clean. This is mindfulness.

Mindfulness versus Concentration

Mindfulness does not mean that you are completely focused on washing the dishes and your concentration is so complete that all else recedes into the background and all that is left is the water and the dishes. Mindfulness means to be aware of everything. Mindfulness is entering into the moment with an awareness of all that surrounds you. When we try to unravel a knot in a thin gold chain, we are concentrating. We are completely focused on the knot—we are not aware of our fingers, our breath, the coolness of the air, or the shaft of sunlight coming in the nearby open window.

Concentration and mindfulness are not the same things, but they work together as a team. In order to have a meditation practice that is working, you must have the power of concentration and the power of mindfulness. Concentration allows you to focus on one thing. Mindfulness allows you to become aware of the focus, and to take note when it strays. Concentration without mindfulness is not a successful meditation practice. Mindfulness allows you to notice that your attention—your concentration—is slipping. Mindfulness is the part of you that notes, "The door is opening, the bird is singing," while you continue to concentrate on one point, whether that be a task, your breath, or your koan.

When we are mindful, we are concentrating. But when we are concentrating, we are not always mindful. We can unravel the knot in a gold chain in a mindful state. But it is much more common for most of us to concentrate without mindfulness. We shut down the parts of us that allow us to be mindful. We shut out the world.

Connection with the World

Mindfulness meditations require that we be open, rather than closed. Through mindfulness, we realize our connection to the rest of the world. We feel a part of the world and are not separate from it. You probably live a good part of your day feeling separate from the rest of the world.

For example, think of a time recently when someone asked for a favor or made a demand of your time. Take note of the example. Now stop and think what your reaction was. Did you tense up and feel like receding from the person? Did you feel that you would gladly do this favor, but it put restraints on your own time? Did you feel that you never have enough time as it is and this was going to make you more crowded than ever? Did your muscles tense and your fatigue level increase?

"The most precious gift we can offer others is our presence. When mindfulness embraces those we love, they will bloom like flowers." —Thich Nhat Hanh

You might often react this way to what you perceive as demands on your time. Many of us live life by dividing it into time segments. Perhaps your day is made up of time you have to shower, time you have to drive, time you have to do the household chores, time you have to spend with your spouse, to work, make food, then, at the end of the day, perhaps time you have for yourself. Perhaps you feel you have very little time for yourself and the rest of your day is taken up with time you must "donate" to others. Through mindfulness, you can participate fully in each part of the day, leaving no part out as a "donation" you make to another. In other words, you can learn to live every moment of your life, instead of relegating part of your time each day as "lost time" you give up in order to maintain certain parts of your life.

Thich Nhat Hanh

Zen master Thich Nhat Hanh is well known for his work on Zen and mindfulness training—as well as his tireless efforts to promote peace in the world. Mindfulness is often more emphasized in the Buddhism of insight meditation than it is in Zen, but Thich Nhat Hanh has always emphasized mindfulness in his Zen teachings.

Who Is He?

Thich Nhat Hanh (known as Thây, or "teacher," to followers and friends) is a poet, scholar, Vietnamese Buddhist monk, and peace activist, well-known for his peace efforts during the Vietnam War. During the war, he founded the Unified Buddhist Church in France. Thây was born in 1926 in Vietnam, and he was a Buddhist monk by the time he was sixteen years old. When war broke out in his homeland, he worked tirelessly to promote peace, and his efforts ended in his being exiled from his homeland by both the Communist and noncommunist governments. At the age of forty, he found himself without a homeland. He went to the United States on a humanitarian visit to try to promote peace in Vietnam. He spoke on behalf of Buddhist monks, and eventually his efforts resulted in accords between North Vietnam and the United States. He continued to assist Vietnamese citizens by helping them escape from their oppressed homeland well into the 1970s. To this day, he is exiled from Vietnam, where he is considered a risk to the status quo there.

Thây's lifelong efforts to promote peace caused Martin Luther King, Jr., to nominate him for a Nobel Peace Prize in 1967 and have won him a steadfast and loyal following the world over.

His Life Today

Today, Thây lives in Plum Village, France, the center he set up in the southwestern part of that country. The center is home to many monks and nuns, and every year thousands of visitors flock to Plum Village to practice with Thây. He spends a lot of time in the United States at his various centers, holding guided retreats for people interested in practicing with him.

His Teaching

Thây's practice is unique and open-armed. In his book *Living Buddha, Living Christ,* Thây writes about the similarities between Jesus and Buddha, erasing the lines in the sand drawn hundreds of years ago and every day since by religious intolerance. He tells us that the spirit of Jesus and Buddha cannot be found in their names, nor can they be found only by only evoking their names as a means of spiritual awakening. The spirits of Jesus and Buddha can be found in practicing the actions they took in their own lives: by becoming a *living* Jesus and a *living* Buddha ourselves. Both men showed us how to live by the actions each took in his own life.

This kind of open-hearted teaching has allowed many Westerners to practice Thây's particular brand of peace and mindfulness with love and diligence. He is said to have both Buddha and Jesus statues on his altar in Plum Village, practicing what he preaches in his daily life.

FACT

Thich Nhat Hanh also founded the Van Hanh Buddhist University in Saigon and the School for Youths of Social Services in Vietnam. In 1998, Thich Nath Hanh brought his practice to the United States, when the Maple Forest Monastery was set up in Woodstock, Vermont, followed by the Green Mountain Dharma Center nunnery in Hartland-Four-Corners, Vermont. Most recently, in May 2000, Deer Park Monastery was established in Escondido, California.

Miracle of Mindfulness

Of the seventy-five or so books that Thây has authored, one of the brightest gems is *The Miracle of Mindfulness*. The stories and exercises in this small guide to mindfulness meditations are accessible and easy to practice. It is a wonderful guide for the beginning practitioner and the seasoned one.

Returning to the Breath

In *The Miracle of Mindfulness,* Thich Nhat Hanh reminds us to return to the breath when our mind becomes scattered. He tells us that it is easy to practice mindfulness when walking alone, watching your breath, but add a friend into the mix and the practice gets harder. "If, in your mind, you think, 'I wish this fellow would quit talking, so I could concentrate,' you have already lost your mindfulness," Thây says. "But if you think, 'If he wishes to talk, I will answer, but I will continue in mindfulness, aware of the fact that we are walking along this path together, aware of what we say, I can continue to watch my breath as well.'"

We cannot be mindful when we are panicked or confused, so use the breath to bring yourself back to center. Then stay with the breath in order to stay mindful and aware.

Thus we remain mindful and alive. To be stuck in the thought, "I wish this fellow would quit talking," is to take yourself out of mindfulness and the present moment. If you are not in the present moment, you are dead. The present moment is missed—you have not lived the moment at hand.

The Miracle of Mindfulness contains many exercises that can help you learn to focus on the time at hand. Thich Nhat Hanh relates how to get intimate with your breath. If you can focus on your breath, you can bring yourself to mindfulness.

Practicing Mindfulness Every Day

Practice mindfulness in your daily life outside of your seated meditation. You cannot stop with your morning meditation and then live in confusion, anger, and haste the rest of the day. You must be mindful all day long. When you shower, you must shower with your whole being, as if your very life depended on the shower. Your very life *is* the shower, and that is all the life you ever have: that one moment that you are living right there. When you eat breakfast, eat your breakfast with your whole mind and body. Do not think about the day to come, the meeting at ten o'clock, the haircut appointment at noon, the dinner date at 7 P.M. Eat your breakfast and focus on the tastes in front of you, the sounds of the morning, the light of the early day. Practice this kind of mindfulness at every opportunity.

Relax Your Muscles

Set aside a period of time in your day to devote to getting to know your breath. To make sure you have some privacy and quiet; retire to a room where you will not be disturbed.

Lie down on your back on the floor, and concentrate on relaxing each of the muscles in your body. Start with your feet. Focus on your feet and relax each of the muscles until you feel your feet let go a little bit and release any tension you are holding there. Move on to your ankles and calves. Tighten your calves, and then release them, taking a deep breath. On the out-breath, feel your calves both relax. Move on to your knees. Check the tension in your body, and when you breathe out, push the tension away from yourself. Do not move on to a new part of your body until you feel the muscles you are working on completely release themselves and unknot any tension they are holding.

Throughout the day, come back to the breath. As you are washing the dinner dishes, focus on the breath as you scrub. Through the breath, you can enter mindfulness and learn to be alive, truly alive each moment.

Focus on Your Breathing

Do this all the way up your body until you have reached your head. When your head, shoulders, and neck are relaxed, focus in on your breath.

Breathe in naturally. Feel where the breath is going. Feel the breath go down your nasal passages into your throat and lungs. Allow yourself to breathe normally for a few minutes, just watching the breaths move in and out. Now take a deep breath. Notice how on your in-breath your stomach moves in, and on your out-breath your stomach moves out. Put your hand on your stomach and feel your body move as you take deep breaths. Notice how your breath involves more of your body than just your nose and lungs. As you breathe in, watch your breath. As you breathe out, watch your breath. Feel the rhythm of the natural breathing and the rhythm of the deep breathing. Do this every day until you feel comfortable with the natural rhythms of your breathing. We rarely pay attention to the basic rhythm of our own living; each and every breath we make, we take for granted.

Slow down! You cannot live the moments of your life if you are rushing around trying to save the world. Take a deep breath, and slow down.

Practice Moving Meditation

It is helpful to then move on to a moving meditation. Try to do a walking meditation or a form of exercise such as yoga that you can do mindfully. As you move, pay attention to the breath. If you are walking, breathe in and step, breathe out and step. Focus on the breath and the movement of the body as you walk. Do this for ten minutes so you can bring mindfulness into an activity. Yoga is a wonderful moving meditation. Focus on your breath as you move through your yoga routine. Become one with the exercises as you focus on your breath, moving smoothly from one position to the next. First we breathe, and then we breathe and start to move through the day, bringing our mindfulness into action.

Staying in the Moment

When you find yourself lost in the future or the past, gently return to the breath and come back to the moment at hand. This is the essence of mindfulness, the essence of Zen. You only live your life one moment at a time: To try to do otherwise is to not live at all. Do not miss the moments of your life. They are precious and beautiful. Every moment is a miracle. Wake up to the miracle of life—breathe in and out.

Meditation on Interdependence

Just by paying attention to your breath you will realize the connectedness you have your interdependency. You cannot breathe without the oxygen, the atmosphere, the plants that provide for you. Your very being is dependent upon so many essentials. Every breath you take is a meditation on interdependence. And when you realize your interdependence, you start to wake up.

"Everything we do is an act of poetry or a painting if we do it with mindfulness." —Thich Nhat Hanh

Most of us want to live in the world of ideas and are sure that if we stumble upon the right set of ideas, we will find the answers we are looking for. To practice mindfulness is to give up on the world of ideas. The world of ideas will not lead you to an awakened life. You will not wake up by thinking about the interdependence of all things, or by reading hundreds of books on Buddhism. If you wash your plate and are present while you wash your plate, you are on the path to enlightenment. When you realize that life is washing plates, wiping noses, getting dressed, and scrubbing floors, you are on the path to awareness. You will never see into your true nature by holding on to concepts. So take a shower, eat your lunch, vacuum the living room. This is life.

Mindfulness and Peace

Many of us hunger for peace in the world. When we look to the future, we can become frightened. The world seems unstable, and the people in it volatile. We hear about the possibility of nuclear devastation when we pick up the paper and turn on the news. We hear about civil unrest, bombings, war, famine. We see the unhappy faces of children, widows, and soldiers on the covers of our magazines and books. And we hear the grief of our own community members as we live with the devastating after-effects of terrorism in our homeland.

What can we do to promote peace in the world? Is it futile to hope that we can have a peaceful world? Perhaps you are overwhelmed and helpless; you have given up on peace. But peace is possible, it just has to start at home. As Confucius said:

> *When things are investigated, then true knowledge is achieved;*
> *When true knowledge is achieved, the will becomes sincere;*
> *When the will becomes sincere, then the heart is set right;*
> *When the heart is set right, then the personal life is cultivated;*
> *When the personal life is cultivated, then the family life*
> *is regulated;*
> *When the family life is regulated, then the national life is orderly;*
> *And when the national life is orderly, then there is peace in*
> *the world.*

During his Nobel lecture, on December 11, 1989, the Dalai Lama said much the same thing:

> *Responsibility does not only lie with the leaders of our*
> *countries or with those who have been appointed or elected to*
> *do a particular job. It lies with each of us individually. Peace,*
> *for example, starts within each one of us. When we have inner*
> *peace, we can be at peace with those around us. When our*
> *community is in a state of peace, it can share that peace with*
> *neighboring communities, and so on. When we feel love and*
> *kindness towards others, it not only makes others feel loved and*
> *cared for, but it helps us also to develop inner happiness and*
> *peace. And there are ways in which we can consciously work*
> *to develop feelings of love and kindness.*

Practice Peace

We cannot change the heart of another person; we can only change ourselves. If we despair of the possibility that the world will ever find peace, we can start to practice peace ourselves. How can we expect to have peace between nations when we do not have peace in our own homes? If you cannot spend a peaceful day with your own family, how can you expect entire countries with different backgrounds and beliefs to get along better than you do?

Put aside your sweeping statements, your ideas, and your despair. Start to practice peace yourself. But do not bite off more than you can chew. The best way to defeat yourself is to try to take on too much. Start with your meditation practice, and strive to find peace in your own heart for twenty or so minutes per day.

When you have spent months and years on your own practice, try to bring that practice out into the living room and the kitchen of your own house. Practice peace by listening instead of talking, by understanding instead of seeking to be understood. When someone is angry, hear what they have to say instead of defending yourself. Practice love, compassion, and peace. Instead of yelling at your dog for jumping on the counter, praise him for sitting away from the counter where he cannot get to the food. Practice tolerance, and look to identify with others instead of comparing yourself to them. See how you are alike, instead of how you are different.

The way to a peaceful home is through a peaceful heart. And a peaceful heart can be found by searching yourself for compassion and love.

You must find the peace in your own heart and mind before you can expect others to find it. If you cannot hold an angry tongue at work, how can you look for world peace? Be a messenger for peace in your own community before expecting others to be messengers of peace for you. Start the inquiry into self. Become intimate with yourself and your own heart. You might be surprised that you have a great wealth of love and compassion at your disposal—inside yourself, not outside of yourself.

Acknowledge Suffering

Thich Nhat Hanh has spread his message of peace across the world one person at a time. He knows that with deep listening, compassion, and loving speech, we can promote peace wherever we are.

In order to realize peace, however, we must be willing to acknowledge the suffering that exists instead of turning our backs on those who suffer, ignoring the pain that is hard to bear witness to. If you practice Zen, and practice daily, you will find the strength to face the horrors of war and the other negative experiences that afflict so many. You will be able to summon the patience, compassion, and open heart needed to listen deeply to anger. If we do not listen to anger, we only add fuel to its fire. We do not have to agree with the people who spread anger, fear, and terror in the world. But we can listen to what is important to them and try to hear where their pain and suffering is coming from. But we cannot do this if we do not first have peace in our own hearts. You will have to practice peace to promote peace.

Sit for Peace

We live in a world where practice is so very important. It is a matter of life and death—your life and death. Zen practice is a gateway to compassion and love—both at home and in the larger world. It is very hard work to practice mindfulness. It is hard work to get up every morning and sit zazen. It is hard to be present when the whole world screams for our attention elsewhere. But slow down, and give yourself a wonderful gift. Give the world a gift as well. Sit for peace. Sit for all sentient beings. Sit for yourself. Just sit. (E)

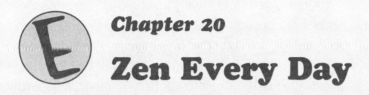

Chapter 20

Zen Every Day

Zen is a way of life. If you just sit for twenty-five minutes a day, you will see changes in yourself before very long. Whether you consciously take your practice into your life or you just sit once a day and watch the practice grow naturally out of zazen, the Zen way of life will grab you and start to change you. Just keep sitting.

A Day in the Life of the Zen Practitioner

Let's walk through a day in the life of a person who is practicing Zen and making an effort to be conscious of practice as often as possible. What opportunities are available in the day to bring attention back to the moment? How can a student of Zen bring mindfulness into daily life? Let's assume that this student is you. You have found a place to practice—through your searches online, you came across a local sitting group that meets at your local college on Thursday evenings. You make a commitment to yourself to make it to every Thursday sit you possibly could. The leader of the group is a Zen master—you have found someone to assist you on the path of practice you have chosen.

Let's walk through a typical day, assuming you go to work and live with either family or friends.

Waking Up

When you wake up each morning, immediately get out of your bed and leave it behind. Do not hesitate as you rise. Just wake up, get up, and move on. We find this is the best way to start the day. If we don't get up immediately, we might fall back to sleep again. After you do this for a while, it will become automatic, and you will just jump out of bed when the alarm sounds. Once up, the cushion looks more inviting than it does from the comfort of your bed!

FACT

A friend told us once that the first thing he does every morning is make his bed. That way, if the entire day turns out horribly he has at least made one good move. This is a wonderful plan you can apply to your Zen practice.

Start Your Day with Zazen

Often, the day can get away from you, and plans can go astray. Before you know it, the time you set aside for zazen is taken up with a sudden emergency, work interference, or a friend in need. If you find that your schedule is already tight, make a conscious effort to wake up half an hour early and do your practice early in the morning.

Jacky was always a late-night person until she started her Zen practice. She started rising at 5:00 A.M., so she could sit before work. What are the consequences of rising at 5:00 A.M.? What did she miss out on? To rise a half hour earlier you might have to go to bed half an hour earlier. What will you miss? Many of us might just miss out on some television, but when you think about it, weighing enlightenment versus half an hour of television isn't really much of a choice. Nowadays, Jacky has no problem arising early, and never once has she felt left out for missing that extra episode of her favorite show or the late news.

It is up to you how long you decide your daily zazen session should be. Twenty-five minutes is a good amount of time, but more or less time might work better for you.

By sitting before you leave the house, you are giving yourself a wonderful gift. You are giving yourself twenty-five or so minutes of quiet. You can approach your day with a peaceful mind instead of jump-starting your brain with thoughts of the day's agenda. If, during your zazen session, you find your thoughts are gripping you, pulling you to the same thought over and again, take note of the thought. Perhaps you have something you need to address. Continually go back to the breath.

So, when you awake, jump in the shower and take care of your morning ritual. Then put on some comfortable clothes and do your daily zazen. Or, jump straight from bed to the cushion. There is no right way to starting your daily zazen, as long as it's daily. Now, whatever happens the rest of the day, you will have started your day in a positive way and done something wonderful for yourself.

"There is only one time that it is essential to awaken. That time is now."
—Buddha

Breakfast and Other Meals

Let's assume you eat your breakfast before leaving the house. Are you eating mindfully? Do you prepare your meals consciously, with some gratitude for the sustenance that allows you to continue your practice? Most of us eat on the run. Fast food is so convenient that we just grab what we can and shove it in. As a result, our pharmacies are bustling with constant business as people run in for heartburn remedies, aspirin, and Tums.

Eating Healthy

As part of your Zen practice, you should make an effort to eat mindfully. Consider the food you are putting in your body. Perhaps dairy food leaves you congested and stuffed up. Note how you feel after your meals, and you will be able to feed yourself the foods that help you feel your best.

As you eat, think this to yourself: I am grateful for this food. Notice the movement of your jaw as you chew. Notice what happens when you swallow. Think of the food you are ingesting and where it came from. Feel your connection to the earth that provided the food you are eating.

If you start eating mindfully, you'll probably notice that a healthy, mindful breakfast doesn't have to take a lot of time. Making an effort to eat a morning meal doesn't mean you have to prepare a three-course extravaganza. It simply means that whatever your food choice, whether it's a bowl of cereal, toast with jam, or soft-boiled eggs, it should be eaten slowly, carefully, and mindfully.

Treat your body well. Your mind will be clearer, and your concentration will be better. If you pay attention to what you are eating, as well as to how you are eating it, you will start to notice what foods affect you negatively.

Cleaning Up

When you clean up after your meal, mindfully wash the dishes or put away the remains of the meal. Notice the water washing over your hands.

Notice how it feels, what the texture is like, how hot or cold it is. Look at the dish in your hands and study it. Is it smooth or rough? Listen to the sound as you put the dish away in the cupboard. Listen to the sound of your footsteps on the floor as you cross the room. Be mindful of the swing of your arms as you walk through the house. Pay attention to your breath. Breathe in, breathe out.

While reading this, you probably think that you certainly don't have time to add mindful eating and washing into your routine, but does it really take much longer than the routine you normally have? You might already rinse out your coffee cup or cereal bowl. If that's the case, continue to do so, but do it mindfully.

Leaving for Work

The journey to work is filled with opportunities to wake up to the present moment. A traffic jam is a wonderful opportunity to practice. A traffic jam allows you to stop and regroup, to re-enter the moment if you have been lost in thoughts of your day, rushing to get to the job. Most of us get angry and frustrated when stuck in traffic. We feel that we are "wasting" our time. In Zen, we slow down.

A traffic jam is a good time to breathe and be mindful of yourself, your surroundings, your hands on the steering wheel, your feet in their shoes.

If you commute to your job, take the opportunity on the train or bus to practice. We often fly through our lives, missing many of the moments that make up a day. We judge our time, saying "*This* time is time well spent. *This* time is a waste of my time." However, all time is time. There is no good time and no bad time. It is all the moments of your life. The dying know this. They can feel each moment they are living. How many people, faced with a terminal illness, say they never felt so alive? The moment becomes crystallized and separate from the moment before. A traffic jam, a stop sign, a yield sign, a pedestrian crossing in front of our car . . . these are all opportunities the world is taking to tell us: Wake UP! Pay attention to these moments. The world wants you to wake up. Everything in the world is rooting for you to wake up *right now*. Don't let these precious moments pass you by. Live them.

"To set up what you like against what you dislike . . .
This is the disease of the mind." —Seng T'san

On the Job

As Shunryu Suzuki said, "Zen is not some kind of excitement but concentration on our everyday routine." When we take Zen to work, we concentrate on the same tasks we always do. We do the same job we've always done, but we try to bring a mindfulness to every activity and interaction that we may not have previously had. It is easy to get caught up in circumstances at work that allow us to drop any attempt at mindfulness. The stress of the job can often send your mind into chaos, and then peace disappears.

Find a Moment to Practice

Slow down as much as you can. Take breaks throughout the day that allow you to refocus your attention on the moment. Sit down in a quiet corner for two minutes and breathe, putting yourself back in touch with the rhythm of your life. Keep a book available, such as a daily meditation book, that allows you to read a quick line or two that might help calm you down and reposition your focus.

If you use a meditation book, calendar, or Web site to help bring your attention back to your practice, remember that each of these items lives in the world of concepts. Zen practice is not about ideas. Use these reminders to return to your practice, but thinking about a clever saying is not the same as experiencing the reality beyond the words.

There are quite a few Zen books on the market today that can help you bring your attention back to your practice. A few recommended ones are the following: *Daily Wisdom: 365 Buddhist Inspirations*, edited by Josh Bartok, or *Zen Flesh, Zen Bones* by Paul Reps and Nyogen Senzaki. You can also purchase daily Zen calendars, such as the *Little Zen Page-a-Day*. There are also Internet sites that will send out daily Zen quotes if you sign up, such as ✍ *www.dailyzen.com*.

Leave Behind the Concepts

Zen masters do not run around trying to accomplish numerous tasks throughout the day. Each task they undertake is done with deliberation, slowly and mindfully. In *Zen Keys*, Thich Nhat Hanh says, "In Zen experience there is no longer an object of knowledge." What this means is that in Zen, we do not bring along the concepts of experience to our experience. When we see a pencil, we experience the pencil deeply, as it is. We do not bring along our concepts of a pencil—it has a pink eraser; it is yellow; it has a brown point; it is light and easy to break.

ALERT!

To practice Zen is to leave behind the concepts. For now, just try to stay in the moment and experience your day. Try not to get caught up in your *ideas* about how your day is going, but stick with what is actually happening right now.

Back Home Again

It is never too late to start the day again. If the day gets away from you, as it often can, come back to center at home. Light some incense, sit on your cushion, and go back to the breath. Make a meal mindfully, or clean up your home with great attention to the task at hand. Make your home an oasis where you can come back to the moment again and again. We so often get caught up in the details of life. Most of it is not worth the energy we put into it. Relax, and enjoy just being a part of the big picture. Realize your insignificance and your great importance all at once.

You are like the wave in the ocean. You are distinguishable for a short time and then become one with the rest of the ocean once again.

Become One with Nature

When you are home, sit outside and look at the sky. The sky is awake. It doesn't know it's awake; it just is. Look at the clouds, the trees, the earth beneath your feet. Be still and be a part of all that is. Feel how you are like the wave in the ocean, distinguishable but still the same as everything else. Do not waste a minute of your time. You are alive and can wake up. This is your opportunity to do so. Do not squander this opportunity. Put all of your energies into waking up.

Do One Task at a Time

Be mindful of the choices you make with your time. Do you watch television and read at the same time? Do you talk on the phone and clean house? Do you pay bills while listening to music? Is your mind constantly divided as you attempt to multitask your way through the day? Just slow down. Try to undertake just one task at a time. Everything you do deserves your undivided attention. Pay attention.

Listen to Others

You have to deal with other people all day long. How can you bring your Zen practice into your relationships? Listen deeply to others. Be respectful of others at all times. Be gracious and kind.

When you are home, you probably either talk on the phone or talk with someone at home about your day. As the person you are talking with relates his or her day to you, listen with your whole mind and body. Attend to others as if they are telling you the most important information. Approach everyone with respect and attention. Be kind and be present. It is a great gift both to yourself and to others.

Resting and Zen

At the end of the day, it is time to retire for the evening. Go to bed as you got up. Sleep as if it is the last sleep you will ever get. When we practice the Middle Way, we tend to our health and well-being. Make sure you get plenty of rest.

Do not stay up too late. Set a time that allows you enough rest, and go to bed promptly. Zen practice will help you rest better as your mind is less cluttered.

At the End of the Day

The opportunity to wake up is a wonderful gift. You can spend your life doing many things. You become an expert in the field of your choice. You can become a parent, go on wonderful vacations, and accumulate wealth and possessions. You can have pets, you can ski, you can own your own company. Maybe you have done much of this already. Maybe you are wealthy beyond your wildest dreams. At the end of the day when you ask yourself the question, "Am I happy?" what is the answer?

You might be thinking that we have covered a very light day in the life of a Zen practitioner. There is so much more to life, you say! We passed over so many possibilities!

For instance, you might ask, what should I do if I lose my job? Just sit. What if I have a fight with my spouse? Just sit. What if I find out I am very ill? Just sit. What if my house gets hit by lightning? Just sit. What if I break a nail? Just sit. You see where this is going?

FACT

If you choose to live a life of Zen practice, you will sacrifice many things. You might sacrifice money, time, vacations, family time, possessions, job success, and more. But if you practice Zen, you will most likely find yourself happier. In simplicity there is great beauty.

Ryokan

There is a wonderful Zen story about the Zen master Ryokan. Ryokan lived a very simple life in a tiny hut at the foot of a great mountain. One evening, while Ryokan was out for a walk, a thief came by, hoping to steal something of value. He found there was nothing of value to steal.

Ryokan came back to the hut and discovered the thief. "You may have come a long way to see me," he said to the thief, "and you should not go away empty-handed. Please take my clothes as a gift."

The thief was confused, but he took the clothes and skulked away.

Ryokan sat naked under the stars, watching the moon. "Poor man," he said, "I wish I could give him this beautiful moon."

With Zen you can know the moon. Every day is a miracle of beauty. Our footfalls on the earth are a wonder. Miracles surround us every moment. Zen is about awakening. It is not about being awake or staying awake, it is about becoming awake. It is not about achieving enlightenment, but about realizing it over and over again. We wake up over and over again. We strive to wake up.

An Illness Called Separation

If you keep sitting, little by little—we hope—you will start to wake up. Life will change from the inside out. You will realize the nature of inter-being and interdependence. You will move from the world of concepts to the world of experience. The illusion of separation will disappear. As Bernie Glassman says in his book *Bearing Witness:* "If there's a gash in my left leg and blood is spurting out, my hands don't say, 'Too bad, let the leg take care of itself, we're too busy to take care of it right now.' . . . But that's what happens in life, in society. And it happens only because we have an illness called separation. If we don't see that the hands, legs, feet, head, and hair are all one body, we don't take care of them and we suffer. If we don't see the unity of life, we don't take care of life and we suffer."

The Unity of Life

If you practice, you will start to see the unity of life. All it takes is great faith, great doubt, and great determination. We assure you of one thing: Practicing Zen is never a waste of time. The worst that can happen is you will feel a little more peaceful and a lot less dissatisfied. But Zen practice is not about reading books. The only way to practice Zen is to sit zazen. So get off the couch and onto a zafu. You can do it, we know you can. It is not easier for others than it is for you. No one is going to try to sell you on the premise that Zen practice is easy and effortless. And if you think you know Zen because you read a book about it, you are wrong. Zen is your experience. Zen cannot be captured in the pages of this book. This is the concept of Zen. Get up and go: *do* Zen now.

As the old Zen saying goes: It is never too late to do nothing.

As Dogen once said, "To study Zen is to study the self. To study the self is to forget the self. To forget the self is to be illuminated by the ten thousand things."

Appendices

Appendix A

Glossary

Appendix B

American Zen Practice Centers

Appendix C

Additional Resources

Glossary

Ascetic: One who believes that spiritual growth can be obtained through extreme self-denial and the renunciation of worldly pleasures. Ascetics often practice poverty, starvation, and self-mortification.

Bodhi tree: Tree of Wisdom; a fig tree.

Bodhisattva: A person who has already attained enlightenment, or is ready to attain that state, but puts off his or her own final enlightenment in order to re-enter the cycle of *samsara* and save all sentient beings.

Brahmin: The priests and the highest class of the hereditary caste system of India. The Brahmins were those motivated by knowledge.

Buddha: The Fully Awakened One. From the Sanskrit *budh,* which means "to awaken."

Buddha-nature: Our true nature, our original nature before we became who we are today. Buddha-nature is that which is within us that gives us the ability to attain enlightenment.

Burmese style: A position of meditation in which the meditator sits cross-legged while both feet and calves remain on the floor, unlike in lotus position.

Ch'an: Literally, meditation. A school of Buddhism started in China in the sixth century by Bodhidharma. Known in Japan as Zen.

***Daikensho*:** Enlightenment.

Dharma: The Path, the teachings of the Buddha. What is, and what should be. Dharma is everything: truth, the teachings, all things and states conditioned and unconditioned, nature, morality, ethics, and that which helps one achieve nirvana, that which is virtuous and righteous.

Dharma wheel: The wheel symbolizes the Buddhist cycle of birth and rebirth. The wheel often has eight spokes, symbolizing the Eightfold Path.

Dokusan: A private encounter with a Zen teacher.

Duhkha: Dissatisfaction, suffering, disease, or anguish caused by attachment and desire.

Dhyana: Sanskrit word for meditation.

Eightfold Path: The path to enlightenment: Right Understanding, Right Thought, Right Speech, Right Action, Right Livelihood, Right Effort, Right Mindfulness, and Right Concentration.

Five Houses of Zen: Guiyang school, Caodong school, Linji school, Yunmen school, and Fayan school.

Five Precepts: Buddhist guidelines for conduct and ethical living. In order, they are: Do not destroy life. Do not steal. Do not commit sexual misconduct. Do not lie. Do not take intoxicating drinks.

Four Noble Truths: The heart of the Buddha's teaching, the truths are as follows: Life is filled with suffering. Suffering is caused by desire. Desire can end. The way to end desire is to follow the Eightfold Path.

Gassho: To place two palms together.

Haiku: A Japanese poem traditionally containing three lines of five, seven, and five syllables. Most commonly, haikus are about everyday life and nature.

Half-lotus position: A meditation position. The legs are crossed with one foot on the thigh of the opposite leg. The other foot is under the opposite thigh, unlike the full lotus position in which both feet are on the thigh of the opposite leg.

Karma: The force generated by action and intention that affects one's quality of life in the next life. Good intention can lead to a good life in the next life via karmic implication. Negative intention can lead to a harder life in the next life via karmic implication.

Kensho: Enlightenment, but not as strong as *daikensho* or *satori.*

Kinhin: Walking meditation in Zen practice.

Koan: Questions that cannot be answered by the rational mind but that are answered as one pushes closer to enlightenment. The most famous koan is "What is the sound of one hand clapping?"

Lotus position: A position used for meditation practice. Lotus position entails sitting cross-legged with the top of your left foot on your right thigh and the top of your right foot on your left thigh.

Mantra: A mantra is a mystical incantation used during meditation.

Middle Way: The peaceful way between two extremes: neither excessive pleasure nor excessive pain. The Middle Way is the path to enlightenment.

Mindfulness: Being aware of things as they are and as they happen. Living in the moment.

Monkey mind: The action of your mind as it jumps from thought to thought, as a monkey jumps from tree to tree. To have monkey mind is to have a cluttered, jumbled, unserene mindset.

Mumu: No-thing, no, nothingness; the most famous Zen koan.

Nirvana: The cessation of suffering by the elimination of desire. Nirvana is not a place separate from us but that lies in each of us; it is the very still center at the core of our beings.

Paranirvana: The attainment of nirvana plus the total extinction of the physical self. When the Buddha died, he reached paranirvana.

Prajna: Wisdom.

Prana: Breath, life force.

Rinazi School of Zen: Rinzai is the school of Zen that emphasizes koan practice.

Roshi: A title given to a Zen master, under whom a student must study if he or she hopes to reach enlightened mind. In Japanese, it means "venerable master."

Samadhi: A profound meditative state.

Samsara: The infinite repetitions of birth, death, and suffering caused by karma.

Sangha: Community of Buddhists. Traditionally, it could be defined as a community of monks, but the contemporary definition includes any Buddhist community of followers.

Satori: Enlightenment.

Seiza: A meditation position in which the meditator sits on his cushion while kneeling with his knees on the ground. The majority of the body weight rests on the cushion.

Sesshin: A Zen meditation retreat in which intensive zazen practice takes place.

Shikantaza: "Just sitting." Sitting without breath practice or any other directed concentration.

Shunyata: Emptiness.

Soto School of Zen: School of Zen Buddhism that emphasizes silent sitting meditation.

Sutra: The collection of teachings of the Buddha: discourses and dialogues.

Teisho: A presentation of insight from a teacher to students. Often the subject of a *teisho* will be a koan or koans.

Three Jewels: Buddha, dharma, *sangha*.

Zabutan: A large flat pillow that fits under the zafu so that your knees do not scrape the floor.

Zafu: A round cushion used for meditation.

Zazen: Seated meditation; total concentration of mind and body.

Zen: A school of Buddhism that emphasizes seated meditation and seeing directly into Buddha-nature.

Zendo: The Zen meditation hall.

Appendix B

American Zen Practice Centers

P ROVIDED HERE IS A SMALL SAMPLING of the Zen centers located in the United States. This list is by no means comprehensive, but it is gathered together to illustrate the diverse cities and towns containing Zen facilities. To find facilities most convenient to you, we suggest either contacting the International Research Institute for Zen Buddhism or searching online. A good place to start online is with the Open Directory Project Web site, at ✍ *http://dmoz.org*. From there, choose the Society link, then Religion and Spirituality. Click on the Buddhism link, then Lineages, Zen, then Centers, then United States (or whatever area you are interested in).

Alabama

Green Mountain Zen Center
Huntsville, AL
www.gmzc.us

Zen Center of Huntsville
Huntsville, AL
www.garply.com/~jjacks/Zen

Alaska

Anchorage Zen Center
Anchorage, AK
Tel: (907) 248-1049

Anchorage Zen Community
Anchorage, AK
www.alaska.net/~zen/

Cold Mountain Zen Centers
Fairbanks, AK
*www.geocities.com/
coldmountainzencenter*

Arizona

Desert Lotus Zen Sangha
Chandler, AZ
www.vuu.org/zen/

Haku-un-ji Tempe Zen Center
Tempe, AZ
www.zenarizona.com

Zen Desert Sangha
Tucson, AZ
*www.delegation.org/lame/zds/
index.html*

Arkansas

Little Rock Zen Group
Little Rock, AR
www.geocities.com/arkansaszen

Morning Star Zen Center
Fayetteville, AR
Tel: (501) 521-6925

Zen Center of Hot Springs
Hot Springs, AR
Tel: (501) 767-6096

California

City of Ten Thousand Buddhas
Talmage, CA
www.drba.org

Community of Mindful Living
Berkeley, CA
www.iamhome.org

Dharma Zen Center
Los Angeles, CA
www.dharmazen.com

Fruitvale Zendo
Oakland, CA
Tel: (510) 532-5226

Harbor Sangha
San Francisco, CA
www.zendo.com/~hs/harbor.html

Hartford Street Zen Center
San Francisco, CA
www.hartfordstreetzen.com

Hazy Moon Sangha
Los Angeles, CA
www.hazymoon.com

Jikoji Zen Mountain Retreat Center
Los Gatos, CA
www.zendo.com/~jikoji/jikoji.html

Kannon Do Zen Center
Mountain View, CA
*www.zendo.com/~kannondo/
kdo.html*

Mahayana Zengong
El Monte, CA
www.zengong.org/

San Francisco Zen Center
San Francisco, CA
www.sfzc.com

Shasta Abbey
Mount Shasta, CA
www.shastaabbey.org

Zen Center of Los Angeles
Los Angeles, CA
www.zencenter.org

Colorado

Crestone Mountain Zen Center
Crestone, CO
www.manitou.org

Great Mountain Zen Center
Boulder, CO
www.gmzc.org

Springs Mountain Sangha
Colorado Springs, CO
www.pcisys.net/~sms.zen

Zen Center of Denver
Denver, CO
www.zencenterofdenver.org

Connecticut

Mindfulness Sangha
New Britain, CT
www.haianpagoda.org

New Haven Zen Center
New Haven, CT
www.newhavenzen.org

Delaware

Buddhist Association of
Wilmington
Wilmington, DE

Delaware Valley Zen Center
Newark, DE
www.dvzc.com

Florida

Brevard Zen Center—Kuge-in
Zen Temple
Cocoa, FL
www.brevardzen.org

Cypress Tree Zen Group
Tallahassee, FL
www.tfn.net/~cypress

Gainesville Zen Center
Gainesville, FL
www.gatelessgate.org/gzc/gzc.htm

Gateless Gate Zen Center
Alachua, FL
*www.gatelessgate.org/ggate/
AboutUS.htm*

Jacksonville Zen Sangha
Jacksonville, FL
www.unf.edu/~zlewis/homepage/

Zen Meditation Center
Hollywood, FL
Tel: (30) 285-2000

Georgia

Atlanta Soto Zen Center
Atlanta, GA
www.aszc.org

ZenSpace
Atlanta, GA
www.zenspace.org

Hawaii

Diamond Sangha
Honolulu, Hawaii
www.ciolek.com

Hsu Yun Temple
Honolulu, HI
www.hsuyun.org

Kaua'i Zen Community Soto
Zen Temple
Hanapepe, HI
www.geocities.com/zenshuhji

Idaho

Beginner's Mind Sangha
Boise, ID
Tel: (208) 336-1525

Mindfulness Sangha
Moscow, ID
Tel: (208) 883-3311

Illinois

Buddhist Temple of Chicago
Chicago, IL
www.budtempchi.org

Chicago Zen Center
Chicago, IL
www.chicagozen.com

Heartland Sangha
Evanston, IL
www.heartlandsangha.org

Prairie Zen Center
Champaign, IL
www.prairiezen.org

Sangamon Zen Group
Springfield, IL
www.sangamonzen.org

Indiana

Indianapolis Zen Center
Indianapolis, IN
www.ameritech.net/users/indyzen/izg.html

Zen Center of Bloomington
Bloomington, IL
www.bloomingtonzen.org

Iowa

Cedar Rapids Zen Center
Cedar Rapids, IA
http://avalon.net/~crzc

Iowa City Zen Center
Iowa City, IA
www.jccn.iowa-city.ia.us/~iczen

Kansas

Kansas Zen Center
Lawrence, Topeka, Kansas City, and Manhattan, Kansas
www.kansaszencenter.org

Kentucky

Furnace Mountain Zen Center
Red River Gorge, KY
www.zenmind.org/fm.html

Lexington Zen Center
Lexington, KY
Tel: (606) 277-2438

Louisiana

American Zen Association
New Orleans, LA
http://home.gnofn.org/~aza

Blue Iris Sangha
New Orleans, LA
http://home.bellsouth.net/p/s/community.dll?ep=16&groupid=45151&ck=

Maine

Meetingbrook Dogen and Francis Hermitage
Camden, ME
www.meetingbrook.org

Morgan Bay Zendo
Surry, ME
http://w2.downeast.net/zbme/zendo

Maryland

Burning House Zen Community
Baltimore, MD
http://burninghousezendo.org

Stillwater Mindfulness Center
Silver Spring, MD
www.stillwatermpc.org

Zen Community of Baltimore
Clare Sangha
Baltimore, MD
www.zcbclaresangha.org

Zen Peacemaker Community
Baltimore, MD
www.peacemakercommunity.org

Massachusetts

Cambridge Zen Center
Cambridge, MA
www.cambridgezen.com

Clear Light Society
Cambridge, MA
www.clearlightsociety.org

Hopping Tree Sangha
Amherst, MA
*http://hometown.aol.com/
clothsack*

Pioneer Valley Zendo
Charlemont, MA
Tel: (413) 339-4000

Michigan

Buddhist Society for
Compassionate Wisdom
Ann Arbor, MI

Lake Superior Zendo
Marquette, MI
Tel: (906) 226-6407

Minnesota

Clouds in Water Zen Center
St. Paul, MN
www.cloudsinwater.org

Compassionate Ocean Dharma
Center
Minneapolis, MN
www.oceandharma.org

Mississippi

Starkville Zen Dojo
Starkville, MS

Missouri

Boonville One Drop Zendo
Columbia, MO
http://zen.columbia.missouri.org

Missouri Zen Center
Webster Groves, MO
www.missourizencenter.org

Montana

Zenno Ji
Missoula, MT
www.zennoji.org

Nebraska

Nebraska Zen Center
Omaha, NE
www.prairiewindzen.org

Nevada

Great Bright Zen Center
Las Vegas, NV
www.greatbrightzen.com

New Hampshire

Southern New Hampshire Zen
Group
Hillsborough, NH
www.nhzen.org

New Jersey

Barnegat Bay Zen Group
Barnegat Bay, NJ

Mid-Jersey Zen Group
Lawrenceville, NJ

Morning Star Zendo
Jersey City, NJ

The Zen Society
Cinnaminson, NJ
www.jizo-an.org

New Mexico

Albuquerque Zen Center
Albuquerque, NM
www.azc.org

Mountain Cloud Zen Center
Santa Fe, NM
*http://members.tripod.com/
~mczc/Home.html*

New York

Clear Mountain Zen Center
Hempstead, NY
http://lizen.homestead.com/

Dharma Drum Retreat Center
Pine Bush, NY
www.chan1.org/ddrc/ddrc.html

Empty Hand Zendo
Rye, NY
www.emptyhandzen.org

Rochester Zen Center
Rochester, NY
www.rzc.org

Zen Center of New York City
Fire Lotus Temple
New York, NY
www.mro.org/zcnyc/firelotus.shtml

Zen Mountain Monastery
Mt. Tremper, NY
www.mro.org

North Carolina

Chapel Hill Zen Center
Chapel Hill, NC
www.intrex.net/chzg

Charlotte Community of Mindfulness
Charlotte, NC
*www.coe.uncc.edu/~billchu/
sangha*

Ohio

Zen Center of Cleveland
Cleveland, OH
www.cloudwater.org

Oregon

Ashland Zen Center
Ashland, OR
www.gmrdesign.com/sangha

Dharma Rain Zen Center
Portland, OR
www.dharma-rain.org

Zen Community of Oregon
Corbett, OR
www.zendust.org

Pennsylvania

Blue Mountain Zendo
Summit Hill, PA
www.bluemountainzendo.org

Laughing Rivers Sangha
Pittsburgh, PA
www.laughingrivers.org

Mt. Equity Zendo Jihoji
Pennsdale, PA
www.mtequity.org

Stillpoint
Pittsburgh, PA
http://trfn.clpgh.org/stillpt

Rhode Island

The Kwan Um School of Zen
Cumberland, RI
www.kwanumzen.com

Providence Zen Center
Cumberland, RI
www.kwanumzen.com/pzc

South Carolina

Charlestown Zen Center
Charlestown, SC
*www.geocities.com/
chaszencenter*

South Dakota

Laughing Teabowl Zendo
Rapid City, SD

Tennessee

Nashville Zen Center
Nashville, TN
www.nashvillezencenter.org

Texas

Austin Zen Center
Austin, TX
www.austinzencenter.org

Maria Kannon Zen Center
Dallas, TX
www.mkzc.org

Northwoods Sangha
Zen Mind Buddhist Sangha
The Woodlands, TX
*www.optimlator.com/hzc/
northwoods.htm*

Utah

Kanzeon Zen Center
Salt Lake City, UT
www.zencenterutah.org

Vermont

Unified Buddhist Church,
Inc.
Hartland-Four-Corners, VT
www.plumvillage.org

Vermont Zen Center
Shelburne, VT
www.vzc.org

Virginia

Ekoji Buddhist Sangha of
Richmond
Richmond, VA
www.ekojirichmond.org

Washington

Cloud Mountain Zen Center
Castle Rock, WA
www.cloudmountain.org

Dai Bai Zan—Cho Bo Zen
Temple
Seattle, WA
www.choboji.org

Dharma Sound Zen Center
Seattle, WA
www.dharmasound.org

Wisconsin

Dragon Flower Ch'an Temple
Rhinelander, WI
www.dragonflower.org

Appendix C
Additional Resources

Books and Magazines

Asking About Zen, by Jiho Sargent (Weatherhill Books: New York, 2001).

Awakening of Faith in the Mahayana and Its Commentary: The Principle and Practice of Mahayana Buddhism, by D.T. Suzuki (Oriental Book Store: 1990).

Awakening to Zen, by Philip Kapleau (Scribner Books: New York, 1997).

Be Still and Know: Reflections Living Buddha, Living Christ, by Thich Nhat Hanh (Riverhead Books, New York), 1996.

Blooming of a Lotus: Guided Meditation Exercises for Healing and Transformation, The, by Thich Nhat Hanh (Beacon Press: 1993).

Breath Sweeps Mind, by Jean Smith, ed. (Riverhead Books: New York, 1998).

Buddha, by Karen Armstrong (Viking Penguin: New York, 2001).

Buddhism Without Beliefs, by Stephen Batchelor (Riverhead Books: New York, 1997).

Buddhist Handbook, The, by John Snelling (Inner Traditions: Vermont, 1991, 1998).

Complete Idiot's Guide to Understanding Buddhism, The, by Gary Gach (Alpha Books: New York, 2002).

Complete Idiot's Guide to Zen Living, The, by Gary McClain, Ph.D., and Eve Adamson, MFA (Alpha Books: New York, 2001).

Crooked Cucumber: The Life and Zen Teachings of Shunryu Suzuki, by David Chadwick (Broadway Books: New York, 1999).

Daily Wisdom: 365 Buddhist Inspirations, by Josh Bartok, ed. (Wisdom Publications: Massachusetts, 2001).

Eight Gates of Zen, The, by John Daido Loori (Dharma Communications: New York, 1992).

Essays in Zen Buddhism, by D.T. Suzuki (Red Wheel/Weiser: 1991).

Everyday Mind: 366 Reflections on the Buddhist Path, by Jean Smith, ed. (Riverhead Books: New York, 1997).

Five Houses of Zen, The, by Thomas Cleary (Shambhala: Massachusetts, 1997).

Gateless Barrier: Zen Comments on the Mumonkan, The, by Zenkei Shibayam (Shambhala: Massachusetts, 1974).

Healing Breath, by Ruben L. F. Habito (Orbis Books: New York).

Instructions to the Cook: A Zen Master's Lessons in Living a Life That Matters, by Bernard Glassman and Rick Fields (Bell Tower Books: New York, 1996).

Introduction to Zen Buddhism, by D. T. Suzuki and Carl Jung (Grove Press: New York, 1991).

Manual of Zen Buddhism, by D.T. Suzuki, ed. (Grove Press: New York, 1987).

Miracle of Mindfulness, The, by Thich Nhat Hanh (Beacon Press: Massachusetts, 1976).

New Buddhism, The, by James William Coleman (Oxford: New York, 2001).

One Bird, One Stone, by Sean Murphy (St. Martin's Press: New York, 2002).

Pure Heart, Enlightened Mind: The Zen Journal and Letters of Maura "Soshin" O'Halloran (Riverhead Books: New York, 1994).

Radiant Mind, by Jean Smith, ed. (Riverhead Books: New York, 1999).

Sacred Hoops: Spiritual Lessons of a Hard Wood Warrior, by Phil Jackson (Hyperion Books: New York, 1996).

Subtle Sounds: The Zen Teaching of Maurine Stuart, by Roko Sherry Chayat, ed. (Shambhala: Massachusetts, 1996).

Teach Yourself Yoga in 24 Hours, by Linda Johnsen (Alpha Books: New York, 2002).

There Is Nothing Wrong with You, by Cherie Huber (Keep It Simple Books: 1993).

Three Pillars of Zen, The, by Philip Kapleau (Anchor Books: New York, 1980, 1965, 1989, 2000).

Verses from the Center by Stephen Batchelor (Riverhead Books: New York, 2000).

Way of Zen, The, by Alan Watts (Vintage: New York, 1957, 1985).

What the Buddha Taught, by Walpola Rahula (Grove Press: New York, 1959, 1974).

What Would Buddha Do? by Franz Metcalf (Ulysses Press: Berkeley, California, 1999, 2002).

Zen Buddhism: Selected Writings of D. T. Suzuki, by William Barrett, ed. (Doubleday: New York, 1956).

Zen Doctrine of No-Mind, by D.T. Suzuki (Red Wheel/Weiser: 1991).

Zen Flesh, Zen Bones, Paul Reps and Nyogen Senzaki, eds. (Tuttle Publishing: 1998).

Zen Keys: A Guide to Zen Practice, by Thich Nhat Hanh (Image Books: New York, 1974).

Zen Mind, Beginner's Mind, by Shunryu Suzuki (Weatherhill Books: New York, 1970).

Zen's Chinese Heritage, by Andy Ferguson (Wisdom Publications: Massachusetts, 2000).

Zen Teachings of Bodhidharma, The, translated by Red Pine (Farrar, Straus and Giroux: New York, 1987.)

Buddhism-Related Web Sites

Buddha 101: The History, Philosophy and Practice of Buddhism

✍ *www.buddha101.com*

A worthwhile site devoted to discussion about subjects such as the following: The Four Noble Truths, Dependant origination, the Eightfold Path, the three characteristics of existence, the Three Jewels and the Five Precepts, Karma and intention, Rebirth and nirvana, the history of Buddhism, the practice of Buddhism.

BuddhaMind

✍ *www.buddhamind.info*

A Web site dedicated to all things Buddhist.

BuddhaNet

✍ *www.buddhanet.net*

A "cyber-sangha" designed to link up people so they can share information about their beliefs and practices.

Buddhism Today

✍ *www.buddhismtoday.com*

A Web site devoted to the study of Buddhism.

A Call for Reckoning: Religion and the Death Penalty

✍ *http://pewforum.org/deathpenalty/resources/internetresources.php3*

A Web site devoted to discussion of religion and public life.

Crooked Cucumber

✍ *www.cuke.com*

A site dedicated to the life and teachings of Shunryu Suzuki, including interviews, encounters with his students, and information on the book *Crooked Cucumber*.

DharmaNet

✍ *www.dharmanet.org*

Among other things, DharmaNet is a wonderful place to find Buddhist resources for the socially engaged.

The Greyston Bakery and Greyston Foundation

✍ *www.buycake.com/Glassman.html*

Web site of Bernard Tetsugen Glassman and the Greyston Foundation.

Holistic Online

✍ *www.holistic-online.com*

A Web site devoted to alternative and integrative medicines.

The Nobel e-Museum

✍ *www.nobel.se*

Educational Web site about Alfred Nobel, the Nobel Foundation, and the Nobel Prize.

The Peacemaker Community

✍ *www.peacemakercommunity.org*

The Web site for the global, multi-faith community of peacemakers around the world, started by Bernie Glassman and Sandra Holmes.

Primary Point

✍ *www.kwanumzen.com/primarypoint*

A archive of articles on Zen practice.

The Pluralism Project

✍ *www.pluralism.org*

A site dedicated to the study and documentation of the growing religious diversity of the United States.

The Right Livelihood Foundation
www.rightlivelihood.se
The Web site for the Right Livelihood Award, which is given each year to a person or organization that has performed outstanding work on behalf of our planet and its people.

Shambhala Sun Online
www.shambhalasun.com
An online magazine about Buddhism and waking up. Site of Andrew Cooper's article, "In the Zone: The Zen of Sports."

Today's Quote
www.todaysquote.com
A site filled with interesting information on a variety of subjects.

Upaya
www.upaya.org
Web site for the Buddhist study center nestled in the foothills of New Mexico's Sangre de Cristo Mountains, with Roshi Joan Halifax.

Zen Mountain Monastery: The Mountains and Rivers Order
www.mro.org
Web site for the Zen Mountain Monastery and John Daido Loori.

Zenshuji
www.zenshuji.org
The Web site for Zenshuji Soto Mission in Los Angeles—the first Sotoshu Zen Temple established in North America.

Zen Stories to Tell Your Neighbors
www.rider.edu/users/suler/zenstory/zenstory.html
This Web site offers a nice selection of Zen stories.

Online Meditation Supply Stores

Here are a few selections—there are many more options available to you.

The American Zen Association
www.gnofn.org/~aza/supplies.html

Dharma Crafts
www.dharmacrafts.com

Four Gates
www.fourgates.com

Samadhi Store
www.samadhicushions.com

Shasta Abbey Buddhist Supplies
www.buddhistsupplies.com

Zen Center of Los Angeles
www.zencenter.org

Zen Mountain Monastery
www.mro.org

Index

A

Abortion, 53–54
Acceptance, 139–41
 of change/impermanence, 43,
  155–56
 of death, 128, 155–56
 defined, 139–40
 learning, 140–41
 looking inside for, 141
 of suffering, 122
Action (Right), 44, 46
Aitken, Robert, 227–28
Altars, 59, 158–60
American Zen, 27–39
 Beat culture and, 35–36
 centers, 33–34, 37–38, 225, 232,
  241, 266–72
 D. T. Suzuki and, 29–32
 origin, 28–29
 Shunryu Suzuki and, 32–35
 traditions, 34–35
Arrogance. See Stink (of Zen)
Art, 182–83
Asceticism
 defined, 18, 50, 262
 monastic life and, 170
 Siddhartha (Buddha) and, 17–18,
  50
Athletics, 195–208
 competition, 201–2
 losing self in, 200–201
 martial arts and, 23, 202–5
 mental focus and, 198
 peak performance in, 199–201
 respecting body and, 196–97
 wrestler example, 198–99
 yoga and, 205–8
 Zen benefits, 197–98
 the zone and, 4, 199–201
Attire, 38–39, 60, 161–63
Awareness, in martial arts, 203–4

B

Baker, Richard, 34–35, 229–30
Basho, 192
Bastis, Rev. Madeline Ko-i, 235
Beat culture, 35–36
Beck, Charlotte Joko, 230–31
Beginner mind, 5–6, 32–33
Being with the Dying Program, 118,
 232–33
Benefits
 in athletics, 197–98
 of pain, 65–66, 101–3
 of practice, 39, 257, 259
 sesshin, 220–21
 of yoga, 207–8
Bodhidharma, 22–23, 24
Bodhisattva
 activities of, 116–17
 defined, 262
 goal of, 118
 modern examples, 117–18
Bodhi tree
 Buddha and, 2, 19
 defined, 19, 262
Body
 intoxicants and, 51–52
 respecting, 196–97, 252
Books. See Resources
Bowing, 62, 165–66
Brahmin caste, 14, 262
Breathing
 counting and, 63
 following, 63–64
 hara focus and, 63
 mindfulness and, 242, 243–44, 245
 in yoga, 206–7
 in zazen, 63–64
Buddha-nature
 defined, 3, 262
 recognizing, 3, 156
Buddha(s)
 defined, 262
 multiple, 21

offerings to, 160
statues, 59, 159
within, finding, 3, 156
Zen origin and, 2–3
See also Siddhartha Gautama
Buddhism, 2, 6–7
 in China, 22–25
 Hui'ko and, 24–25
 in Japan, 25–26
 origins. See Siddhartha Gautama
 overview, 13
 schools of, 21–22
 spread of, 21–26
Buddhist Peace Fellowship, 228
Buddhist Society, 29
Burmese style, 62, 262

C

Calligraphy (zenga), 187–89
 beginning, 189
 origins, 188
 precision/unity of, 187, 188–89
Candles, 59, 159–60
Caodong school, 24
Career. See Job/Career
Chadwick, David, 33, 34
Ch'an, 2, 262
Change/impermanence
 accepting, 43, 155–56
 Buddhism and, 34
 death and. See Death
 gardening symbolizing, 184,
  186–87
 listening and, 87
 marriage and, 94
 of "me", 136–38
 nature of, 129–30
 positive outlook on, 131
 Siddhartha observations, 19
 suffering and, 43, 131
 understanding, 130–31, 132
Channa, 15–16
Children, 87–89

Chores, 153–55
Cleaning
    after meals, 252–53
    house, exercise, 147–48
Clothing, 38–39, 60, 161–63
Commitments
    significant others, 90–92
    to teachers, 100
Compassion
    attitude of, 178–80
    manifesting, 138–39
    in marriage, 94
    peace/harmony and, 84–85,
        150–53
Competition, 201–2
Concentration (Right), 45, 46
    in meditation, 47
    mindfulness vs., 238–39
    at work, 179
Concepts, leaving behind, 255
Confronting yourself, 7–8
Confucius, 246
Connectedness. See Mindfulness
    (Right)
Cooking, 154–55
Creative visualization, 57
Creativity, 181–93
    art practice and, 182–83
    calligraphy and, 187–89
    discovering, inside, 182–83
    expressing, options, 192–93
    flower-arranging and, 189–90
    gardening and, 183–87
    mindfulness training and, 183
    opening dharma eye, 193
    poetry and, 190–92
    unlimited, 192–93

D

Daikensho. See Enlightenment
Daily Zen, 11–12, 249–59
    after work, 255–57
    job and. See Job/Career

listening and, 256
meals and, 252–53
mindfulness and, 256
optimizing, 257–58
resting/sleep and, 257
unity and, 259
waking up and, 250–51, 258
zazen, 250–51
See also Home life
Dalai Lama, 246
Death
    accepting, 128, 155–56
    Being with the Dying Program,
        118, 232–33
    confronting fear, 127–28
    facing, 127–28
    future after, 142–44
    impermanence and, 126, 129–31
    meditation and, 127
    Partners Program, 233
    reincarnation and, 142–44
    releasing emotions, 127
    worrying about, 142
    Zen view, 52–53, 129
Deception, 50–51
Decisions, difficult, 53–54
Desire
    blinding nature of, 43–44
    distinctions and, 171–72
    eliminating, 9–10, 44
    Four Noble Truths and, 42, 43–44
Dharma, 5, 262
Dharma combat, 80
Dharma eye, 193
Dharma transmission, 2–3
Dharma wheel, 45, 263
Dhyana, 2, 263
Diamond Sangha, 228
Discipline. See Mental discipline
Distinctions, 171–72
Dogen, 2
Dokusan, 78–79, 215–17, 263
Dualistic thinking
    cause of, 109

eliminating, 65, 103, 109
pain and, 103
Duhkha, 17, 263. See also Suffering

E

Eco-friendly environment, 150
Effort (Right), 44, 46, 47, 179
Ego
    compassion replacing, 138–39
    dropping, 110, 138–39
    illusion of, 137–38
    stink of Zen and, 155–56, 165–66
    See also Self
Eightfold Path, 44–47
    awakening and, 109, 258
    categories, 45
    defined, 263
    dharma wheel and, 45, 263
    Four Noble Truths and, 42–44
    mental discipline and, 46–47
    morality and, 46
    steps, 44–45
    wisdom and, 45–46
Eight Gates of Zen, 233–34
Elitism. See Stink (of Zen)
Emotions
    death and, 127
    painful, 102
    releasing, 127
Empty mind, 64–65, 176–77
Engaged Buddhism, 226, 228
Enlightenment, 107–19
    activities after, 115–18
    as awakening, 109, 258
    Bodhidharma on, 23
    Buddha realizing, 2
    ceasing suffering and, 9
    conceptualizing vs. experiencing,
        113–14
    defined, 9
    desire and, 9–10
    discussing, 112
    dropping ego for, 110

Enlightenment, *(continued)*
  Eightfold Path and, 109
  experiencing, 109, 112–13, 258
  Four Noble Truths and, 109
  meditation and, 2
  mystery of, 111–14
  nirvana and, 3, 9, 108
  nonattachment for, 110–11, 155–56
  now vs. future, 108
  other words for, 3, 9
  personality flaws in, 35, 230
  reaching, 140
  road map to, 97, 100–101
  Siddhartha finding, 18–21
  sitting as, 34, 108, 114–15
  stink of, 155–56, 165–66
  teacher experience of, 96–97
  as Zen purpose, 3, 258
Ethics. *See* Eightfold Path
Euthanasia, 53–54
Evil (Mara), 19–20
Experience
  enlightenment and, 109, 112–13, 258
  importance of, 30–31
  three parts of, 65

F

Fayan school, 24
Fear
  confronting, 66–67, 127–28
  of death, 127–28
Finding yourself, 7
Five Houses of Zen, 24–25, 263
Five Precepts, 47–52
  defined, 47–48, 263
  destroying life and, 48–49
  intoxicants and, 51–52
  lies/deceit and, 50–51
  list of, 48
  in perspective, 51–52
  sexual misconduct and, 50
  stealing and, 49–50
  Ten Commandments vs., 52

Flower-arranging, 189–90
Flowers, 59, 159–60
Food
  daily meals, 252–53
  mindfulness and, 252–53
  respecting body and, 197, 252
  sesshin meals, 218–19
Four Great Vows, 94
Four Noble Truths, 42–44
  awakening and, 109, 258
  defined, 42, 263
  four signs and, 15–16
  list of, 42
  See also Desire; Eightfold Path;
    Suffering

G

Gardening (Zen), 183–87
  characteristics, 184
  equipment, 184–85
  impermanence and, 184, 186–87
  landscaping and, 185
  spiritual experience of, 186
Gassho, 32, 62, 165–66, 263
Gay/lesbian lifestyles, 53
Glassman, Bernie, 226–27, 234
Greystone Foundation, 227
Guiyang school, 24. *See also* Soto
  School of Zen
Gung Fu, 23

H

Haiku, 191–92, 228, 263
Hair, 162
Hakuin, Master, 71
Hakuyu Taizen Maezumi, 233, 234
Half-lotus position, 61, 263
Halifax, Joan, 117–18, 232–33, 234
Hara, 63
Harmony, 84–85. *See also*
  Compassion
History (Zen), 2–3, 13–26
  Bodhidharma and, 22–23, 24

Buddhism schools and, 21–22
Buddhism spread and, 21–26
  in China, 22–25
  Five Houses of Zen, 24–25
  in Japan, 25–26
  of koans, 70–72
  in Western civilization, 26
  See also American Zen;
    Siddhartha Gautama
Home life, 145–56
  chores and, 153–55
  cleaning exercise, 147–48
  cooking and, 154–55
  eco-friendly environment, 150
  laundry and, 153–54
  meditation space, 146–47
  simple spaces in, 148–49
  sitting group and, 167–68
  time management and, 149–50
  zendo for, 166–68
  See also Daily Zen
Hui'ko, 24–25

I

I. *See* Ego; Self
Ikebana, 189–90
Illness
  death and, 52–53, 126, 127–28,
    129–31
  of family/friends, 125–27
  stress of, 125
Impermanence. *See*
  Change/impermanence
Incense, 59, 159
Interdependence, 19, 64
  kindness and, 89–90
  meditation on, 245
  in relationships, 84–85, 89–90
  Siddhartha discovering, 19
  at work, 179
Intoxicants, 51–52

J

Jesus Christ, 241
Jikijitsu (jikido), 160–61, 163, 164
Job/Career, 169–80
  attitude toward, 178–80
  commuting to, 253–54
  distinctions and, 171–72
  Eightfold Path and, 178–80
  empty mind and, 176–77
  losing self in, 176–77
  in military, 175
  mindfulness vs. mindlessness
    and, 176–77
  opinions and, 172–73
  relationships, 180
  Right Livelihood and, 44, 46,
    173–75
  selecting, 174–75
  stress of, 177–78
  zazen breaks, 177–78
  Zen at, 171–73, 254–55
Judgment, 65

K

Kapleau, Philip, 224–25
Karesansui, 185
Karma
  defined, 263
  reincarnation and, 142–43
Kerouac, Jack, 31, 35, 36
Kinhin, 57
  advantage of, 57
  defined, 217, 263
  practicing, 217–18, 244
Koans, 69–81
  collections of, 71
  defined, 70, 263
  dharma combat and, 80
  discussing, 73, 77–81
  dokusan and, 78–79
  examples, 70, 74–76
  historical perspective, 70–72

mondo and, 80–81
moving beyond, 72–73
Mu, 76–77
purpose, 72–73
requirements, 74, 81
Rinzai Zen and, 26, 69, 264
samadhi for, 74
in sesshin, 211
Soto Zen and, 69
teisho and, 79–80
as tool, 72–73
working with, 73–76
Kyosaku, 103, 164

L

Landscaping. See Gardening (Zen)
Laundry, 153–54
Lesbian/gay lifestyles, 53
Life, not destroying
  abortion and, 53–54
  as precept, 48–49
Linji school, 24, 25. See also Rinzai
  School of Zen
Listening, 86–87, 256
Literature. See Resources
Livelihood (Right), 44, 46, 173–75.
  See also Job/Career
Living Buddha, Living Christ, 241
Living in moment, 3–4
  ceasing desires and, 9–10
  with children, 88–89
  enjoying now, 10–11
  impermanence and. See
    Change/impermanence
  judgment and, 65
  mindfulness and, 244–45
  quieting mind and, 4–6
  relationships and, 91–92
  suffering and, 122–23
  zazen and, 65
Loori, John Daido, 233–34
Lotus position, 61, 263–64

Love
  commitments and, 90–92
  marriage and, 92–94
  See also Relationships
Lying, 50–51

M

Magazines. See Resources
Mahakashyapa, 2–3
Mahayana Buddhism, 21–22, 29
Mandalas, 57–58, 166–67
Mantras, 57, 264
Mara (evil), 19–20
Marriage
  ceremonies, 92–94
  Four Great Vows, 94
  respect in, 94
  Rinzai Zen weddings, 93–94
  Soto Zen weddings, 93
Martial arts, 202–5
  awareness and, 203–4
  history, 23, 202
  mental training, 203
  samurai and, 25, 204–5
Masters. See specific master names;
  Teachers
Meals. See Food
Meditation
  creative visualization, 57
  death and, 127
  on interdependence, 245
  mandalas for, 57–58
  with mantras, 57, 258
  other words for, 2
  purpose, 2
  types, 2, 56–58
  walking (kinhin), 57, 217–18, 244,
    263
  Western style, 56–57
  yoga as, 206
  See also Sitting; Zazen
Mental discipline, 45–47

Middle Way
  defined, 264
  Siddhartha recognizing, 18
Military careers, 175
Mind
  empty, 64–65, 176–77
  focusing, 198, 256
  martial arts and, 203
Mindfulness (Right), 45, 46, 237–48
  being present and, 244–45
  breathing and, 242, 243–44, 245
  concentration vs., 238–39
  connectedness and, 239
  in daily life, 256
  defined, 47, 237, 264
  eating and, 252–53
  exercises, 242
  interdependence and, 245
  mindlessness vs., 176–77
  moving meditation and, 244
  openness and, 239
  peace and, 245–48
  practicing daily, 242–44
  relaxing muscles and, 243
  of Siddhartha, 18–19
  single tasks and, 256
  Thich Nhat Hanh and, 117,
    240–42
  during tragedies, 123
  training, art as, 183
  at work, 176–77, 179
Miracle of Mindfulness, 241–42
Moment, living in. *See* Living in
  moment
Monastic life, 170
Mondo, 80–81
Monkey mind
  defined, 4, 264
  quieting, 5
Morality, 46
Moving meditation. *See* Kinhin
Mu, 76–77
Mumonkan, 71
Muscle relaxation, 243

N
Nature, communing with, 256
Nirvana
  defined, 3, 108, 264
  path to, 9
  See also Enlightenment
Nonattachment, 110–11, 155–56
Now, 10–11. *See also* Living in
  moment

O
Offerings, 160
O-nami, 198–99
Ordinary Mind School of Zen,
  230–31
Organization
  of house, 147–49
  simplicity in, 148–49
  time management and, 149–50
Oryoki, 158

P
Pain, 101–3
  benefits of, 65–66, 101–3
  emotional, 102
  in lotus position, 61
  in zazen, 62, 65–66, 101–3
Paranirvana, 264
Parents, 85–87
Parliament of World Religions, 28
Partners Program, 233
Peace, 84–85, 150–53
  acknowledging suffering and, 248
  mindfulness and, 245–48
  practicing, 247
  sitting for, 248
  See also Compassion
Peaceful Dwelling Project, 235
Peacemaker Order, 227
Pets, 146–47
Poetry, 190–92
  of Basho, 192

haiku, 191–92, 228, 263
  of Robert Aitken, 228
Practice
  art as, 182–83
  attire, 38–39, 60, 161–63
  benefits of, 39, 257, 259
  chores as, 153–55
  concepts and, leaving, 255
  defined, 8–9, 43
  enlightenment and. *See*
    Enlightenment
  environment, 38–39
  family schedule and, 146
  at home. *See* Home life
  locations, 37–38, 60, 146–47
  pets and, 146–47
  reasons for, 6–8
  rules, 8–9
  unity of life and, 259
  at work. *See* Job/Career
  See also Sitting; Zazen
Practitioners, 6
Present, living in. *See* Living in
  moment
Priests. *See* Teachers
Prison Project, 233

Q
Quieting mind, 4–6

R
Reasons, for practice, 6–8
Reincarnation, 142–44
Relationships, 83–94
  being present in, 88–89, 91–92,
    256
  challenges in, 151–52
  with children, 87–89
  commitments and, 90–92
  illness and, 125–27
  interdependence in, 84–85, 89–90
  listening and, 86–87, 256
  living separately together, 91

marriage, 92–94
with parents, 85–87
peace/harmony in, 84–85, 150–53
respect in, 84–85
with teachers. *See* Teachers
during tragedies, 123
at work, 180
worship focus and, 85–86
Resources
literature, 36–37, 224, 228, 231,
232, 235, 255, 273–76
Online supply sources, 280
Web sites, 234, 255, 277–80
Respect
for body, 196–97, 252
in marriage, 94
for others, 84–85
Resting, 257
Retreats. *See* Sesshin
Retreat Without Walls, 235
Right actions/wisdoms/disciplines.
See Eightfold Path
Rinzai School of Zen, 24–26, 264
in America, 34
beliefs, 25–26
D. T. Suzuki and, 34
history, 24–26
koans and. *See* Koans
weddings, 93–94
Rochester Zen Center, 225
Roshi, 96, 264. *See also* Teachers
Rules, 8–9, 158, 163–65. *See also*
Eightfold Path; Five Precepts
Ryokan, 258

∫

Samadhi, 74, 264
Samsara
defined, 17, 264
reincarnation and, 142–44
Samurai, 25, 204–5
San Francisco Zen Center, 33–34
Sangha, 33, 220–21, 264

Satori. *See* Enlightenment
Scandals, 34–35, 230
Schools
of Buddhism, 21–22
of Zen, 24–25
Self
accepting, 139–41
as aggregate, 136–37
changing nature and, 136–38
compassion replacing, 138–39
discovering, 135
identifying, 134
illusion of, 137–38
losing, 4, 176–77, 200–201
See also Ego
Self-realization. *See* Enlightenment
Sensei. *See* Teachers
Separation, 258. *See also* Dualistic
thinking
Service, 118–19. *See also*
Bodhisattva
Sesshin, 209–21
behavior, 213–14
benefits, 220–21
closed environment, 210–11
daily schedule, 212–13, 214–15
defined, 65–66, 264
dokusan during, 215–17
exhaustion from, 214–15
kinhin during, 217–18
koans and, 211
meal practice, 218–19
overview, 210–11
pain and, 65–66
preparing for, 211–14
sangha unity, 220–21
supplies, 211–12
work practice, 219–20
Seung Sahn, Master, 125
Sexuality, 53
Sexual misconduct, 50
Shaolin monastery, 23, 202
Shikantaza, 2, 81, 115, 264. *See also*
Sitting; Zazen

Shoes, 162–63
Shoshan, 80
Siddhartha Gautama, 14–21
ascetic life and, 17–18
becoming Buddha, 20–21
early life, 14–15
enlightenment of, 19–21
four signs for, 15–16
internal battle of, 20
Mara (evil) and, 19–20
mindfulness of, 18–19
predictions for, 14
renunciation by, 16–18
suffering and, 15–17
truth search, 18–19
Silence, with teachers, 99–100
Simplicity, of organization, 148–49
Sitting, 2
at-home group, 167–68
attire, 38–39, 60, 161–63
benefits of, 39
controlling thoughts, 114–15
daily, 249, 250–51, 257
death perspective and, 53
defined, 42
difficult decisions and, 53–54
as enlightenment, 34, 108, 114–15
environment, 38–39
locations, 37–38
for peace, 248
precepts and, 51
Shikantaza and, 2, 81, 115, 264
during tragedies, 123, 257
as Zen emphasis, 42
See also Zazen
Sitting postures
Burmese style, 62, 262
half-lotus position, 61, 263
kyosaku corrections, 103, 164
lotus position, 61, 263–64
pain and, 61, 62, 65–66, 101–3
Sleep, 257
Soen Shaku, 28–29, 30

Soto School of Zen
  in America, 34–35
  beliefs, 25, 26
  founder, 2
  history, 24–26
  koans and. See Koans
  meditation, 2
  Shunryu Suzuki and, 34–35
  weddings, 93
Speech (Right), 44, 46, 50–51,
  178–79
Spiritual elitism. See Stink (of Zen)
Spiritual retreats. See Sesshin
Stealing, 49–50
Stink (of Zen), 155–56, 165–66
Stress
  illness and, 125–27
  practice during, 124
  at work, 177–78
  worrying and, 124
Suffering, 42–43, 122–23
  accepting, 122
  acknowledging, 248
  being present in, 122–23
  cause of, 42, 43, 65
  ending, 9, 43
  Four Noble Truths and, 42–43,
    131
  illness and, 125–27
  impermanence and, 43, 131
  from judgment, 65
  life as, 17, 42–43, 131
  Siddhartha and, 15–17
  sitting during, 123
  worrying and, 123–24
  as Zen motive, 6–7
Supplies
  for home zendo, 166–67
  online stores, 280
  for sesshin, 211–12
  zazen, 58–59, 60, 280
Support groups. See Zen centers
Suzuki, Daisetz Teitaro (D. T.),
  28–32

initial U.S. visit, 28–30
legacy of, 29, 31–32
people influenced by, 31, 35, 36
as student, 30
as teacher, 30–31
tradition of, 34
Zen name, 30
Suzuki, Shunryu
  in America, 33–35
  beginner mind and, 5, 32–33
  biography about, 33, 34
  early life, 32–33
  tradition of, 34–35

T

Tea, 23
Teachers, 95–105
  discussion points, 104–5, 216–17
  dokusan with, 78–79, 215–17, 263
  finding, 97–99
  interacting with, 99–101
  male/female, 96
  meeting, 98–99
  omnipresence of, 98
  pain, learning and, 101–3
  qualifications, 96–97
  questions to avoid, 103–4
  relationship with, 103–5
  road map from, 97, 100–101
  roshis, 96, 264
  silence with, 99–100
  trusting, 105
  worship focus and, 86
  See also specific teacher names
Teisho, 79–80, 265
Ten Commandments, 52
Thangkas, 166–67
Theravada Buddhism, 21, 22
Thich Nhat Hanh (Thây), 117,
  240–42, 248
Thought (Right), 44, 45, 46
Time management, 149–50
Traffic, 253–54

U

Understanding (Right), 44, 45–46
Unity of life, 259

V

Vajrayana Buddhism, 21, 22
Vietnam, 240, 241

W

Walking meditation. See Kinhin
Watts, Alan, 31, 36
Web sites, 234, 255, 277–80
Weddings. See Marriage
Western meditation, 56–57
Western Zen Masters, 223. See also
  specific names
White Plum lineage, 233, 234, 235
Wisdom, 45–46
Work. See Job/Career
Work practice, 219–20
Worrying
  about death, 142
  stress of, 124
  wasting time with, 123–24
Wu-Men, Master, 71, 76

Y

Yasutani, Roshi, 225
Yoga, 205–8
  benefits, 207–8
  breathing in, 206–7
  history, 205
  movement, flexibility and, 206
  as moving meditation, 206
  styles, 205
Yunmen school, 24

Z

Zabutan, 58, 158, 265
Zafu, 58, 158, 265

Zazen, 55–67
- altars for, 59, 158–60
- breathing, 63–64
- children and, 87
- clothing, 38–39, 60, 161–63
- cushion position, 58
- daily, 250–51
- defined, 56, 265
- empty mind and, 64–65, 176–77
- ending, 62
- fear and, 66–67
- length of, 251
- location, 60
- mistakes and, 65
- pain in, 62, 65–66, 101–3
- requirements, 56
- routine, 59–60, 146, 250–51
- sesshin and, 65–66, 264
- sitting postures, 61–62
- stillness in, 65
- supplies, 58–59, 60, 280

- timing, 62, 251
- tips, 59–60
- at work, 177–78

Zen
- daily. *See* Daily Zen
- defined, 2–6, 265
- Five Houses of, 24–25, 263
- history. *See* History (Zen); Siddhartha Gautama
- portability of, 169, 170
- practice, 8–9
- practitioner profile, 6
- purpose of, 3, 258
- reasons for, 6–8
- rules, 8–9, 163–65
- stink of, 155–56, 165–66

Zen centers
- American, 33–34, 37–38, 225, 232, 241, 266–72
- finding, 37
- inquiring about, 37–38

- practitioners and, 6
- support groups, 11

Zendo, 157–68
- altars, 59, 159–60
- attire, 38–39, 60, 161–63
- behavior, 163–65
- defined, 38, 158, 265
- discipline, 103, 160, 164
- gassho and, 32, 62, 165–66, 263
- headmaster (jikijitsu), 160–61, 163, 164
- at home, 166–68
- overview, 158
- rules, 158, 163–65

Zenga. *See* Calligraphy (zenga)
Zen gardens. *See* Gardening (Zen)
Zone, the, 4, 199–201

THE EVERYTHING BUDDHISM BOOK

By Jacky Sach

THE **EVERYTHING BUDDHISM BOOK**

Learn the ancient traditions and apply them to modern life

Jacky Sach

Trade paperback
$14.95 ($22.95 CAN)
1-58062-884-2, 304 pages

Buddhism's principles of nonviolence, mindfulness, and self-awareness resonate with many people who feel distracted and conflicted in their daily lives. *The Everything® Buddhism Book* walks you through the rich traditions and history of the Buddhist faith, while providing a straightforward approach to its ideological foundations. Special features include power of karma, the practice of Zen, the notion of nirvana, the life of Buddha and his influence throughout the world, descriptions of the definitive Buddhist texts and their significance, and Buddhist ceremonies and celebrations.

OTHER *EVERYTHING*® BOOKS BY ADAMS MEDIA

BUSINESS

Everything® **Business Planning Book**
Everything® **Coaching and Mentoring Book**
Everything® **Fundraising Book**
Everything® **Home-Based Business Book**
Everything® **Leadership Book**
Everything® **Managing People Book**
Everything® **Network Marketing Book**
Everything® **Online Business Book**
Everything® **Project Management Book**
Everything® **Selling Book**
Everything® **Start Your Own Business Book**
Everything® **Time Management Book**

COMPUTERS

Everything® **Build Your Own Home Page Book**

Everything® **Computer Book**
Everything® **Internet Book**
Everything® **Microsoft® Word 2000 Book**

COOKBOOKS

Everything® **Barbecue Cookbook**
Everything® **Bartender's Book, $9.95**
Everything® **Chinese Cookbook**
Everything® **Chocolate Cookbook**
Everything® **Cookbook**
Everything® **Dessert Cookbook**
Everything® **Diabetes Cookbook**
Everything® **Low-Carb Cookbook**
Everything® **Low-Fat High-Flavor Cookbook**
Everything® **Mediterranean Cookbook**
Everything® **Mexican Cookbook**
Everything® **One-Pot Cookbook**
Everything® **Pasta Book**

Everything® **Quick Meals Cookbook**
Everything® **Slow Cooker Cookbook**
Everything® **Soup Cookbook**
Everything® **Thai Cookbook**
Everything® **Vegetarian Cookbook**
Everything® **Wine Book**

HEALTH

Everything® **Anti-Aging Book**
Everything® **Diabetes Book**
Everything® **Dieting Book**
Everything® **Herbal Remedies Book**
Everything® **Hypnosis Book**
Everything® **Menopause Book**
Everything® **Nutrition Book**
Everything® **Reflexology Book**
Everything® **Stress Management Book**
Everything®**Vitamins, Minerals, and Nutritional Supplements Book**

All Everything® books are priced at $12.95 or $14.95, unless otherwise stated. Prices subject to change without notice.
Canadian prices range from $11.95–$31.95, and are subject to change without notice.

HISTORY

Everything® **American History Book**
Everything® **Civil War Book**
Everything® **Irish History & Heritage Book**
Everything® **Mafia Book**
Everything® **World War II Book**

HOBBIES & GAMES

Everything® **Bridge Book**
Everything® **Candlemaking Book**
Everything® **Casino Gambling Book**
Everything® **Chess Basics Book**
Everything® **Collectibles Book**
Everything® **Crossword and Puzzle Book**
Everything® **Digital Photography Book**
Everything® **Family Tree Book**
Everything® **Games Book**
Everything® **Knitting Book**
Everything® **Magic Book**
Everything® **Motorcycle Book**
Everything® **Online Genealogy Book**
Everything® **Photography Book**
Everything® **Pool & Billiards Book**
Everything® **Quilting Book**
Everything® **Scrapbooking Book**
Everything® **Soapmaking Book**

HOME IMPROVEMENT

Everything® **Feng Shui Book**
Everything® **Gardening Book**
Everything® **Home Decorating Book**
Everything® **Landscaping Book**
Everything® **Lawn Care Book**
Everything® **Organize Your Home Book**

KIDS' STORY BOOKS

Everything® **Bedtime Story Book**
Everything® **Bible Stories Book**
Everything® **Fairy Tales Book**
Everything® **Mother Goose Book**

EVERYTHING® KIDS' BOOKS

All titles are $6.95
Everything® **Kids' Baseball Book, 2nd Ed.** ($10.95 CAN)
Everything® **Kids' Bugs Book** ($10.95 CAN)
Everything® **Kids' Christmas Puzzle & Activity Book** ($10.95 CAN)
Everything® **Kids' Cookbook** ($10.95 CAN)
Everything® **Kids' Halloween Puzzle & Activity Book** ($10.95 CAN)
Everything® **Kids' Joke Book** ($10.95 CAN)
Everything® **Kids' Math Puzzles Book** ($10.95 CAN)
Everything® **Kids' Mazes Book** ($10.95 CAN)
Everything® **Kids' Money Book** ($11.95 CAN)
Everything® **Kids' Monsters Book** ($10.95 CAN)
Everything® **Kids' Nature Book** ($11.95 CAN)
Everything® **Kids' Puzzle Book** ($10.95 CAN)
Everything® **Kids' Science Experiments Book** ($10.95 CAN)
Everything® **Kids' Soccer Book** ($10.95 CAN)
Everything® **Kids' Travel Activity Book** ($10.95 CAN)

LANGUAGE

Everything® **Learning French Book**
Everything® **Learning German Book**
Everything® **Learning Italian Book**
Everything® **Learning Latin Book**
Everything® **Learning Spanish Book**
Everything® **Sign Language Book**

MUSIC

Everything® **Drums Book (with CD),** $19.95 ($31.95 CAN)
Everything® **Guitar Book**
Everything® **Playing Piano and Keyboards Book**

Everything® **Rock & Blues Guitar Book (with CD), $19.95** ($31.95 CAN)
Everything® **Songwriting Book**

NEW AGE

Everything® **Astrology Book**
Everything® **Divining the Future Book**
Everything® **Dreams Book**
Everything® **Ghost Book**
Everything® **Meditation Book**
Everything® **Numerology Book**
Everything® **Palmistry Book**
Everything® **Psychic Book**
Everything® **Spells & Charms Book**
Everything® **Tarot Book**
Everything® **Wicca and Witchcraft Book**

PARENTING

Everything® **Baby Names Book**
Everything® **Baby Shower Book**
Everything® **Baby's First Food Book**
Everything® **Baby's First Year Book**
Everything® **Breastfeeding Book**
Everything® **Father-to-Be Book**
Everything® **Get Ready for Baby Book**
Everything® **Homeschooling Book**
Everything® **Parent's Guide to Positive Discipline**
Everything® **Potty Training Book,** $9.95 ($15.95 CAN)
Everything® **Pregnancy Book, 2nd Ed.**
Everything® **Pregnancy Fitness Book**
Everything® **Pregnancy Organizer,** $15.00 ($22.95 CAN)
Everything® **Toddler Book**
Everything® **Tween Book**

PERSONAL FINANCE

Everything® **Budgeting Book**
Everything® **Get Out of Debt Book**
Everything® **Get Rich Book**
Everything® **Homebuying Book, 2nd Ed.**
Everything® **Homeselling Book**

All Everything® books are priced at $12.95 or $14.95, unless otherwise stated. Prices subject to change without notice.
Canadian prices range from $11.95–$31.95, and are subject to change without notice.

Everything® **Investing Book**
Everything® **Money Book**
Everything® **Mutual Funds Book**
Everything® **Online Investing Book**
Everything® **Personal Finance Book**
Everything® **Personal Finance in Your 20s & 30s Book**
Everything® **Wills & Estate Planning Book**

PETS

Everything® **Cat Book**
Everything® **Dog Book**
Everything® **Dog Training and Tricks Book**
Everything® **Horse Book**
Everything® **Puppy Book**
Everything® **Tropical Fish Book**

REFERENCE

Everything® **Astronomy Book**
Everything® **Car Care Book**
Everything® **Christmas Book, $15.00 ($21.95 CAN)**
Everything® **Classical Mythology Book**
Everything® **Einstein Book**
Everything® **Etiquette Book**
Everything® **Great Thinkers Book**
Everything® **Philosophy Book**
Everything® **Shakespeare Book**
Everything® **Tall Tales, Legends, & Other Outrageous Lies Book**
Everything® **Toasts Book**
Everything® **Trivia Book**
Everything® **Weather Book**

RELIGION

Everything® **Angels Book**
Everything® **Buddhism Book**
Everything® **Catholicism Book**
Everything® **Jewish History & Heritage Book**
Everything® **Judaism Book**

Everything® **Prayer Book**
Everything® **Saints Book**
Everything® **Understanding Islam Book**
Everything® **World's Religions Book**
Everything® **Zen Book**

SCHOOL & CAREERS

Everything® **After College Book**
Everything® **College Survival Book**
Everything® **Cover Letter Book**
Everything® **Get-a-Job Book**
Everything® **Hot Careers Book**
Everything® **Job Interview Book**
Everything® **Online Job Search Book**
Everything® **Resume Book, 2nd Ed.**
Everything® **Study Book**

SELF-HELP

Everything® **Dating Book**
Everything® **Divorce Book**
Everything® **Great Marriage Book**
Everything® **Great Sex Book**
Everything® **Romance Book**
Everything® **Self-Esteem Book**
Everything® **Success Book**

SPORTS & FITNESS

Everything® **Bicycle Book**
Everything® **Body Shaping Book**
Everything® **Fishing Book**
Everything® **Fly-Fishing Book**
Everything® **Golf Book**
Everything® **Golf Instruction Book**
Everything® **Pilates Book**
Everything® **Running Book**
Everything® **Sailing Book, 2nd Ed.**
Everything® **T'ai Chi and QiGong Book**
Everything® **Total Fitness Book**
Everything® **Weight Training Book**
Everything® **Yoga Book**

TRAVEL

Everything® **Guide to Las Vegas**

Everything® **Guide to New England**
Everything® **Guide to New York City**
Everything® **Guide to Washington D.C.**
Everything® **Travel Guide to The Disneyland Resort®, California Adventure®, Universal Studios®, and the Anaheim Area**
Everything® **Travel Guide to the Walt Disney World Resort®, Universal Studios®, and Greater Orlando, 3rd Ed.**

WEDDINGS

Everything® **Bachelorette Party Book**
Everything® **Bridesmaid Book**
Everything® **Creative Wedding Ideas Book**
Everything® **Jewish Wedding Book**
Everything® **Wedding Book, 2nd Ed.**
Everything® **Wedding Checklist, $7.95 ($11.95 CAN)**
Everything® **Wedding Etiquette Book, $7.95 ($11.95 CAN)**
Everything® **Wedding Organizer, $15.00 ($22.95 CAN)**
Everything® **Wedding Shower Book, $7.95 ($12.95 CAN)**
Everything® **Wedding Vows Book, $7.95 ($11.95 CAN)**
Everything® **Weddings on a Budget Book, $9.95 ($15.95 CAN)**

WRITING

Everything® **Creative Writing Book**
Everything® **Get Published Book**
Everything® **Grammar and Style Book**
Everything® **Grant Writing Book**
Everything® **Guide to Writing Children's Books**
Everything® **Screenwriting Book**
Everything® **Writing Well Book**

Available wherever books are sold!
To order, call 800-872-5627, or visit us at everything.com